# THE PANARE

# THE PANARE

## Tradition and Change
## on the Amazonian Frontier

PAUL HENLEY

YALE UNIVERSITY PRESS
NEW HAVEN AND LONDON
1982

Designed by Caroline Williamson.
Filmset in Dymo Baskerville and printed in Great Britain
by Robert MacLehose & Co. Ltd, Renfrew, Scotland.

Published in Great Britain, Europe, Africa, and Asia (except Japan)
by Yale University Press, Limited, London. Distributed in Australia and
New Zealand by Book & Film Services, Artarmon, N.S.W., Australia; and in
Japan by Harper & Row, Publishers, Tokyo Office.

**Library of Congress Cataloging in Publication Data**

Henley, Paul.
   The Panare, tradition and change on the
Amazonian frontier.

   Bibliography: P.
   Includes index.
   1. Panare Indians.   I. Title.
F2319.2.P34H46      980'.004'98   81-40432
ISBN 0-300-02504-1               AACR2

# CONTENTS

PLATES

## MAPS

## TABLES

# FIGURES

## ACKNOWLEDGEMENTS

This book is based on just over five years of doctoral research (January 1974–March 1979). Three years of this research was funded by the British Social Science Research Council whilst further grants were received from the Horniman Foundation, the Venezuelan Academy of Sciences, the Raúl Leoni Fund, the Corporación Venezolana de Guayana, the Wyse Fund and Queens' College, Cambridge. I would like to thank all these bodies for their support.

The data presented in this book were primarily gathered during the period January 1975–October 1976, which I spent on fieldwork in Venezuela. Prior to my departure for the field, I received help and encouragement from my predecessor amongst the Panare, Jean-Paul Dumont. I hope that he will regard the criticism that I offer here of his work not as a sign of ingratitude but simply as the inevitable corollary of a different point of view.

During my time in Venezuela I received academic or logistical support from the following bodies: the Instituto Venezolano de Investigaciones Científicas, the Fundación La Salle, the Comisión Presidencial del Guaniamo. I am grateful to all these bodies and also to Dra Nelly Arvelo-Jiménez for acting as my local supervisor and to Dr Francisco Kerdel Vegas for supporting my applications to various Venezuelan bodies for funds.

The periods I spend in Caracas were extremely pleasant on account of the good company and unstinted hospitality of Dr Luis Castro, Sra Rebeca Leiva de Castro and their family. I am also indebted to many other friends and colleagues in Caracas, but the help given by Marie-Claude Müller, Domingo Nedelka, Walter Coppens and Roberto Lizarralde was particularly valuable.

In writing up this material, I benefitted greatly from the guidance I received from Professor John Barnes and from Dr Stephen Hugh-Jones, both of whom acted as my supervisor in Cambridge for a period. I am also grateful to Michael Pickering for his astute criticisms of early drafts of my thesis, whilst the comments of my examiners, Dr Peter Rivière and Dr David Lehman, proved stimulating when it came to modifying the final draft for publication.

Many other friends and colleagues provided help and encouragement during my passage through that dreadful limbo between fieldwork and final draft known to all doctoral candidates in anthropology. A list of their names would read like a telephone directory: space precludes mentioning all but Val Curran and Howard Reid, Christine Hugh-Jones, Helen Pickering and Phyllis Lee. Ultimately, however, my greatest debt of gratitude is to my closest kin, 'real' and classificatory: to my parents and to my fictive kin in Amazonia. For without their tolerance and generosity, none of this would have seen the light of day.

# INTRODUCTION

The headwaters of the Orinoco lie about two degrees north of the Equator, and for the first few hundred miles of its course the river flows in a northwesterly direction. Then, skirting the western flank of the Guianese Shield, it passes Puerto Ayacucho and begins to describe a long and leisurely arc towards the north-east, flowing on in this direction until it reaches the sea. It is inland from this arc of the Orinoco that the indigenous people known to the local criollos[1] and the ethnographic literature as the 'Panare' presently live (see Map 1). It is not known exactly where the name came from—the Panare for their part call themselves *e'nyëpa*. With the exception of their southern neighbours, the Hoti, whom they call *onwa*, they apply this term to all indigenous groups. *E'nyëpa* they distinguish from *tato,* i.e. criollos, non-Indians in general.[2]

The cartographical co-ordinates of the area that the Panare inhabit are 5° to 8° North and 65° to 67° West; in contemporary geopolitical terms this area falls within the Cedeño district of Bolivar State, Venezuela. If one drew a line on the map around all the extant Panare communities, it would enclose a roughly triangular area of approximately 20,000 square kilometres. But in actual fact this figure has little real meaning since the area is not continuously settled by the Panare. Large tracts of it remain uninhabited whilst other parts are occupied by criollos who have been living in the rural hinterland of Caicara since at least the beginning of the nineteenth century. Since that time, the two populations, Panare and criollo, have gradually been converging. Whilst the criollos have been pushing their front of colonization southward, the Panare have been migrating northwards, out of their ancestral homeland at the headwaters of the Cuchivero.

1. The policy I have adopted with regard to the use of foreign words in the text is explained in Appendix 1, as is the system of notation used for transcribing Panare words.

2. I use the term 'criollo' to refer to all Venezuelan non-Indians. I believe this term to be less confusing than other possible terms such as 'neo-Venezuelans' or 'whites'. It should be noted however that the term is used of all non-Indians, regardless of social class or ethnic background. It does not therefore have quite the same connotations as the English word 'creole'.

Today most Panare settlements are no more than half a day's walk from a criollo homestead. Only those Panare who still live on the upper reaches of the Cuchivero remain isolated from the criollos, and even they pay visits to criollo settlements further downstream for trade.

Yet despite their close proximity to the criollos, the Panare have retained their distinctive social and cultural traditions to a remarkable degree. This cultural resilience has impressed several of the anthropologists who have visited the Panare during the last twenty years. Reporting on his visit to Panare territory in 1958, Johannes Wilbert wrote '. . . we were surprised to see that, despite their proximity and contact with civilization, the Panare Indians still conserve their aboriginal culture, slightly modified by advances of a material kind' (Wilbert 1961: 23). Following his visit ten years later, Jean-Paul Dumont observed that 'the most striking characteristic of this population may be the strength of Panare cultural resistance to acculturation, particularly when compared to the weak resistance offered by the proselytized Piaroa of the Isla Ratón or with the creolized Makiritare of the Paragua river' (Dumont 1976: 27). More recently, María Eugenia Villalón, who visited the Panare several times between 1969 and 1978, has remarked that 'apart from the adoption of certain items of the white man's technological complex, the *e'nyapa* have shown an almost incredible imperviousness to the influences of the Western world' (Villalón 1978: 12).

In view of recent changes in local criollo society the resistance the Panare continue to offer to the cultural influences of the criollos is now all the more remarkable. Over the last ten or fifteen years, as Caicara and its rural hinterland have been developed economically, the social and technological disparity between the criollos and the Panare has become more marked. When Wilbert visited Caicara in 1958 it was a sleepy little town of approximately 3,000 people, largely unchanged since the beginning of the century. Twenty years later, it is a town of more than 15,000 people, with wide new roads and highways, many new houses, air-conditioned supermarkets and bars, and a café where the fashion-conscious youth of the town listen to a juke-box playing local cowboy music, Caribbean 'salsa' and even Anglo-American rock. In fact, my first encounter with a Panare, far from being, as I had imagined, at some isolated riverside landing-place or clearing in the forest, took place when a young man in a bright red loincloth, his body painted with black geometric designs, strode up to me as I sat in the café and imperiously demanded a soft drink.

The recent history of Amazonia has made one so accustomed to the idea that the indigenous societies of the region are doomed to disintegrate at the first brush with industrial civilization that the resilience of the Panare stands out as an exception worthy of explanation. Indeed, to provide such an explanation is the ultimate objective of this book. However, in the course of doing so, I shall consider both the Panare's internal system of social relations and the external system of relations that they maintain with the local criollos. After two preliminary chapters of a largely descriptive character, the book can be divided into two parts: Chapters 3 to 5 examine the internal organization of Panare society whilst their relations with the criollos are dealt with in Chapters 6 to 8. However, at various points in the book, I shall be concerned to show how the two systems of relations, the internal and the external, articulate with one another. My argument will be that the reasons for the Panare's resilience to outside influences are to be found in the form of this articulation.

In the chapters dealing with the internal organization of Panare society, I will try to show how the various different domains of Panare social life inter-relate so as to form a more or less integrated whole. The analysis builds up gradually, commencing at the most materialistic level. I begin by arguing that the form of the Panare's adaptation to the ecological system in which they live (described in Chapter 2) bears a direct structural relationship to the system of economic relations (Chapter 3), since the latter both determines and is determined by the former. Following a detailed analysis of the kinship system (Chapter 4), I suggest that there may be a similar structural relationship between the latter and the economic system. Finally, I attempt to relate these various domains of Panare social life, which together account for the reproduction of the material infrastructure of the society, to such relatively superstructural features as the political system, certain aspects of the belief system, and ceremonial activities (Chapter 5).

Although the Panare are my central concern in this book, a considerable proportion of the latter half of it is given over to the description of local criollo society. This interest in the criollo 'side' of interethnic relations in Panare territory is a reflection of a general theoretical proposition that underlies this work: namely, that the form that social relations take between indigenous groups and the local representatives of the national societies of Amazonia is primarily determined by the social, economic and other interests of the latter. Since the non-Indians are generally stronger, both in numbers and technology, it is they who set the stage, as it were, on which contact shall take place. The social and cultural characteristics of the indigenous groups with whom they come into contact will influence the way in which both Indians and non-Indians act upon that stage, but the Indians themselves are generally incapable of changing its layout. It seems to me important therefore, in a book such as this, that local criollo society be considered directly as an integral part of the text instead of being merely referred to, as is often the case in the anthropological literature on Amazonia, as a vague but highly menacing threat standing in the wings.

This approach to the study of interethnic relations derives from my reading of *Os índios e a civilização*, Darcy Ribeiro's voluminous study of the relations between the indigenous groups and national society of Brazil between 1900 and 1960 (Ribeiro 1970). Indeed the final three chapters of this book represents as an attempt to apply Ribeiro's approach to the present situation of the Panare. In my view, Ribeiro's work, although deficient in a number of critical respects and now somewhat dated still remains the most comprehensive framework that has so far been developed for the analysis of relations between the indigenous groups and modern national societies of lowland South America.[3] Probably on account of the fact that most of it is available only in Portuguese, Ribeiro's book is little-known amongst English-speaking anthropologists. Elsewhere I have published a 'critical appreciation' of the central ideas and arguments of the book (Henley 1978), but here, for reasons of space, I confine myself to presenting these ideas only in the most summary manner in order to explain the way in which the last three chapters are organized. This summary is to be found at the beginning of Chapter 6.

The first extended study of the Panare was carried out by the French anthropologist Jean-Paul Dumont between 1967 and 1970. The results of this study have been published in a number of articles and two books, listed below in the bibliography. I was able to read most of these publications before I began my own study of the Panare. This reading suggested that our respective studies would complement rather than duplicate one another. In the majority of his writings, Dumont approaches the Panare from a radical if somewhat idiosyncratic structuralist viewpoint, his ultimate aim being to

---

3. The only other author to make a systematic attempt to develop a general theory of relations between the indigenous groups and the national societies of lowland South America is Roberto Cardoso de Oliveira. Cardoso has suggested that Ribeiro's work should be seen 'as a point of departure, not a sign of arrival' (1972a: 128–9) and considers his own theory of *fricção interétnica*, i.e. 'interethnic friction', to be an attempt to break new ground, even though it rests on foundations laid by Ribeiro (Cardoso 1972b: 14). But, whilst there is no doubt that Cardoso's theoretical writings do represent an advance on some aspects of Ribeiro's work, not least in that they have influenced a number of case studies both by Cardoso himself and his followers (notably, Cardoso 1968, 1972a; Melatti 1967; Laraia and Da Matta 1967) which have shown the general scheme presented in *Os índios e a civilização* to be too simplistic, they do not yet have the comprehensive range of the latter.

identify the fundamental categories of Panare thought as manifest in their culture and social life (see, for example, Dumont 1976: 3). In contrast, my own interests were largely confined to the relatively materialistic domains of kinship, economics and interethnic relations, my approach thus having much more in common with the British empiricist tradition than with the rationalist tradition to which the structuralist approach can be said to belong (see Leach 1976: 4–6).

In planning my programme of fieldwork, I proposed to divide my time between two Panare communities, both of which would be in regular contact with the criollo population but which differed from one another in that one would have undergone a significant degree of acculturation whilst the other would still have been relatively traditional. By comparing the data collected in these two communities, I hoped to identify what it was about their respective situations of contact that explained the differences between them. Furthermore, I planned to concentrate the greatest part of my efforts on studying the relations of these communities with the local criollo population, relying on the accounts of Dumont and others to provide me with the necessary ethnographic background.

In the event, my itinerary turned out to be quite different from the one that I originally planned. In total, I spent about 12 months in the field between February 1975 and June 1976. More by accident than design, my bouts of fieldwork were staggered in such a way that I was in the field during at least part of every month of the year except the month of August, the middle of the rainy season. Following a preliminary survey of Panare communities, I established myself in the Colorado valley, in a community that appeared to be amongst the most traditional, at least in superficial traits, but whose members were in regular contact both with North American Protestant missionaries and with local criollo cattle pastoralists. Furthermore, the Panare living in this valley were geographically closely situated and genealogically closely related to the group studied by Dumont a few years previously. (In fact, Marquitos, the headman of the group studied by Dumont, is the son of Arcaño, the first Panare to settle on the valley floor in Colorado at the turn of the century.) Thus I hoped to be able to use the insights offered by Dumont's work to gain a relatively rapid understanding of what was going on there.

I must record however that although Dumont's work did prove very valuable as an introduction to Panare life, it was not as reliable as I had hoped. Any study of the intellectual life of an indigenous group requires a high degree of competence in their language. But it is clear from the linguistic evidence that Dumont cites in support of his arguments that his command of the Panare language was simply not sufficient to sustain a line of analysis as sophisticated as the one that he has attempted in his publications.[4] This fact, along with a number of other practical considerations, led me to abandon my original plan to dedicate most of my time in the field to a study of the criollo population. Instead, I spent well over three-quarters of my time amongst the Panare. Although I did collect information about the local criollo society, I was unable to do this systematically, simply for lack of time. I have therefore had to rely to a considerable extent on official documents and other second-hand sources for information regarding the criollo population. Lack of time was also the reason for the curtailment of my plan to carry out a controlled comparison of two Panare communities. Nevertheless, I did manage to pay visits to the majority of the extant Panare communities, and this enabled me to get a good idea of how representative the data I collected in the Colorado valley were of the Panare as a whole.

Like Dumont, I had to confront serious linguistic difficulties in order to work amongst the Panare. The great majority of the Panare are monolingual speakers of their own language, which, at the time that I was living amongst them, had never been written down. Most Panare men speak a little trade Spanish, perhaps two hundred words, but no more. The Panare who speak Spanish fluently still number less than half-a-dozen and for a number of practical reasons I was very rarely able to use these people as interpreters. One of the factors that inhibited the use of interpreters, also encountered by Dumont, was that the Panare were very reserved in the presence of members of communities other than their own (see Dumont 1978: 24–5). Since none of the Panare in Colorado was bilingual, in order to use an interpreter I would have had to have brought one in from elsewhere. This, I felt, would have created more problems than it would have solved. I was therefore obliged to carry out my research in the Panare language.

I was greatly aided in my attempts to learn the language by Dra Marie-Claude Müller, then of the Universidad Central de Venezuela, who very generously put all her linguistic data at my disposal. However, at the time that I began my fieldwork, she had only recently started to work with the Panare herself and her material consisted

4. For example, in an article originally published in 1974 (but re-published in a slightly modified form in 1977), Dumont tries to show, amongst other things, that in Panare thought, dogs constitute a 'hinge' between nature and culture, whilst stars constitute a 'hinge' between culture and the supernatural. In the course of doing so, he discusses the names that the Panare give to their dogs and provides a list of some eighteen names, none of which, he claims, have any substantive meaning (Dumont 1974c: 646–7; 1977: 91). In fact, at least ten of these names do have meanings, some of them being such simple descriptive terms as 'black', 'grey', 'spotted', 'blind', 'skinny' etc.

Plate 1.   Intyo, the author's 'mother', preparing cassava bread on an iron griddle in her cooking hut. The aluminium pot just behind her was one of the gifts he gave her, whilst the metal box in the background he brought with him to keep his gear in.

primarily of lexical items, including relatively few verb forms. It therefore took me several months of residence in Colorado before I could engage in anything more than a simple conversation. Even by the end of my fieldwork, I cannot claim to have been entirely fluent in Panare. I could understand most things that were said to me, particularly since the Panare learnt to simplify the syntax of what they said and to pronounce words slowly and clearly when speaking to me. But I still found it difficult to understand them when they were talking amongst themselves.

During my first period of fieldwork, my relations with the Panare were uneasy. This was partly due to the fact that, by a stroke of ill-fortune, I had arrived at the beginning of the rainy season, the time when the Panare are short of food. They were therefore not pleased at the prospect of having another mouth to feed even though they greatly appreciated the steel tools and other useful technological items that I had brought with me to give in exchange. Throughout my fieldwork, I was aided and protected by an adult man in his twenties, living uxorilocally, who, although one of the most competent and successful producers in the community, was somewhat more distantly related to the other members of the community than they were to each other.

Towards the end of my fieldwork, he told me that during the first months that I was living in the community the other members had rebuked him for being friendly towards me. The turning point in my relations with the Panare came when Intyo, the woman in whose cooking hut I was living, a widow, declared that I was brother of her son. In response, I began to call her *sanë,* mother. This relationship was consolidated by the preferential exchange of goods: at the beginning of each bout of fieldwork, I would bring her special gifts and she would reciprocate by giving me fruits and other morsels from her garden. Early on in my fieldwork, I was given a Panare name and a nickname. After being adopted by my 'mother', I also had a position in the relationship system which made collecting genealogies much easier since I could use myself as a point of reference.

Although I found it difficult to explain to the Panare my true motives for being amongst them, it was not as difficult as one might imagine. The Panare are interested to know about the world beyond their immediate horizons and I was able to respond to their questions by showing them pictures of my family and illustrated news magazines. They found it quite understandable that I should want to know about a different way of life. What they could not understand was that I should be prepared to spend so much time away from my family in order to do so. Shortly after I arrived, one of the older women asked me if I had a mother back at home. When I said that I did, she asked, 'And doesn't she miss you?' 'Yes,' I replied tentatively. 'Then why don't you go home?' she said in an apparently mystified tone. At that stage of my fieldwork, I was still uncertain about my welcome and I interpreted her questions as a subtle hint that I should leave. Only when I got to know the Panare better did I appreciate that Acim, as she was called, who had had nine children herself, was expressing genuine concern on my mother's behalf. Panare sons doing brideservice elsewhere often return on a visit to their mothers' communities during the dry season, usually bringing a piece of smoked game with them as a present. Acim clearly felt that I ought to do this too.

Once I had been adopted into Intyo's family, my relations with everyone, both men and women, became far more relaxed. But throughout my fieldwork, I made every effort to avoid giving the Panare the impression that I had come to steal one (or more) of their women. The conversation of young local criollos, both amongst themselves and when they talk to the Panare, is often punctuated with sexual references, frequently very graphic ones. To a certain extent this habit is a sign of male camaraderie, and the criollos assume that the Panare will interpret it as such. The Panare men, however, who appear to be far less preoccupied with sex than are the criollos, interpret this habit not as a sign of camaraderie but as a sign of danger. Not entirely without reason, they suspect that, if given half a chance, the criollos would make off with all their womenfolk. So that they should not think that this was my motive, I invented a 'wife' whom I had left behind in England. I thought I might invent some children too, but then decided that the Panare would probably regard a man who left his children behind for so long as totally lacking in decent human feelings. Intyo, my fictive mother, and the other women of the settlement would often ask me when my wife was going to come. I explained that she didn't want to 'because it was too far' or 'because she wasn't used to the food' (playing here on two reasons that Panare women often give for not going to Caicara). But Intyo and her friends were not at all satisfied with these excuses. 'Order her to come here,' they would say, 'we want to see her. Say you'll beat her, with the flat of a machete blade, if necessary!' And everybody would laugh at the prospect of my imaginary wife soon coming round when faced with this sort of threat. The men for their part would taunt me, 'Bring her here, make her come. She'll be getting lonely at home without any children.' The best I could do was undertake to bring her 'next time'. They reluctantly agreed to this but nevertheless relaxed their suspicions of me. By the time of my second bout of fieldwork, the men were sufficiently confident to allow me to stay at home with the women when they had all gone out to hunt or fish, or work in their gardens.[5]

Another factor that made my objectives rather more comprehensible to the Panare was that they were accustomed to the idea of systematic language learning, on account of the presence of missionaries in the valley. For approximately three years prior to my arrival, two families of missionaries had been established there and had been engaged in learning and transcribing the Panare language. Very soon after my arrival, the missionaries and I agreed on a policy of mutual non-interference. Although when the Panare asked me about them, I made my personal disagreement clear, I refrained from any direct criticism. Similarly, although the missionaries would help me with minor logistical problems, they declined to help me in any other way. Although there was always a certain strain in our relations, they were always very courteous to me. I do not believe that they ever actively prejudiced the Panare in their attitude towards me, although it would have been easy for them to have done so.

The Panare are not loquacious informants. In general, they are not

5. Dumont has given an excellent account of what it is like to do fieldwork amongst the Panare in his second book (Dumont 1978).

given to expatiation about their social and cultural institutions, even amongst themselves. Although certain individuals would recount lengthy anecdotes of their daily activities, I never heard anyone recite a myth. Nor are the Panare given to extended discussion of their kinship system. As far as I could tell, the Panare have no explicit, verbal 'social charters' for their behaviour. They do not acknowledge the existence of any supernatural or social sanctions for deviant behaviour except a rather nebulous threat that deviant individuals are likely to die. At first, I found this attitude toward their social institutions rather frustrating and attributed it to their lack of confidence in me. Later, I came to accept it as a distinctive feature of their society.

For example, in collecting genealogies, I found that some Panare claimed not to know the names of such close relations as full brothers of their fathers. One man even claimed not to know the name of his own father, saying that he had died when he, the son, was very small. During my time in the field, I played with three different explanations for this phenomenon: firstly, that the informants did not want to tell *me* these names because I was an outsider; secondly, that the informants would not tell anyone on account of a tabu on naming the dead; or thirdly, that they genuinely did not know, indicating a remarkable lack of interest in genealogical descent. During the early stages of my time in Colorado, I tended to consider the first of these three possible explanations to be the correct one. As my relations with the Panare became easier, I turned to the second as the most likely explanation. But by the end of my fieldwork, whilst not entirely abandoning the second explanation, I had come round to the conclusion that it was, after all, the third that represented the best explanation. In this, at least, both Dumont and I agreed (Dumont 1977: 92).

# CHAPTER ONE

# Past and Present

The area occupied by the modern Panare is divided into two by the new road being built from Caicara to San Juan de Manapiare. From the air, the road is an impressive sight as it zigzags across the savanna south of Caicara, hugging the tracts of high ground to avoid rainy season inundations, before disappearing into the bluish horizon beyond the Guaniamo river. Work began on the road in 1969 under the direction of the government agency the *Comisión para el Desarrollo del Sur* (CODESUR) and was conceived as a means of encouraging the colonization and economic development of the Venezuelan Amazonas. At the time, the infrastructural links between Amazonas and the rest of the country were still very poor. Roads into the area were almost non-existent. Air links were better developed but had the obvious disadvantage for heavy commercial traffic of being very expensive. Most commercial traffic therefore entered Amazonas via the Orinoco. But as a means of access into the heart of Amazonas, the river had serious shortcomings on account of the rapids around Puerto Ayacucho that made certain stretches unnavigable. Cargo had to be unloaded at a point below the rapids and then, having been transported around the rapids by road, it had to be re-loaded again further upstream (see Map 1).

The road from Caicara to San Juan was to provide a much better and more direct means of access to the heart of Amazonas than the Orinoco. It was to be the first stage in a much more ambitious project, a series of roads that would penetrate right to Cucuy at the southern tip of Venezuela and eventually link up with the Brazilian highway, the Perimetral Norte. If this road is ever completed, it is very likely to have the most serious repercussions for the Panare, attracting large numbers of new settlers to the region who will compete with them for control over local natural resources. But after an energetic start, the road-building programme became bogged down in political wrangling. Commercial interest groups in Puerto Ayacucho were strongly opposed to the new road since they feared that it would draw business away from their town, already suffering from serious unemployment. When I left the field in 1976, the road had still not reached San Juan and work on it had slowed almost to a standstill. Much more effort was being expended on the construction of another road, running

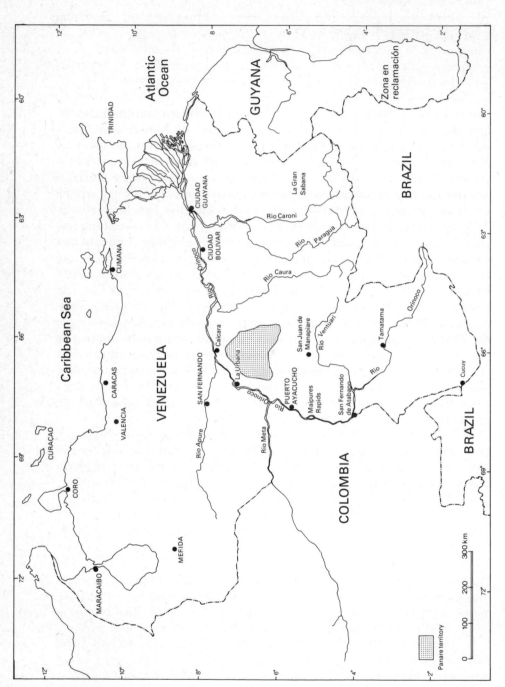

Map 1. The location of Panare territory within Venezuela

more or less parallel to the Orinoco and skirting Panare territory to the west. This suggests that, after all, it will be this route on which government will pin it hopes for the economic development of Amazonas. Whilst this road is also bound to attract new settlers to the region, it will not have such serious repercussions for the Panare as would a road running right through the heart of their territory.[1]

The history of the road to San Juan de Manapiare serves as a reminder of the fact that the fate of the Panare, like that of most other indigenous groups of contemporary lowland South America, is determined by factors that lie far beyond their control and knowledge. Viewed from within the society, these factors seem entirely fortuitous and arbitrary, like 'acts of God'. But however distinctive their way of life may be and however irrelevant the national society and its aspirations might appear as one lives amongst them from day to day, the Panare are ultimately dependent on the national society—not merely in the negative sense that remote powers within the national society decide when and how the region in which they live will be transformed by economic development schemes but also in the sense that for as long as any Panare can remember they have been dependent on the industrially-manufactured goods that they acquire through trade with the local criollos. These goods now form an integral part of their daily life and bind the Panare inextricably not only to the national but to the international economy: until recently, the machetes on which they had come to depend were made in Birmingham, Warwickshire, (they are now manufactured in Venezuela) whilst the beads they cherish for personal adornment come from Italy and Czechoslovakia. In exchange for these goods many Panare used to trade sarrapia a forest fruit which was exported to developed industrial nations and used in the manufacture of toiletries and cigarettes;[2] when the market for

1. It is somewhat ironic, given the way in which the Caicara–San Juan road was hailed as a brave new venture, that it follows very closely the route taken by an eighteenth-century Spanish expedition led by one Miguel Sanchez. The Spaniards wanted to find an overland route to the Ventuari along which to drive cattle. They hoped to be able to supply San Fernando de Atabapo in this way, presumably because they had found the Orinoco unsuitable for this purpose for the same reasons that it is unsuitable for heavy commercial traffic today. Details of the expedition come down to us through the Jesuit chronicler Gilij. He does not give an exact date for the expedition but the expeditionaries stayed at his mission at La Encaramada, a few miles downstream from the present site of Caicara, so it must have taken place some time during Gilij's residence there from 1749 to 1767 (when the Jesuits were expelled from the Spanish Empire). The fate of the eighteenth-century expedition does not represent an encouraging precedent for the present venture: although the expedition reached its goal, San Fernando, most of the cattle the expeditionaries took with them, and many of the men, including Sanchez the leader, died on route or soon after arrival (Gilij 1965, I: 128–31).

this product collapsed, many Panare turned instead to producing decorative baskets that are sold to tourists and visitors from abroad in the gift shops of Caracas and other large urban centres of Venezuela. In short, the Panare as they are today are the precipitate of the history of the colonization of the corner of Guiana where they live and of the relations they have maintained with the colonizers in order to acquire industrially manufactured goods. One cannot therefore begin to understand their present situation without reference to that history. [3]

The first Hispanic settlers arrived in the middle Orinoco region in the seventeenth century. In the absence of written records or archaeological material, the only means available for reconstructing the history of the Panare in earlier periods is speculation on the basis of comparative linguistic data. All modern authorities agree that the Panare language belongs to the Carib family; and if Durbin's theories about the migration of Carib-speakers is correct, the modern Panare live close to the homeland of the original proto-Carib language (Durbin 1977 : 35). However, although there is no doubt that Panare is a Carib language, it manifests certain lexical peculiarities that suggest that it may have been influenced at some stage by a non-Carib language. What this language was and when it influenced the Panare, it has so far been impossible to establish. It does not however appear to be any of the extant non-Carib languages spoken in the immediate vicinity of Panare territory.

As far as the Panare are concerned, their history began when the first people emerged from a mountain at the headwaters of the Cuchivero. But although most modern Panare are aware of this belief, very few can recount any details of the event. The most elaborate account I heard was that of an elderly man of the community of Manteco on the middle reaches of the Cuchivero. According to this informant, all Panare, as well as all criollos and all animals, once lived inside a large mountain overlooking the headwaters of the Cuchivero. For some unspecified reason, the mountain broke open and most of

2. The two species that were mainly sought after in Venezuela were *Dipteryx odorata* (Aubl) *Willd* and *Dipteryx punctata* (Blake) *Amsh*. The beans of this fruit were cured for several days in barrels of strong rum or alcohol, a process which produced a heavy crystalline coumarin deposit on the beans. It is this coumarin that accounts for the characteristic odour and flavour of the bean. In addition to being used in the manufacture of tobacco and toiletries, sarrapia beans were also used in confectionery, liqueurs and as a substitute for vanilla in ice cream and other products. In English, it is often known by the term 'tonka bean'. (See Purseglove, 1974: 258–63; Schnee 1973: 657–8).

3. Throughout this book, unless otherwise stated, I use the term 'Guiana' in its most general sense, i.e. to identify the 'island' formed by the Atlantic Ocean, the Orinoco, the Casiquiare Canal, the Negro and the Amazon.

the occupants emerged. Many criollos came out, but only two Panare, one of whom was called *marioka*. It is for this reason, the informant explained, that there are so many criollos today and so few Panare. He also added that some humans and some animals still remain inside the mountain and that he personally had visited the site of the mountain and had heard the sound of lowing cattle coming from inside. This mythological fragment evidently reflects the recent historical experience of the Panare, appropriately for a society that has been in contact with the criollos for such a long period of time. But although the original myth may have been modified, the localization of the site of origin of the Panare people at the headwaters of the Cuchivero fits well with the indirect evidence that can be gleaned from early documentary sources.

The earliest reference in the historical ethnographic literature to a group by the name 'Panare' is by Codazzi in his *Geografía* published in 1841. There are no references to a group by the name of *e'nyëpa* or any similar name in the literature until the anthropological works of the last decade. Codazzi mentions the Panare on four separate occasions, locating them on the upper Cuchivero and on the Mato river, a left-bank tributary of the Caura that springs in the mountain ridge over-looking the right bank of the Cuchivero. The Panare also appear on the Mato in Richard Schomburgk's map published in 1846, although it is quite possible that Schomburgk merely derived his information from Codazzi (Codazzi 1940, II : 17, 25, 49-50; Grant 1898 : 40).

Although it seems reasonable to suppose that the Panare existed as an identifiable group prior to the 1840s, there is no mention of them in the work of Gilij, the author who was best informed about the middle Orinoco region in the eighteenth century.[4] Gilij's account of the region and its inhabitants is copious, and with regard to the parts of it he knew personally, generally reliable. But in listing the indigenous groups who inhabited the Cuchivero at that time, he does not mention a group by the name of Panare. One can think of various reasons why Gilij should have omitted to mention the Panare—he may not have

---

4. I am indebted to Professor Johannes Wilbert for looking through his copies of archival materials from Seville, unfortunately in vain, for references to a group by the name of 'Panare'. The Panare are mentioned by none of the Jesuit chroniclers (cf. Del Rey Fajardo 1971). Nor are they mentioned in the diary of Padre Bueno, the Franciscan missionary in La Urbana from 1801 to 1804 who was visited by Humboldt, himself yet another author who fails to mention the Panare (cf. Bueno 1933; Humboldt 1942). Since the Jesuits and the last two authors are generally the best informed about the Cuchivero–Suapure region for the period prior to that of Codazzi, I suspect that any further ferreting in the ethnohistorical literature for references to the Panare is bound to be fruitless.

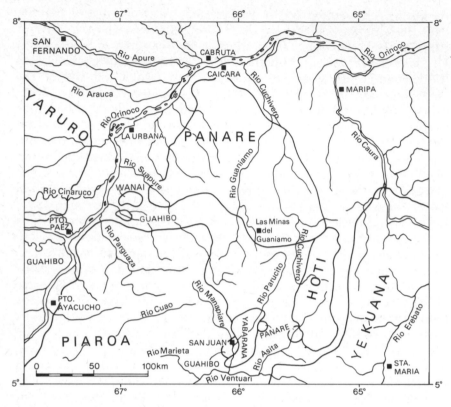

Map 2. The location of the Panare relative to neighbouring indigenous groups

known about them, they may have lived elsewhere, he may have forgotten about them—but the most likely is that they are recorded in the list of groups inhabiting the Cuchivero under another name. Of the groups mentioned in the list, those most likely to be forbears of the modern Panare are the Aquerecoto, the Oye and the Payuro, all located on the middle or upper Cuchivero, the area the modern Panare consider to be their ancestral homeland, and all belonging to the Carib language family (Gilij 1965, I : 131-2; III : 174). But apart from this linguistic affiliation and their geographical location, there is no further evidence for associating the Aquerecoto with the ancestors of the modern Panare. The only further evidence that Gilij provides for identifying the Payuro with the Panare are three Payuro words, which although resembling their Panare equivalents, are no more similar than one would expect of words from two neighbouring languages of the same language family (Gilij 1965, III : 172).

Gilij's chronicle provides better evidence for associating the Panare with the Oye. Gilij speaks highly of the Oye and singles them out as the only group on the Cuchivero that was not 'insolent and ferocious'. He explains however that his opinion of them was formed not so much from personal contact as from the account he was given of them by the Tamanaco who lived in his mission. The Tamanaco, he says, always assured him of the Oye's 'friendly disposition', a view he found to be confirmed by his acquaintance with a handful of Oye who visited his mission in person. Elsewhere Gilij informs us that the Tamanaco word for 'friend' was *panari* and given that the Tamanaco regarded the Oye as friendly, it is possible that they referred to the Oye by this name (Gilij 1965, I : 61; III : 136, 303). In the course of colonization, the Spaniards borrowed many indigenous words to describe Guianese phenomena that were new to them; and the Tamanaco, being one of the indigenous groups of the Orinoco that were in closest contact with the Spaniards, were one of the sources of these loan-words. Thus it is not unreasonable to suggest that the Spaniards came to adopt the Tamanaco word *panari* as the name to be applied to the group whom Gilij knew as the Oye. Some confirmation for this suggestion is to be found in the fact that the modern Ye'kuana, the Panare's neighbours to the east, call the Panare *eyei* (Villalón 1978 : 7). [5]

5. There is another, though less likely, origin for the name 'Panare' which is worth recounting for its own intrinsic historical interest. Like the Tamanaco, the Kariña word for 'friend' is *panari* (Gilij 1965, II: 57). Today, the Kariña, known as 'Caribs' in the Jesuit chronicles, have no contact with the Panare but it is possible that in the eighteenth century they did have. In Gilij's time, the Kariña lived between the mouth of the Caura and the Orinoco delta, and used to raid the Arawak-speaking Maipure on the Ventuari for slaves which they took back and sold to Dutch and French slavers operating on the lower reaches of the Orinoco. At first, they used to gain access to the Ventuari *via* the Orinoco but from the 1740s onwards this way became blocked to them due to the presence in the middle Orinoco of a number of Spanish garrisons and the Guipunave, allied to the Spanish, whom the Kariña feared greatly (Del Rey Fajardo 1971: 56; Gilij 1965, I: 62). Rather than give up the slave trade, the Kariña used another route to penetrate the Ventuari, described with great precision by Gilij on the basis of an account given to him by one Francisco Veniamari, a Tamanaco who had lived for many years with the Kariña (Gilij 1965, I: 135). This description allows one to reconstruct this route with reasonable confidence, and it is plotted on Map 3. As the map shows, the slave route would have passed through or very close to the traditional Panare homeland in the upper Cuchivero basin. Although Gilij attributes the small populations of the indigenous groups living on the Cuchivero in his time to the depredations of the Kariña, the principal targets of these long-range trips were the Maipure of the Ventuari (Gilij 1965, I: 131, 133). This being the case, it is possible that the Kariña refrained from raiding the inhabitants of the upper Cuchivero and preferred to establish friendly relations with them in order to ensure a safe passage through their territory. In these circumstances, the Kariña would have referred to the inhabitants of the upper Cuchivero as *panari*. Subsequently the inhabitants of the upper reaches of the Cuchivero could have become generally known by this name.

The grounds for associating the Oye of Gilij's chronicle with the forbears of the modern Panare are admittedly no more than circumstantial. But this circumstantial evidence, the Panare's own oral tradition and the first unambiguous reference to the Panare by Codazzi all point to the upper Cuchivero as their ancestral homeland. It appears to have been only since Codazzi's time that the Panare began to expand out of this region to occupy their present territory, which stretches as far north as the banks of the Orinoco and as far west as the middle reaches of the Suapure. In recent years, one small group of Panare has migrated south of the area they traditionally occupied and has settled on two small tributaries of the Ventuari. By combining evidence from the ethnographic literature with the accounts of elderly informants, both criollo and Panare, it is possible to reconstruct the history of this expansion.

In expanding out of the upper Cuchivero basin, the Panare appear to have split into two branches after crossing the Guaniamo. One branch followed the Guaniamo north-eastward and settled in the mountains to the west of the criollo village of El Tigre. The other branch expanded westward, settling in the serranía, or mountain ridge, that separates the Guaniamo from the Orinoco floodplain. This branch appears to have split into two once again, one group settling to the north in the so-called Serranía de Chaviripa, close to the criollo settlement of Mundo Nuevo and the other continuing further west to settle in the Serranía de la Cerbatana overlooking the criollo village of Túriba (see Map 3). Not all Panare took part in this migration, and a certain proportion of the population still lives to the south of the Guaniamo.

This diffusion appears to have been completed by the early years of the present century. The earliest reference to the Panare north of Guaniamo is to be found in Chaffanjon's account of his travels in the region. In 1885, this author visited the criollo village of Cuchivero on the right bank of the lower reaches of the river of the same name. He reports that the Panare used to bring their agricultural produce to the village for exchange with the criollos. Chaffanjon is often an unreliable source of information, but this reference bears credence since it is indirectly corroborated by the testimony of the oldest living criollos of the village of El Tigre. These informants, some of whom are in their seventies and have lived in El Tigre all their lives, say that the Panare have 'always' lived in the countryside around the village. They could not recall their fathers telling them of the time when the Panare first arrived in the region. This suggests that the Panare were well established around El Tigre by the turn of the century. Thus it is quite feasible that fifteen years earlier when Chaffanjon was there the

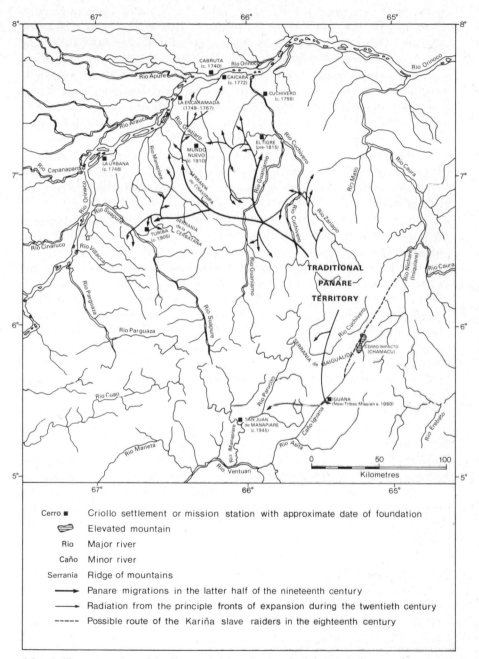

Map 3. The expansion of the Panare in the nineteenth and twentieth centuries

Panare were already making visits to the criollo village of Cuchivero as he claims. [6]

The earliest reference in the literature to a group of Panare inhabiting the mountain ridge that separates the Guaniamo from the Orinoco floodplains is in a book by Bartolomé Tavera Acosta. This author reproduces a short and badly-transcribed vocabulary that he had had collected for him in 1921 'amongst the Indians living in the Colorado mountain, in the jurisdiction of La Urbana'. Tavera Acosta explains that he had been unable to go to the region himself and had had the vocabulary collected by a worthy of La Urbana because he was afraid that the Panare might become extinct at any moment. At that time, he claims, there were only 'three or four' families living a nomadic existence on the 'Uainiamu' (presumably the Guaniamo) and the other small tributaries of the Cuchivero (Tavera Acosta 1930 : 173 – 6). The 'Colorado mountain' to which Tavera Acosta refers is most probably a reference to the section of the Serranía de la Cerbatana from which the Colorado river flows into the valley where I spent most of my time in the field. According to the local criollos, the Panare settled in this valley some time before 1921, more or less contemporaneously with the foundation of the village of Túriba in 1905. The small number of Panare families that Tavera Acosta claims existed in 1921 probably includes only those that had settled in the Serranía de la Cerbatana. Moreover, he was clearly wrong in his pessimistic prognosis for the Panare since there are now 44 conjugal families living in the valley of Colorado, numbering a total of 226 people.

The first specific reference in the ethnographic literature to groups of Panare settled further to the north in the Serraní de Chaviripa dates from 1944 (Lopez Ramírez 1944 : 254-255). However an old Panare of the community of El Pajal, now probably in his seventies, claims that he lived in the Serranía de Chaviripa as a boy and used to visit the criollo hamlet of Mundo Nuevo to trade with the criollos. This suggests that the Panare established themselves in the Serranía de Chaviripa more or less at the same time as they populated the Serranía de la Cerbatana.

There appear to have been both internal and external reasons for the Panare expansion. An old man of the Mata Brava community explained to me that his father had migrated from the region of the Guaniamo river to the Colorado valley in order to get away from other Panare who were constantly fighting with one another. He was unable

6. Chaffanjon 1889: 73. There are two other references to the Panare in Chaffanjon's book, but for reasons too lengthy to go into here, these do not bear credence (1889: 116, 168).

to give any reason for this warfare apart from the fact that in former times the Panare were *wasupe*, fierce. Whatever the internal reasons for the migration, the Panare expansion also appears to have been motivated by a desire to get closer to the criollo population, and hence to the source of steel tools and other goods, since all three fronts of Panare expansion converged upon criollo settlements: Túriba in the west, Mundo Nuevo in the north and El Tigre in the east. The Panare expansion was no doubt facilitated by the disappearance of the groups that formerly occupied the area between the Guaniamo and the Orinoco, notably the Tamanaco and the Pareca. These groups appear to have become extinct during the latter half of the nineteenth century or to have retreated to the headwaters of the Suapure, thereby leaving a vacuum for the Panare to move into Codazzi 1940, II : 17).[7]

The present distribution of Panare communities is the product of radiation from the nineteenth-century fronts of migration and from the nucleus of the Panare population that remained to the south of the Guaniamo (see Map 3). As one might expect, given the relatively recent date of this dispersal, there is very little cultural variation in the modern Panare population. As one proceeds from north-west to south-east, one encounters a progressive dialect variation, but this is not sufficient to prevent mutual comprehension between individuals from opposite ends of Panare territory.[8] There is also a number of small differences in kinship terminology: the terminology used by the Panare living south of the Guaniamo river involves a greater number of terms used exclusively for address and does not include certain reference terms used by the Panare of the northwestern sector. The terminology of the Panare of the eastern sector appears to be slightly different again. I am insufficiently familiar with the eastern and southern groups to say whether these terminological differences have any practical consequences in terms of marriage patterns or other aspects of the kinship system. I suspect not, but this topic merits further investigation.

7. See Henley 1975 for further details of the history of the indigenous groups of this region.

8. Some Panare claim that they are unable to understand the speech of Panare from communities located a long way from their own. However I put this claim down to regional chauvinism rather than to a genuine inability to understand. Although obviously far less competent than any Panare in the language, I was able to understand the speech of informants from all regions of Panare territory. Furthermore, I understand from the missionaries of the New Tribes Mission that a Panare man from Colorado whom they took on a visit to Caño Iguana, at the opposite extreme of Panare territory, was capable of engaging in long conversations with his hosts.

Plate 2.   A man from the settlement at Tiro Loco (Southern Panare territory) about to set out on a peccary hunt with his lance and his hunting dogs.

Variation in styles of dress from one region to another is similarly minor. All over Panare territory, except in the areas closest to Caicara, where criollo styles have been adopted, a man will wear a bright red loincloth, dyed with onoto, rectangular in shape with a tassle at each corner. It is passed between the legs and held up by a belt. It is doubled over the belt at the front, and when there is no danger that it will drag on the ground, it is allowed to hang down at the back so that the tassles reach to the level of the back of the knees. Otherwise, the loincloth is tucked up into the belt at the back as well, in such a way as to form a pouch in which a knife, a box of matches and other small articles may be carried. Around the lower leg, above and below the calf, Panare men often wear gaiters of human hair. (In western Panare territory, they shave their heads once a year, as a prophylactic measure against lice. This shaven hair is subsequently twisted into twine for the gaiters by the women.)

The tassles on the loincloths of the western Panare are larger and more flamboyant than in the southern and eastern groups and their gaiters are wider. All Panare men wear beads, but whereas the western Panare wear them only in the form of armbands around their biceps, the men of the other areas wear them either criss-crossed bandolier-fashion across the torso, or more rarely in the form of wristbands. In western Panare territory, men wear only blue and white beads: elsewhere, they are less choosy. Young men throughout Panare territory also wear red cotton bandoliers, fringed with tassles that hang just below the ribs; as in the case of loincloths, the western Panare's tassles are larger. Western Panare men wear their hair in characteristic Amerindian fashion, long at the back with a fringe cut across the forehead. In other parts, men wear their hair much shorter, probably in imitation of criollo fashion.

Women's styles of dress and body adornment vary less as one passes from one region to another within Panare territory. Like men, women wear bright red loincloths, but theirs are much smaller, barely covering the pubis in front and the natal cleft behind. This scant garment is held up by a thin string around the waist, from which two tassles hang down in the rear, one tassle resting on each buttock. These tassles are also more flamboyant in western Panare territory than elsewhere. Around their necks, all Panare women wear beads (though only blue and white ones in western Panare territory); unmarried girls wear them bandolier-fashion whilst older women wear them in the form of necklaces. Panare women often wear large quantities of beads, representing a considerable economic investment in trade with the criollos (up to £50 in some cases). All Panare women, regardless of area, cut their hair in the Amerindian style and all women sometimes wear hair gaiters, though these are rarely as wide as those of the men. Finally, most Panare women own a piece of cloth, also acquired through trade with the criollos, which they use to wrap around themselves when non-Panare visitors arrive in their settlements or when they go on a visit to a criollo homestead.

The only other significant regionally variable cultural feature that I noted concerned ceremonial activities. The Panare living to the south of the Guaniamo carry out a ceremony in connection with female puberty which the groups north of this river do not. On the other hand, the groups north of the Guaniamo carry out a more elaborate series of rituals in connection with male initiation. There are also certain differences in the funeral ceremonies of the two sectors of Panare territory. But none of these regionally variable features is important enough to define cultural subdivisions within the Panare population, and they should be considered as no more than variations on an essentially uniform cultural theme.

The Panare can be readily identified as a unitary ethnic group on the basis of a common language and culture shared by all members. Yet from a sociological point of view their society is highly atomistic. They recognise no descent groups nor any ego-focus corporate kin groups. They recognize neither age grades nor age sets. In fact, the only social group to which a Panare speaker might refer is the group of people who inhabit the same settlement site. Such a group may be referred to by the name of their settlement (if it has one, for not all do) with the suffix -mënë added, meaning 'the one(s) of'. Alternatively, they may be referred to by a personal name with the addition of the suffix -piyaka, which in this context means 'of the same kind as'. The personal name used will be that of a relative of the speaker or of a headman or some other senior man living in the settlement. By definition, these names refer only to particular groups and they are very rarely standardized. To the best of my knowledge, the Panare language does not permit one to talk about a residential group in the abstract.[9]

A Panare settlement typically consists of about forty people. This residential group is the largest group that acts collectively in everyday life in Panare society; only on certain ceremonial occasions does a

9. Dumont (1978: 71 and *passim*) uses the Panare term *tapatakyen* as an abstract category to refer to the 'residential group . . . that is, the members of the local group'. But, strictly speaking, this term is not a noun denoting a social group as such but rather an adjective describing a person or persons (or any living entity including animals and spirits) who have a home of some sort. One can also refer to a residential group by adjoining the suffix *—makun* to the name of a member thereof. However, this usage implies that the other members of the group are subservient to the person named and it is therefore regarded as somewhat belittling.

Plate 3. Houses of the 'ship's hull' variety in the Colorado valley, December 1980.

larger group ever act in concert. A settlement is usually located either in a clearing in the forest or at a point where the forest meets a stretch of savanna. Most settlement sites contain one or two large collective residential houses and a number of smaller structures that are used for cooking by the women of the group. The residential houses are of two basic forms. The most common form has a rectangular floor plan and when viewed longitudinally, an A-shape elevation. It is thatched with one or more of four types of palm leaf, normally reaching right to the ground on both sides of the house. One or both ends of the house may be closed by bays, through which one enters by means of a small opening about 1.25 m high. When a house has a bay at each end, it resembles a ship's hull, and is cool and dark inside since there are no windows of any kind. The other type of house form is simply conical. Like the ship's hull variety, the conical house form has palm thatch reaching to the ground on all sides, no windows and only the smallest of entrances. The collective houses that I encountered in 1975–6 varied considerably in size: the largest of the ship's hull form had a floor plan of approximately 12m by 15m and was 10m high, whilst the largest of the conical variety had a diameter of approximately 25m across the floor and was about 12m high. At the other end of the scale, the smallest houses with a rectangular floor plan were no more than 3m by 4m and 3m high, whilst the smallest conical house I saw was only 5m high and about 7m in diameter. In the settlements located close to centres of criollo population, there is a tendency for the place of the large collective houses to be taken by a number of smaller dwellings, each housing no more than one or two conjugal families. In these settlements, the houses are often built in the criollo style with mud walls, small porches and zinc roofs.

A settlement group is recruited on the basis of kinship ties, but in everyday life it is primarily as an economic group that it acts collectively. This collective economic behaviour takes place principally in the sphere of distribution and consumption. In the great majority of subsistence activities, a conjugal family goes about producing food independently, but under normal circumstances contributes the greater part of its daily product to a food pool that is consumed collectively in the form of two communal meals, one for men, the other for women and children. Every member of the settlement group, regardless of his or her contribution to the food pool, has a right to participate in these daily communal meals, which usually take place at dusk.

But although a settlement group has a practical function in Panare society as the largest collective economic unit, it is often difficult to define its social boundaries. Panare settlements are not evenly distributed over the area they occupy, and one frequently encounters two or more settlements within a few minutes' walk of one another. In some places, one finds clusters of as many as ten settlements within a radius of an hour's walk. Such is the case for example in the Colorado valley, where this clustering effect is the consequence of the presence of a New Tribes Mission station established in 1972. There is another large cluster of settlements around the criollo village of El Tigre. Although such closely-situated settlement groups may operate as separate economic entities there is a constant passage of conjugal families between them throughout most of the year. Furthermore, on the comparatively rare occasions when the Panare engage in collective subsistence ventures, such as fish-poisoning or a collective hunt, it is common for the members of closely-situated settlement groups to collaborate. Generally speaking, however, each group takes the meat that it has captured back to its own settlement site for distribution and consumption. At the height of the dry season, on the other hand, it is not unusual for two or more settlement groups to become a single economic entity, not merely in the sphere of production but in the sphere of distribution and consumption as well. At this time of year, it becomes hot and stuffy in the palm thatch houses, and it is the Panare's habit to move out and sling their hammocks in the open air of the forest. On these occasions, the members of closely-situated settlement groups often set up camp together and pool the food they produce.

Thus although the settlement group forms the largest collective group of everyday life, it is rather artificial for simple descriptive purposes to distinguish between all the various settlement groups one finds in a cluster, since the members of these groups are in almost daily social contact with one another. Yet it is equally artificial to distinguish between a cluster of settlements and a single settlement that remains relatively isolated from others of its kind. As we shall see in Chapter 5, it often occurs that some members of an isolated settlement group will break off from the main group and build themselves another house at a point that is sufficiently distant for them to act as an independent economic unit but sufficiently close to remain in regular social contact with the parent group. Thus a settlement group that is not a cluster at any given moment in time may well become one at some point in the future. For these reasons, I have used the catch-all term 'community' to describe all Panare social conglomerations that remain isolated by a distance of approximately half a day's walk from another, regardless of the number of discrete settlement groups this conglomeration embraces.

At the time that I carried out my fieldwork, I estimate there to have been approximately 1700 Panare distributed between 38 communities. These communities are listed in Table 1 with estimates of the population of each. The wide variation in size of these estimates is a function of the way I have used the term 'community' of any social conglomeration without regard to the number of settlement groups it includes. Thus Colorado, the largest community with 226 people, embraces ten independent settlement groups, whilst most of the communites in the Table involve no more than one or two. Of the total of thirty-eight extant communities, I was able to visit at least one settlement site or dry season camp-site of twenty-five. These communities are marked with an asterisk in the penultimate column of the Table. Information concerning the communities I did not visit myself came from a number of secondhand sources: other anthropologists, missionaries, Panare, local criollos. Although these sources are probably reliable as to the existence and geographical location of communities, the population estimates they gave are less trustworthy. Even the data I collected myself are of variable quality. For this reason, I have classified the population estimates in the Table into five 'levels of confidence', each involving a different estimate margin of error. The basis on which these levels of confidence were defined is explained in Appendix 2.

The geographical location of all communities extant at the time of my field work is shown in Map 4. The geographical distribution of communities has no doubt changed considerably since the data were collected, since a settlement site usually lasts no more than three or four years. Since these changes of settlement site are often the occasion for a change in residential associations, the size of these communities is bound to have changed considerably as well. (This aspect of Panare residential organization will be discussed in greater detail in Chapter 5.) In the map, all sites are identified by criollo names since the Panare generally do not give their own names to their settlement sites, a fact which could be considered as an apt expression of their impermanance. But then they are not much given to naming the features of the natural environment either. Over the years, certain well-known spots acquire names that most Panare would recognize, and settlements located close to these spots will be referred to by the same name. Such is the case with the spot known as *kuruwata* in the Colorado valley. This is the name given to an extensive stand of coroba palms (*Jessenia sp.*) and is composed of the Panare word for coroba palm, which is *kuruwa* and the suffix -*ta* which in this context means 'the place where'. But settlement sites with Panare names are exceptions to the general rule, and when referring to a settlement site amongst themselves the Panare will do so by means of identifying a relative in the settlement in question. Thus if a man has a son called To'se in a particular settlement group, he will refer to the site of his settlement as *To'sewo'ya*, literally 'the place where To'se lives'. This way of referring to settlement sites can sometimes lead to confusion since *To'sewo'ya* can denote not only the settlement in which To'se normally resides but also the place where To'se happens to be at the time of speaking. If To'se happens to be temporarily camped out in the forest, the term *To'sewo'ya* could well refer to his campsite and not to the settlement where he is normally resident. I found that if one wanted to avoid unnecessary journeys it was essential to make sure exactly what such terms denoted. One way of clarifying the issue was to refer to the terms used by criollos, who, in sharp contrast to the Panare, are disposed to name every nook and cranny of the topography, regardless of whether they actually inhabit them or not. It is these criollo names that are used to identify Panare communities in Map 4.

Criollo names are used in the Table for the same reason. The names that appear in parentheses are either alternatives that are frequently used either by the Panare or by the criollos or they are the names given to secondary settlement sites or campsites. Generally speaking however, for reasons of space, I have indicated each community by a single triangle on the map. That is, I have made no attempt to represent every discrete settlement group. There are two exceptions to this procedure, both involving communities with settlement sites that

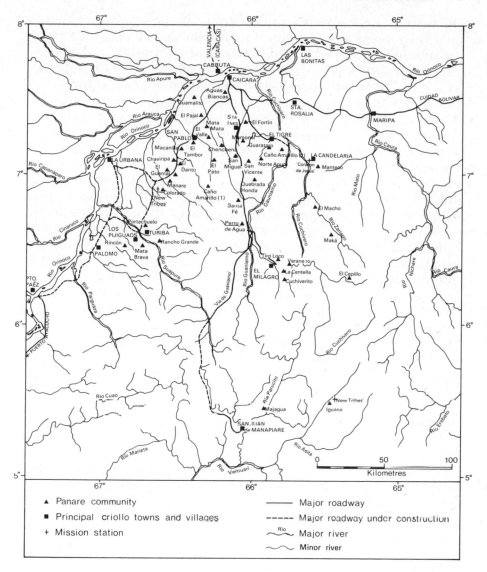

Map 4. The present distribution of the Panare

during the period 1975 – 6 were situated at abnormally large distances from one another. The first of these involves the community that until May 1976 was located at El Tambor (approximately 7° 15′ N, 66° 25′ W). At this time, at the behest of the Archbishop of Cuidad Bolivar, the whole community was moved by truck to a site much further to the south, Perro de Agua (approximately 6° 40′ N, 66° 05′ W). The background to this move will be discussed in detail in Chapter 7. The other exception involves the community whose principal settlement site at this time was at Caño Amarillo (approximately 6° N, 66° 15 W).[1] This community had a second settlement site close to Caicara at Aguas Blancas, where the member of the group would stay whilst they were on visits to the town. I have subsequently heard that since I left, this group has also moved south to the area around Perro de Agua.

In order to aid in the identification of communities, the names of prominent men in most of the communities are given in the Table. Here too it is convenient to give Spanish names since the range of possible names in Spanish is greater.[10] The Panare names of these individuals , if known, are given in parentheses. These individuals are often referred to as *capitanes* by the local criollo population. The political authority of *capitanes* is often over-estimated by the criollos who speak of such men as having the rest of their communities '*a su mando*': literally, 'at their command'. However, as we shall see in Chapter 5, the formal political authority of such men is very limited, if it is recognized at all by the members of their own community.

In the Table, the thirty-eight extant Panare communities are classified into three regional populations defined on the basis of the historical reconstruction of Panare migrations offered above: the contingent of the population that has remained to the south of the Guaniamo is referred to as the Southern Panare; that descended from the population that settled in the Serranía de la Cerbatana and the Serranía Chaviripa has been classified as the Western Panare, whilst those who are descended from the population that settled around El Tigre are classified as the Eastern Panare. At the present time, there are no known genealogical links between the Southern Panare and the other two regional populations. The genealogical break between the Eastern and Western groups is not so absolute but there are very few cases of intermarriage between them. It should be emphasized

10. The Panare have only six personal names for adult men (Nahtë, Tëna, Manyën, Puka, To'se, Wënye) and four for adult women (Acim, Intyo, Atun, Matë). There is however a long list of children's names, some of which are quasi-descriptive. Despite the paucity of adult names, there is very little confusion in practice since kinship terms, teknonyms, and nicknames are frequently substituted, both in reference and address. The fact that the Panare have so few adult personal names is obviously consistent with their reluctance to give names either to geographical sites or social groups. However I must confess that I have no ready explanation for this phenomenon. Dumont (1974c, 1977) has analyzed naming among the Panare from a structuralist viewpoint, but I am not entirely convinced by his arguments, partly because his data are shaky. This is clearly a topic that deserves more attention than I have so far been able to give it.

however that these 'regional populations' are merely a descriptive device and do not correspond to any association of communities to which the Panare themselves would give linguistic recognition.

The data available on the Panare population are not sufficient to allow one to draw any incontrovertible conclusions about demographic trends. Previous estimates are not precise nor detailed enough to permit comparison with my own estimate. Nor is it possible to assess demographic trends on the basis of the data I collected myself, since these did not include information that would allow one to calculate rates of natality and mortality with any degree of precision. The data I collected in Colorado were sufficient only to identify the distribution of the population of the valley by age. These data are presented in the form of Figure 1. The manner in which the ages of the individuals in the sample were calculated is explained in Appendix 2.

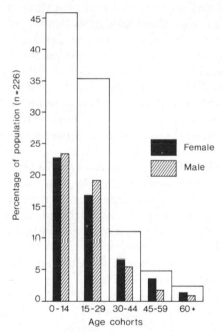

Figure 1. The age structure of the Colorado Panare

In the absence of quantitative data, one is obliged to rely mostly on the testimony of informants. Taking this testimony at face value, it would appear that the Panare population, considered as a whole, is on the increase. The criollos living in the vicinity of Colorado claim that when the Panare first settled in the valley around the turn of the century there were only 'six or seven families' living there. When the local criollos speak of 'families' they mean conjugal families and, as already noted, at the present time there are forty-four conjugal families in the Colorado valley. Although some families have moved into the valley during the present century, more families have migrated out of the valley than have migrated into it. All this suggests that the population of the valley is on the increase, a conclusion that is not incompatible with the age structure of the population as shown in Figure 1. It also fits with the presence of several very large families in the valley: there are fifteen women in the valley with six or more children each and six men, alive or recently dead, who have more than ten children by various wives. One of these men, the *capitán*, has twenty-one children by three wives and his father, who died some time ago, now has over eighty living grandchildren either in Colorado or in neighbouring communites.

The fact that the Panare of the Colorado valley appear to be on the increase would suggest that this segment of the Panare population at least has built up some immunity over the period of contact to the diseases introduced by the criollos in the course of colonization. Although it was my impression that the Panare of Colorado were more severely affected by the common cold and diseases such as malaria and measles than the local criollo population, they have not suffered, in the period covered by living memory, from a sudden and drastic population decline of the kind registered in many lowland South American groups following an epidemic of introduced diseases. If the Panare ever did suffer decimation by disease, this must have occurred in the early years of contact, a century or more ago. In showing a tendency now to increase, the population of Colorado conforms with a pattern frequently encountered in Amerindian groups that have managed to survive the first impact of introduced diseases. [11]

It still remains to be considered to what extent the Colorado population can be taken as representative of the Panare as a whole. They number 226 individuals, representing 26.7 per cent of the estimated Western regional population and 13.2 per cent of the estimated total Panare population. But beyond this simple statistical measure, it is difficult to say how representative the Colorado Panare are. In the Western Panare region generally, informants tended to agree that there were more Panare now than there had been in the past. The

11. It is not always the case that the indigenous groups that survive the initial impact of introduced diseases recuperate their numbers. In fact, the reaction of indigenous populations to introduced diseases has been very variable and the determinants of this reaction are not well understood (see Ribeiro 1970: 287 ff).

same was true of informants in the Eastern Panare region. This suggests that, like the Colorado Panare, the remainder of the population living north of the Guaniamo river has built up some immunity to criollo diseases. On the other hand, the data available on the Southern Panare suggest that if this regional population is growing at all, it is growing at a slower rate than the Colorado population. I did not record any informants' views about the demographic trends in the Southern Panare population but the genealogical data collected in six Southern Panare communities, which represent just over half the estimated population of this region, indicate that the ratio of children to parents in the conjugal families is generally lower than it is in Colorado.

In the absence of more complete data, it is difficult to account for this apparent difference in demographic trends. One of the reasons may be the degree of contact with the criollos that the various regional populations have sustained. Although the Southern Panare population has been in contact with criollos since the early years of this century, this contact has never been as intense as it has been further north in Panare territory. But in recent years, Southern Panare territory has been invaded by a large number of individuals both from other parts of the country and from abroad. This influx is mostly accounted for by the people who have come to work in the newly-opened diamond mines situated just south of the Guaniamo and around which four of the six Southern Panare communities in which genealogical data were collected are currently situated. It is quite probable that this population has introduced diseases against which the local Panare have no biological defence and which, by producing a higher mortality rate, would therefore account for the apparent difference in growth rate between the Southern Panare and the two more northerly regional populations.[12]

At the present time, the contact that the Panare maintain with other indigenous groups is no more than sporadic. The area lying between the Ventuari and the upper reaches of the Cuchivero and the Guaniamo is often identified as the territory of little known and isolated groups. This area may once have been inhabited by such groups, but they must either have become extinct or have migrated out of the area; they no longer live there now. The only groups that occupy this region today, other than the Panare themselves, are the

12. The biological effects of these diamond mines on the local Panare populations is further discussed in Chapter 7 when the general social and economic effects of the mines are dealt with.

Hoti and one or two acculturated communities of Piaroa and Yabarana (see Map 2).[13]

The most southerly Panare communities make occasional trading expeditions to the Hoti, whom they refer to as *onwa*. In the past, the Panare used to act as intermediaries between the Hoti and the criollo settlements on the Cuchivero. They would acquire items such as steel tools, cloths, beads, aluminium pots and dogs, and take them south to Hoti territory where they would exchange them for blowguns. Although the Hoti and the Panare are very similar in their dress and technology, and there have been one or two isolated cases of marriage between them in the recent past, they speak very different languages. The Hoti language has not been classified as a member of any major language family but it seems unlikely that it is Carib (M. Durbin, personal communication, 1976). Certainly it is incomprehensible to the Panare. Although the Panare fear the Hoti on account of their reputation as shamans, they treat them in the most imperious and authoritarian manner.[14] Even when they are in Hoti settlements they order the Hoti around and help themselves to local natural resources. The Hoti for their part seem ready to adopt this subordinate role whenever the Panare are present.

Until very recently, the Panare represented one of the very few channels of contact that the Hoti maintained with the criollo world. Another was the mixed Yabarana – Piaroa community at Majagua, just north of San Juan de Manapiare, at the junction of the Parucito and Majagua rivers (see Map 4). But from 1969 this began to change following the establishment of a New Tribes Mission station on the Caño Iguana in the southern sector of the area occupied by the Hoti. This station soon became an alternative source of goods for the southernmost Hoti, thereby ending their dependence on the community of Majagua. Not long afterwards, in 1974, a group of Panare from the Upper Cuchivero region decided to make the trip south to the new mission station. Once installed there, they began to subject the Hoti to various abuses including stealing food from their gardens

13. It has commonly been asserted that the headwaters of the Cuchivero is the location of a group called 'Mapoyo'. This group is sometimes identified with another group of the same name, living between the Suapure and Villacoa rivers further to the west on the banks of the Orinoco. However the so-called 'Mapoyo' of the upper Cuchivero are merely a subgroup of Panare who are linguistically, culturally and socially quite different from the Mapoyo living between the Suapure and the Villacoa. In order to avoid further confusion, I have proposed elsewhere that this latter group be referred to from now on by their own name for themselves, Wánai. This is the name that I have used in Map 2 (see Henley 1975).

14. Much of the ensuing account of Panare–Hoti relations is derived from a personal communication by W. Coppens (1976).

and threatening to make off with the women. It also appears that the Panare brought with them a virulent form of malaria previously unknown in Hoti territory but with which the latter soon became infected. It was not long therefore before the Hoti who had settled in the mission station withdrew, retreating to the headwaters of the Asita river. Subsequently, following some internal dispute, the Panare group at Iguana split into two, one half taking off to Majagua. The other half of the group remained in the mission station and the missionaries, who had never had much success getting the Hoti to collaborate in teaching them their language, now turned their attention to learning Panare instead.

There is some evidence that the Panare once maintained a more extensive trade network with the groups to the south of them than they do now, but if so, this network has fallen into disuse. According to Wilbert (1959 : 48), the Panare used to maintain 'intensive' trade relations with the Yabarana and used to penetrate as far south as the Ventuari in order to do so. Although elderly informants in the Southern Panare region confirmed that the Yabarana occasionally visited Panare communities on the upper Cuchivero, they denied that they ever used to go down to the Ventuari to trade themselves. The Panare also appear to have had some sort of contact with the Ye'kuana since the latter have a name for them, *eyei*. (The Panare however have no special name for the Ye'kuana; they merely refer to them as *e'nyëpa* or by the same term as the local criollos do, 'Makiritare'). But if the two groups were in direct contact in the past, they are no longer so now. The only case of trade between them that I heard of was that engineered by the Orinoco River Mission in Caicara in the 1960s: Ye'kuana from the Caura brought blowguns to the mission and the missionaries would re-sell them to the Panare. It was by means of these blowguns that the missionaries were first able to establish some sort of relationship with the Panare. However the Orinoco River Mission in Caicara was primarily concerned to work on the criollo population and never made any systematic attempt to evangelize the Panare (see Dumont 1978 : 179 – 82).

Although the Panare occasionally run across Guahibo and Wánai, the only group living to the south-west of them with whom they have trading relations is the Piaroa. During the dry season, itinerant Piaroa come to Panare settlements in the south-west and trade blowguns and blocks of *peramán* (a resinous gum used for waterproofing binding and as a general adhesive) for curare. From the perspective of the ethnography of the indigenous trade network of this part of Guiana, it is most interesting that it should be the Panare who give the Piaroa curare rather than *vice versa* since the Piaroa are commonly regarded as the masters of curare manufacture in the middle Orinoco region. Relations with the Piaroa occasionally go beyond the purely commercial. When I visited the Panare community of Mata Brava, I discovered two Piaroa girls living there, both of them dressed in the Panare style and one of them married to a Panare. In another settlement of the same community, a Piaroa man and his family lived in a mud house of the criollo style, situated right alongside a traditional Panare collective house of the conical type.

But like the trade network to the south-east, the trade relations the Panare maintain with the Piaroa appear to be on the decline. Although Piaroa traders still visit Panare settlements, they do not do so as frequently as they did in the past. In Colorado, for example, the Panare lament that sometimes a whole dry season will go past without a visit from the Piaroa. It is said that the reason for this decline is that the Piaroa who used to go on trading expeditions now dedicate their energies to cash-cropping and wage labour instead. Whatever the reasons, the result for the Panare is to make it increasingly difficult to get hold of blowguns. They claim that they cannot make them themselves since the appropriate materials are not available in their territory. Many Panare have therefore felt themselves obliged to replace their worn-out blowguns with shotguns bought from the criollos, thereby increasing their dependence on the latter.

Even before the indigenous trade network began to decline, the relations that the Panare sustained with other indigenous groups were far less important in both an economic and a social sense than the system of relations they maintained with the criollos. The history of the relations they have sought with the criollos in order to acquire industrial goods explains their distribution today. These industrial goods are integral to their present way of life, as are introduced crops to their diet. The plantain is second only to manioc as the Panare staple; in many communities, rice is also important; in most communities, sugar cane forms the basis of the beer that is drunk in vast quantities at ceremonials. In simple material terms, it is difficult to imagine Panare society without these items derived from contact. In this sense, the Panare are no different from most indigenous groups of contemporary lowland South America, even the most isolated.

Since the present condition of the Panare cannot be dissociated from the history of their contact with the criollos, the term 'traditional' can be applied to Panare communities only in a relative sense. A 'traditional' community is not one that has preserved some pure Panare tradition since time began, but rather one that, despite having undergone a certain degree of modification as a result of contact, continues to practise a way of life that is distinct from that of the local criollos. Nevertheless, when one bears in mind the length of the Panare's history of contact, one cannot help being struck by how 'traditional' the Panare are, in this relative sense. Almost by any criterion one might choose—physical type, language, dress, residential arrangements, marriage rules, economic behaviour, supernatural beliefs—almost all Panare communities can be easily distinguished from the local criollo population.

There are signs however that the Panare as a whole are in the process of losing their cultural distinctiveness, abandoning their own customs and adopting those of the criollos instead. This acculturative trend has become marked only over the last decade, and is immediately apparent only in the communities closest to Caicara. And yet, despite this incipient process of cultural convergence between the two ethnic groups, there is no indication that the social boundaries between them have begun to diminish. If anything, these boundaries have become more sharply defined as a result of disputes between the two groups of a kind unknown in earlier periods of contact. I will discuss the reasons for these changes going on both within Panare society and in their relations with the criollos in the last three chapters of this book. But first, I must examine the internal relations of Panare society. These form the subject matter of the next four chapters.

*Table 1. An estimate of the Panare population* (1975–6)

A. The Southern Panare

| Community | 'Capitán' | Population | Level of Confidence† | Margin of Error (±) |
|---|---|---|---|---|
| 1. Majagua | ? | 30 | (D) (1) | 6 |
| 2. Iguana | ? | 30 | (D) (1) | 6 |
| 3. Cepillo | Augusto | 50 | (D) (1) | 10 |
| 4. Maká | Teodoro (Puka) | 35 | (E) | 9 |
| 5. El Macho (Sto. Domingo) | Juan Gonzalez | 30 | (B) | 3 |
| 6. El Manteco (La California, Dos Indios) | Domingo (Wĕnye) | 90 | (B) * | 9 |
| 7. Cuchiverito | ? | 50 | (B) * | 5 |
| 8. La Centella | Francisco (Tĕna) | 19 | (A) * | – |
| 9. Veranero | Valentín (Tĕna) | 25 | (B) | 2 |
| 10. Tiro Loco (Bicicleta) | Vicente (Tĕna) | 42 | (A) * | – |

† see Appendix 2      Total:    401         ± 50

* visited by the author

*Table 1* (continued)

## B. The Eastern Panare

| Community | 'Capitán' | Population | Level of Confidence† | Margin of Error (±) |
|---|---|---|---|---|
| 1. Caño Amarillo (El Tigre, El Rosario) | Castro | 130 | (C) * | 20 |
| 2. Guarataro | Jesús (Nahtë) | 40 | (B) * | 4 |
| 3. Norte Apure | ? | 30 | (C) * | 5 |
| 4. El Fortín | Bastardo | 50 | (B) * | 5 |
| 5. Santa Fé | Mendoza (Nahtë) | 50 | (C) * | 7 |
| 6. Quebrada Honda (Čerro Pelón) | ? | 40 | (E) | 10 |
| 7. San Vicente | ? | 25 | (E) | 6 |
| 8. San Miguel | ? | 25 | (E) | 6 |
| 9. Mamonal | ? | 30 | (C) * | 5 |
| 10. Chenchena (Camaguán) | Manuel Angel | 40 | (B) * | 4 |
| | Total: | 460 | | ± 72 |

## C. The Western Panare

| Community | 'Capitán' | Population | Level of Confidence† | Margin of Error (±) |
|---|---|---|---|---|
| 1. Guamalito | Beltrán (Wěnye) | 40 | (B) * | 4 |
| 2. El Pajal | Ramón Grande (Puka) | 45 | (C) * | 7 |
| 3. Matamata (Corozito) | Manuel García | 25 | (E) | 6 |
| 4. El Valle | ? | 25 | (E) | 6 |
| 5. El Tambor (Perro de Agua) | Manuel Castro (Manyěn) | 35 | (C) * | 5 |
| 6. El Pato (Guaratarito) | Manuelito | 25 | (C) | 4 |
| 7. Caño Amarillo | Algota | 38 | (B) (2) * | 4 |
| 8. Macanilla (El Sapo) | Nicanol | 40 | (C) * | 6 |
| 9. Chaviripa (Pata del Chivero) | Perez (Puka) | 30 | (B) * | 3 |
| 10. El Danto (La Raya) | Medina | 50 | (B) (3) * | 5 |
| 11. El Guamal (El Escondido) | Pedro (Wěnye) | 35 | (B) * | 3 |
| 12. Rancho Grande | Guariqueño | 25 | (E) | 6 |
| 13. Manare (Corozal) | Mendoza (To'se) | 23 | (A) * | – |
| 14. Colorado | Avila (Nahtë) | 226 | (A) * | – |
| 15. Portachuelo (Charal, Túriba) | Casanova (Wěnye) | 90 | (B) (3) * | 9 |
| | subtotal | 752 | | ± 68 |

| Community | 'Capitán' | Population | Level of Confidence† | Margin of Error (±) |
|---|---|---|---|---|
| 16. Carta (Los Pozos) | Tosta (Manyën) | 25 | (B) (3) * | 2 |
| 17. El Rincón (Trapichote) | Domingo Barrios (Tëna) | 30 | (C) * | 4 |
| 18. Mata Brava | Marquitos (Wënye) | 40 | (C) * | 6 |
| | Total | 847 | | ± 80 |

## D. The total population

A. Southern Panare    401 (±50)
B. Eastern Panare    460 (±72)
C. Western Panare    847 (±80)

Total    1708 (±202)

† see Appendix 2
* visited by the author

# CHAPTER TWO

# Ecology and Subsistence

Panare territory lies at the junction of two major eco-systems.[1] To the south and east lies the Guianese Shield, a massive block of pre-Cambrian rock, broken up by erosion and tectonic action, whilst to the north and west lie the vast series of plains that stretch from northern Venezuela to southern Columbia, known in both countries as the 'Llanos'. Although Panare territory is actually cut off from the main bulk of the Llanos by the Orinoco, on the right bank of the river there is a belt up to 30 kms wide where the ecological features of the Llanos still predominate: an undulating terrain, covered with a savanna vegetation and crossed by numerous meandering streams and rivers lined with clumps of gallery forest. Here and there, the savanna is studded with large outcrops of eroded rock, outposts of the scarp slopes of the Shield (or *serranías*, as they are called by local Spanish-speakers). During the rainy season large stretches of the savanna are inundated by the rivers and streams as they overflow their banks, yet most of them are too small and too shallow to be navigable. In the dry season many of them dry up completely. Only on the lower reaches of the three major rivers of Panare territory, the Cuchivero, the Guaniamo and the Suapure, is navigation possible. Further upstream, it is impeded by rapids and waterfalls. However the Panare themselves are not a river-going people and use canoes only for ferrying themselves across minor rivers and streams.

In north-western Panare territory there is a sharp contrast between this flat and monotonous landscape and the mountain ridges of the Guianese Shield. Most of the savanna lies less than 100m above sea level, and from this altitude the mountains rise almost in one step to 250m, in many places assuming the form of imposing grey-black cliff faces denuded of vegetation. Above 250m the topography levels out and the bare slopes give way to a forest vegetation. The altitude of the mountain ridges continues to increase gradually to about 1000m,

1. Unless otherwise stated, the technical information in this chapter concerning the natural environment in Panare territory was taken from an official publication of the *Comisión para el Desarollo del Sur* (CODESUR 1970). The authors of this publication warn that some of the information it contains is based on preliminary studies that require further confirmation before they can be accepted as authoritative.

Plate 4. A stretch of the Rio Guaniamo (see Map 4) demarcating the point where the Guianese Shield ends and the Llanos begins.

eventually reaching 1300m in the extreme west of Panare territory. In the south-eastern sector of Panare territory, south of the Guaniamo river, the contrast between savanna and mountain is not so marked: here stretches of undulating savanna are found along the banks of the major rivers but they are narrow compared to those of the north-west. Otherwise the terrain is more broken and rocky and generally more elevated than it is north of the Guaniamo. The mountains reach to over 1000m at many points and even to over 2000m just south of Panare territory in the Serranía de Maigualida from which the Cuchivero springs. The vegetation in this sector is more silvine than in the north but alternates with patches of savanna at all altitudes up to 500m.

The climate in Panare territory reflects its position as a transition zone between the Llanos and the Guianese Shield. The annual average rainfall in Panare territory is about 2400mm, a figure which is closer to the annual average for the Guianese Shield as a whole (over 3000mm) than it is to that of the Llanos (varying between 1000 and

1800mm). On the other hand, the distribution of rainfall over the course of a year in Panare territory resembles the pattern of the Llanos rather than that of the Guianese Shield. As in the Llanos, there is a marked dry season, if a somewhat shorter one, lasting only from December to May. The annual average temperature is about 25°C but the dry season is decidedly hotter than the rainy season. At this time of the year, it becomes hot and stuffy inside the Panare's houses, and they move out into the forest to set up camp there. Temperature also varies with altitude in Panare territory but neither this nor seasonal variation is as great as the diurnal variation in temperature. At night, particularly during the rainy season, it becomes quite cold and it is unpleasant to sleep without a blanket. If the Panare do not have blankets, they light fires beneath their hammocks to keep themselves warm.

The Panare subsistence economy is based on swidden (slash-and-burn) agriculture, fishing, hunting and gathering. The natural environment of their territory provides them with three distinct natural resource zones: the savanna, the rivers and the forest. The most abundant forest in north-western Panare territory is found on the summits of the mountains at 250 m and above. Forest is also encountered in a less developed form at the level of the plains, in clumps at the base of the slopes and in the form of gallery forest. South-eastern Panare territory is generally more silvine, but even there the forest becomes more abundant the higher one goes. The forest is the richest resource zone for the Panare: it is here that they cut their gardens and do most of their hunting. It is also the richest source of wild fruits and the raw materials used to make artifacts. The rivers provide the Panare with large quantities of fish, particularly during the dry season when the waters are low. In the north-western sector of Panare territory, the steep slopes of the mountains prevent all but the smallest fish from reaching the headwaters of the rivers, and the Panare who live in this sector are therefore obliged to do most of their fishing on the plains. Compared to the other two resource zones, the savanna is relatively unimportant for the Panare, providing them with only a few game animals and some fruits of minor importance to their diet. In summary therefore, the ecological adaptation of the Panare is primarily silvine, secondarily riverine and only marginally savanna-oriented. Thus when the Panare settle on the plains, it is the pockets of forest and the rivers that they exploit to meet their subsistence needs rather than the savanna itself.

As described in Chapter 1, the Panare have engaged in economic exchanges with the local criollos for at least a century, if not more. Nowadays the Panare acquire a wide range of industrial goods from the criollos including steel tools which form an integral part of their ecological adaptation. The most important of these trade goods are listed in Table 2. In effect, the criollo settlements constitute a resource zone that is as essential to the Panare subsistence economy as the three natural zones distinguished above. However, although I will refer to the Panare's economic exchanges with the criollos in this and the following chapter, I will leave direct consideration of this topic until Chapter 8.

The dispersion of resource zones in the north-western sector of Panare territory often makes it impossible for the members of a community to locate their principal settlement site at a point that is simultaneously close to the richest variant of each. The forest occurs both on the plains and in the mountains but it is the mountainous variant that is the richest: there is more game to be hunted, more wild fruit and raw materials to be collected and, according to the Panare, the gardens cut in the forest in the mountains are more productive than those cut in the pockets of forest on the plains. On the other hand, the richest riverine resources lie on the plains, usually at least half a day's walk from a settlement located in the mountains. Furthermore, the source of industrial technology and other trade goods, the criollo settlements, also lies down on the plains, usually in open savanna.

In the south-eastern sector of Panare territory where savanna and forest alternate at greater altitudes and the change from plains to mountains is not so abrupt, the physical dispersion of the three natural resource zones is not so great as in the north-western sector. Nevertheless, when establishing a new settlement, the members of the communities located in the south-eastern sector still face a choice of strategies similar to that confronted by members of the communities of the north-western sector. In all parts of Panare territory, the members of a community have to decide whether to locate themselves close to the criollos and hence to the source of goods and medicines or at some distance away where the natural resource zones are generally more plentiful since they are less intensively exploited.

Panare communities overcome the problem of dispersed resource zones by means of a semi-nomadic settlement pattern. This semi-nomadism takes a variety of forms but for present purposes can be reduced to three basic types. In the past, a community usually built its principal settlement in the mountains and its members would make sorties from there to the plains in search of fish and trade goods. These expeditions could last several weeks and during this time they would build themselves a temporary shelter, or simply camp out in the pockets of forest on the plains. Some communities still follow this strategy, but it is becoming increasingly frequent for a community to build its principal settlement down on the plains from whence its members make periodic sorties to the mountains in search of game, wild fruits or to pick over old garden sites. Permanent settlements on the plains are generally located close to a pocket of gallery forest or a stretch of forest at the foot of the mountains in which the community will be able to cut its gardens. The Panare of these plains settlements may have to compensate for the poverty of the local forest by making sorties to the mountains, but their richest source of fish, the rivers meandering across the plains, and their only source of trade goods, the criollo settlements, are closer to hand. Some communities even have two permanent settlement sites, one in the mountains, the other on the plains, and the members of these communities move between them as their subsistence needs require. Generally speaking though, one of these settlements will be larger and more important than the other. The Panare give various reasons for the change that is taking place in their settlement pattern but undoubtedly the most important of these is the desire to have readier access to industrially produced goods and medicines.

Most of the information on Panare subsistence activities presented in the remainder of this chapter is based on notes made in the community of Colorado of Western Panare territory between February 1975 and June 1976. This community is located in an oval-shaped valley, about 15 km long and 6 km wide at the widest point. The entrance to the valley is very narrow whilst the other end of the valley is closed by the mountains that encircle it. The natural environment in the valley is typical of this part of Panare territory, featuring a marked contrast between flat, undulating plain on the valley floor, covered with a savanna vegetation, and steep mountain slopes.

At the time of my fieldwork, the Colorado community consisted of ten independent settlements located around the edges of the pockets of forest found on the floor of the valley. Despite regular contact with criollos since the turn of the century, the Colorado Panare have retained a basically 'traditional' way of life. But in one important respect, the situation in the valley has changed markedly in recent years. Until five years ago, a large proportion of the present community lived in dispersed settlements up in the mountains as much as two days' walk away from the heart of the valley where they live now. Although this process of moving from the mountains to the plains is happening all over Panare territory, in the case of Colorado the process has been catalyzed by the presence of a New Tribes Mission station which was first established there in 1972. Although the Panare were very wary of the mission station at first, they have gradually brought their houses closer to it, attracted, in the first instance at least, by the various goods and medical services it provides. By 1976, the majority of the Colorado Panare community were living within a stone's throw of the mission station.

As a result of this change in settlement pattern, there are two ways in which the Colorado Panare can no longer be said to be representative of Panare communities in general. Firstly, the density of settlement in the valley is unknown anywhere else in Panare territory with the possible exception of the Panare settled around the criollo village of El Tigre in the Eastern Panare region. Secondly, although there is now a general tendency amongst Panare communities to establish themselves on the plains, as the Colorado community has done, there are still some communities who continue to live in a more silvine environment either up in the mountains of the northern sector or in the more southerly sectors of Panare territory. In the ensuing account, I will point out when these two features make the subsistence activities of the Colorado Panare atypical of those of the Panare in general.

The nature of the subsistence resources that the Panare exploit varies significantly with the passage of the seasons. Although it is conventional amongst Spanish-speakers to divide the year in this part of the world into two seasons, the wet and the dry, the Panare divide it into four. The first part of the rainy season, from May to about August, is referred to as *kano'kampe*. The period from September to November, when the rains are less heavy, is referred to as *kanonya*. The interstadial period between the wet and the dry season which corresponds roughly to the period mid-December to mid-January, the Panare refer to as *serainpe*, whilst the dry season proper is referred to as *kamawë*. *Kamawë* is also the term by which the Panare refer to the annual cycle as a whole, thus 'next year' would be *tyako kamawë*, literally 'the other summer'. The passage of time is assessed primarily by the position of two constellations: the Pleiades and Orion's Belt. This technique is supplemented by observations of changes in the local flora and fauna. For example, the Panare know that when the chaparro (Latin: *Byrsonima* sp.; Panare: *takïco*) flowers and the *wocin* and *woromin*, two species of bird, descend from the mountains to the plains the rains will not be long in coming.

Although the relative importance of the various sectors of the Panare economy varies with the seasons, agricultural produce forms the basis of the Panare diet throughout the year. The Panare agricultural year could be said to begin when they cut their gardens in March or April. The fallen trees and debris are then left lying on the ground to be dried out by the hot dry season sun. Shortly before the rains begin, the debris is fired. There is a certain amount of luck involved in selecting the right moment for firing. The longer the debris is left to dry, the better the firing will be but if the rains come earlier than expected, a good firing is difficult, if not impossible. According to both the Panare and the local criollos, the rains have not been as predictable in Panare territory over the last few years as they were in the past, with the result that a number of swidden agriculturalists have been badly caught out. For example, in 1976 many Panare men in the Colorado valley abandoned plans to cut new gardens for the following year when the rains arrived at the beginning of April, about a month ahead of schedule. Once the firing has been carried out, the small debris that still remains is chopped up and cleared away to the perimeter of the garden. Most of the larger trunks and branches are left where they have fallen but the area around them is carefully weeded. Once the garden has been cleared, planting can begin.

The Panare cut their gardens with steel axes and clear the debris with machetes. The machete and another tool, known in Spanish as the *chícora,* a sort of adze with a steel head, are used during the planting of a garden. Although the Panare may haft these tools themselves, the steel heads all come from trade with the criollos. Nowadays no one can remember a time when the Panare did not use these tools and no one knows how to manufacture tools with stone heads. It is impossible therefore to come to any certain conclusions as to the effect of the introduction of these tools on Panare subsistence activities. However Harner's study of the effects of steel tools on the Eastern

Plate 5.    A garden, recently burnt, in the process of being cleared before planting.

Jívaro and comparable material from societies in other parts of the world with subsistence practices similar to those of the Jívaro and the Panare, provide one with a few clues.[2] In the first place, there is no doubt that steel tools must have greatly reduced the amount of time required to carry out most subsistence activities. But they have probably had the most dramatic labour-saving effect on the clearing of gardens since it is in this subsistence activity that steel tools are most intensively used. Secondly, comparative evidence suggests that in societies with the same general type of social and economic organization as the Panare, the time saved by the introduction of steel tools is used, not for increasing food production but for increasing the amount of leisure time. If this was so in Panare society, then the introduction of steel tools would have increased the leisure time of men more than that of women since the activity on which steel tools have probably had the most effect, the clearing of gardens, is primarily a male activity. This may serve to explain, at least in part, why men work less hard than women in Panare society, particularly during the dry season which is the period when gardens ought to be cleared.

The introduction of steel tools may also have served to increase the economic autonomy of the conjugal family in the sphere of production. Once again, I reach this conclusion on the basis of comparative evidence. In his article, Harner quotes a passage from Up de Graff, who lived amongst the Jívaro in the late nineteenth century before they had steel tools. In this passage, de Graff describes teams of six to eight men working together to fell large trees, not so much by cutting them as by reducing the trunks to pulp with their stone axes—a feat, as de Graff observes, 'more of patience than of skill'. Harner, for his part, reports that today it is common for a single Jívaro, equipped with a steel axe, to fell a large tree in a matter of hours (Harner 1968: 372). It seems quite likely that prior to the introduction of steel tools the Panare were obliged to fell trees in the way described by de Graff. But today, although two or three men may collaborate when they are clearing adjacent gardens, this is by no means a universal practice. Although it may be more enjoyable, and possibly more efficient, for a man to collaborate with others when clearing a garden, a modern Panare armed with a steel axe is not absolutely dependent on the collaboration of others as his forefathers probably were.

The gardens of the modern Panare are of three basic types:

i) *Mixed gardens* Most new gardens are of this type. Table 3

2. Harner (1968) shows his conclusions about the Jívaro to be similar to those arrived at by Sharp and by Salisbury in their well-known works on the effect of steel tools on Australian and New Guinean societies respectively.

provides a list of the principal plants cultivated in Colorado and a rough measure of their relative importance in terms of their frequency in daily communal meals.[3] A similar complex of plants would be found in the mixed gardens of most modern Panare communities. But in one respect the Colorado gardens are atypical of Panare gardens in general, since rice plays a very important part in the Colorado diet, particularly during the rainy season. The oldest members of the Colorado community acknowledge that rice was introduced by the criollos but claim that they have 'always' planted it. But in most Panare communities, even those that are neighbours to Colorado, rice is either of very little importance or even not planted at all. In these communities on the other hand, it would appear that bitter manioc is a more important crop than it is in Colorado (Dumont 1976: 46). This suggests that rice may have taken over to some extent the position of bitter manioc and its derivative, cassava bread, in the Colorado diet.

Apart from rice, the most important crops in the Colorado mixed gardens are sweet manioc and a diverse range of bananas. One or both of these foodstuffs form part of every major Panare meal. The Panare distinguish linguistically between bitter and sweet varieties of manioc but it requires considerable experience to distinguish between them in practice. Many young adult men were unable to do so and in such instances they would refer me to the old women of the community who were generally regarded as the most knowledgeable on this matter. In addition, within the categories bitter (uto'nye) and sweet manioc (amaka), the Panare distinguish a number of sub-varieties, but given that even the general categories of bitter and sweet manioc are now commonly regarded by botanists as members of a single species, these sub-varieties must be nothing more than cultivars. Similarly, although the Panare distinguish between some fifteen different varieties of banana, in view of the fact that recent botanical research indicates that even the conventional species distinction between M. paradisica and M. sapientum is not valid genetically, these too must correspond to nothing more than distinctions between cultivars (Purseglove 1968: 173, 1972: 349–50).

Figure 2 represents a typical Colorado mixed garden just after it has been planted. Manioc, both bitter and sweet, takes up roughly

3. The botanical identifications in this Table and in Table 6 (Edible Wild Fruits) I made myself with the aid of Schnee (1973) and Perez-Arbeláez (1956). A number of identifications in Table 7 (Useful Wild Plants), I also made myself but the majority were made by a professional botanist, Mary Kalin of the Universidad Central de Venezuela on the basis of dried samples I brought from the field. Apart from these latter identifications, which are marked with an asterisk in the Table, the botanical identifications in the Tables must be regarded as tentative.

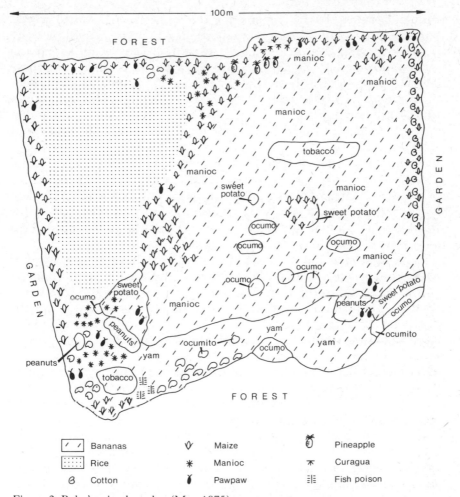

Figure 2. Puka's mixed garden (May 1975)

half the area of the garden. This area is broken up by clumps of other roots such ocumo, sweet potato, yams, etc. More extended patches of these latter roots are found around the edge of the garden. A swathe of maize divides the manioc from the rice section which takes up about a quarter of the area of the garden. Most of the other crops, both edible and inedible, are planted around the perimeter of the garden or along-side the fallen trunks and branches that were too big to clear before planting began. Tobacco, on the other hand, which is highly valued and consumed throughout the year by most Panare men and even some older women, is accorded pride of place in the midst of the manioc patch. The dotted lines running across the diagram represent rows of bananas. In the sections devoted to manioc and other tubers, banana stumps are planted in rows, about 5 m apart, simultaneously with the tubers, at the beginning of the rainy season. In the case of the sections devoted to maize and rice however, it is only once these original crops have been harvested, in August and November respectively, that these sections are planted with bananas, and sometimes with manioc also.

A mixed garden rarely lasts more than two years. The root crops with which the garden is first planted can be harvested after about nine months, although they are generally left longer. In the second year, certain sections of the garden may be replanted with root crops or a small extension may be added on to the side of the main garden. Normally however, a new mixed garden is opened every second or third year and the old garden is given over entirely to bananas which by this time have come into full production.

ii) *Banana gardens* Gardens of this type are in fact merely mixed gardens at a later stage of development. The longevity of a banana garden depends on the variety of *Musaceae* it contains and where it is located. The Panare report that some varieties grow better on the damper soils of the mountains than they do on the savanna and *vice versa*. In all cases however, the productivity of banana gardens is said to decline after the first two or three years. Nevertheless some of the older men of the Colorado community claimed that they had banana gardens in the mountains which were still producing a little fruit even though they had been opened when the men concerned were first married, some thirty or more years previously.

iii) *Sugar cane gardens* According to the Panare, the best soil for a mixed garden is what they call *miciripe,* which is of a sandy, gravelly texture. Sugar cane on the other hand does better on what they call *ano'nye*, which has a more clay-like texture. Ideally it should also be *kuhpëpe,* that is, damp. Consequently a man's sugar cane garden is often found at some distance from his main mixed garden, usually on the edge of a small stream. Sugar cane is planted in rows, frequently interspersed with rows of rice and/or maize. Panare sugar cane gardens come into production within a year of planting and rarely last more than about three years.

Most Panare men have their own gardens from which they expect to support themselves and their families and to contribute to the food consumed by the settlement group in communal meals. The size and number of gardens that an individual man has vary according to age. For social reasons discussed in the following chapter, a Panare man is at his greatest productive capacity between the ages of about twenty-five and forty-five years of age. A new mixed garden belonging to a man between these ages is usually about 0.75 of a hectare, whilst a new sugar cane garden is normally somewhat smaller, being about 0.35 hectares. By the standards of some lowland South American indigenous group, as well as by those of the local criollos, the Panare's gardens are small, but it should be remembered that at any given moment a Panare man at full productive capacity will usually have at least three gardens producing food: one mixed garden in the first or second year; a sugar cane garden between one and three years old and one or more old banana gardens.

A fully productive Panare man normally cuts a new mixed garden every other year. In the intervening years, he may cut a sugar cane garden or put an extension on his mixed garden of the previous year. Alternatively, or in addition, he may replant sections of this old mixed garden. Thus every year, come the rainy season, a Panare man enlarges the area he has under cultivation. In order to illustrate how the process of garden-making is staggered from one year to the next, I reproduce the record of the gardening activities of one of the most industrious men in the Colorado valley:

*in 1972,* he opened a mixed garden of about 0.75 hectares at about fifteen minutes walk from his house.

*in 1973,* he put a small extension on this mixed garden, planted the extension with manioc, allowing bananas to take over the remainder of the garden.

*in 1974,* he cleared another large mixed garden of about 0.75 hectares, planting most of it with manioc and rice.

*in 1975,* he replanted the section of the 1974 garden dedicated to rice with manioc. At the same time, he opened up a new sugar cane garden about half-an-hour's walk from his manioc and banana gardens and established a new house next door to it. The sugar cane garden was also planted with a small amount of rice.

*in 1976,* shortly before I left the field, he was opening a new mixed garden close to his new house and extending his sugar cane and rice garden.

Although agricultural produce forms an important part of the Panare diet throughout the year, a meal is not considered a proper meal unless it contains meat. Over the course of a year, the Colorado Panare derive most animal protein from fishing. Fishing is particularly important during the dry season, whilst hunting is more of a rainy season activity. The predominance of fish in Colorado Panare diet is a reflection of the community's savanna location and in communities in more silvine locations, notably those in south-eastern Panare territory, it was my impression that game played a comparatively more important part in the diet.

The Panare employ two basic methods of fishing. The traditional method is to infuse small creeks with one of two principal varieties of poison. The other involves the use of hook and line. The traditional method can be properly employed only during the dry season when the waters are low. Although it is also used at the beginning and end of the rainy season, when the waters are somewhat higher than the ideal, it is usually of only limited success at this time of year. Of the two varieties of poison most commonly used to poison fish, one is wild and the other domesticated. The wild variety is derived from a liana that grows in the mountains and which is known to the Panare as *enërima* (possibly *Lonchocarpus* sp.). The domesticated variety, known as *kayin* (probably *Tephrosia purpurea*) is a plant resembling a nettle. Although it is grown in Panare gardens, it is also found growing wild. Of the two, *enërima* is by far the more potent and therefore preferred but, being wild, it is less readily available.

A fishing expedition is invariably a collective affair but men and women carry out different tasks during the course of it. If the poison to be used is *kayin*, it is first pounded with poles by some of the men before being put into baskets and immersed in the water. *Enërima* is also pounded, though not as much as *kayin*, before being immersed. Whilst some of the men are preparing the poison, others together with the women and children station themselves at various points downstream. As the poison begins to take effect, the fish rise to the surface, their gills flapping frenetically. At first they appear to want to get out of the water and some of them succeed in leaping out on to the bank where they are picked up by children. The fish that remain in the water are speared with hand-held spears by the men or chopped over the back of the head with machetes or knives by the women. When the creek has become completely saturated with the poison, it is even possible to pick the fish out by hand. Apart from those already mentioned, no other items of technology are used in fish poisoning. Occasionally the Panare dam the creek with a crudely-made barrage of palm leaves and branches but they use neither the basketwork traps nor the nets that have been reported amongst some Guianese indigenous groups.

At the height of the dry season when the waters are low, poisoning can produce vast quantities of fish for a minimal input of labour. If *enërima* is to be used, one or two men have to go to the mountains in search of it, whilst *kayin* has to be brought from the gardens and then pounded. But apart from this, there is no drudgery involved in fish poisoning. Everyone enjoys a collective fishing expedition and there is always much laughing and joking. I was never able to weigh the exact amount that a fishing expedition of this kind produced but as a rough

Plate 6. A group of Panare return from a fishing expedition across the savanna during the dry season. Behind them they are burning off the grass in order to keep the foot paths clear and reduce the mosquitoes.

guide I can cite the occasion that I accompanied about fifteen men on a fishing trip in the middle of March 1976. On that occasion, the women were preparing beer for a forthcoming dance so there were only men on the trip. Between us, from a creek that was only knee-deep and no more than five to eight metres wide, we captured about 75 kg of fish! There were still fish floating about helpless in the creek when it was decided that we had caught enough and that it was therefore time to go home and sample the newly-made beer.

Fish poisoning is prohibited by Venezuelan law on the grounds that it drastically and permanently reduces the fish population of a river. Nowadays the Panare are afraid to use poison outside their own valley because they know that it will anger the local criollos and, worse still, it will bring the National Guard after them. Therefore, during the dry season, when they go ranging across the savanna outside the valley in search of fish, they generally take with them only their hooks and lines.

Although the practice of fishing with hook and line was probably copied at some time from the criollos, the Panare have fished in this way as long as anyone can remember. Even if they did manufacture the equipment for themselves in the past, nowadays they use nylon lines and steel hooks which they purchase from the missionaries or from the criollos. They do not use rods of any description and merely throw the line out on to the water by hand, relying on the weight of the bait or a piece of shot threaded on to the line to give it momentum when it is cast. Nor do they use floats, with the result that the line gradually sinks to the bottom of the river where, as often as not, it gets entangled in sunken logs and branches. Nevertheless when the fish are biting, this method can be very effective and has the advantage over poisoning that it can be employed by a single man on his own. Furthermore, during the *kanonya* (that is, the latter half of the rainy season) when the waters are not quite low enough for poisoning, one can still catch fish with hook and line.

A diverse range of fish and other reptiles is available in and around the creeks and rivers of Panare territory. In Colorado, I compiled a list of about thirty edible varieties of fish plus about a dozen more that were regarded as inedible. No specific tabu was attached to the latter—they were merely said not to taste good. The most important of the edible varieties are listed in Table 4, along with the local criollo names and, in some cases, tentative zoological classifications.[4] In addition to fish, the Panare also hunt for small caimans, terrapins and eels in and around the larger rivers of their territory. According to Dumont, the Panare also eat certain forms of frogs and crustacea although I never came across this myself (Dumont 1976 : 52–3). On the other hand the Panare never eat stingrays, freshwater dolphins or water snakes, all of which are readily available in the rivers. Once again, no specific tabu was attached to these animals, although stingrays and water snakes were regarded, with good reason, as physically dangerous.

The indigenous technology that the Panare employ in hunting is only slightly more complex than their fishing technology. Until recently they used lances for hunting larger game such as tapir and peccary, and blowguns for birds and monkeys. The manufacture of both these traditional weapons was dependent on trade relations with non-Panare. A lance consisted of a pliable bamboo-like switch hafted with steel blades fashioned from old machetes which had been acquired originally from the criollos. Blowpipes were acquired from

4. These fish identifications must be regarded as extremely tentative since they are based on the descriptions given by Röhl (1956) which are fragmentary. His descriptions of land animals are generally fuller and these coupled with the descriptions provided by Tello (1979) and with the ornithological work of Ginés and Arveledo (1958), have been used to make the identifications in Table 5 (Game Animals).

neighbouring indigenous groups, although both the darts and the poison with which they were painted were manufactured by the Panare themselves. The bow and arrow were also used traditionally, but it appears to have been a stop-gap weapon used when the supply of blowpipes was interrupted for one reason or another. Over the last few years however, many Panare have acquired shotguns, usually secondhand from the criollos. These are now used for most land game, monkeys and larger birds. The Panare still prefer to use blowpipes for hunting smaller birds since a shotgun blast tends to rip them to shreds. Furthermore, some Panare still prefer to use lances for hunting peccary because, as they would explain in dramatic detail, it is much more thrilling to chase a peccary through the undergrowth and then stab it in the neck with a lance than it is to fell it with a shotgun blast. A number of other items acquired from the criollos have also modified Panare hunting techniques. The acquisiton of battery-operated torches makes hunting of the paca and other nocturnal creatures easier; large fishing hooks are used to pull tortoises out from under large boulders. The dog, an essential part of Panare hunting methods, must also have been introduced from the outside originally but this probably took place even before the Panare left the upper Cuchivero.

Although the technology employed may be comparatively simple, a great deal of skill and experience is required to hunt successfully. In the first place, one has to know where to find game. This requires a knowledge of the habits of the hunted species, in particular of the foods they eat, the times of year these are available and where they are to be found. Certain points in the forest or on the savanna are known to be spots favoured by certain species at certain times of the year. Taking into account these factors of seasonal availability, a hunter will generally have a rough idea of the sort of animal he is after and will take with him the appropriate weapon. This does not mean, of course, that he will be averse to bagging an agouti when he is out looking for peccary, say, or a bird if he is after monkeys, but the range of possible animals that he will return with is limited both by the weapon he takes with him and the place to which he chooses to go. Once he reaches his destination, the hunter needs to know how to detect the presence of the animal he is after. If it is a land animal, the most obvious indicator of its presence is its tracks, but the Panare also use a number of other clues such as the way in which the undergrowth has been disturbed and whether or not the fruits on the forest floor have been gnawed. The next stage—running the animal to ground or bringing it out into the open so that it can be killed—is perhaps the most difficult. If it is a land animal that he is after, a Panare will usually rely on his dog to do this; if it is a bird he will try calling it. Monkeys can be persuaded to come down from the canopy of the trees by waggling the branches lower down the tree on which they are sitting. It seems that their curiosity to find out what is going on is sometimes greater than their instinct to flee. If the hunter is convinced that the animal he is after is present but has taken fright, he may build himself a hide and return to the same spot on another day.

Table 5 gives a list of the principal animals hunted by the Panare. Taking the year as a whole, the game animal that features most frequently in the Colorado Panare diet is undoubtedly the agouti.Not so common, but also eaten throughout the year are peccaries and tapirs. Other animals are eaten frequently only at certain times of year. The toucan and the macaw form a recurrent part of the Panare diet towards the end of the rainy season in November and December. These birds come down from the mountains to seek out certain fruits that are available on the savanna only at this time of year. Another reason for hunting them then is that their feathers and beaks are needed to manufacture various articles of ritual gear and the *cirisko,* a percussive instrument used in the dances which begin about the same time. For the same reason, the capuchin monkey, whose canine teeth are used in the manufacture of necklaces worn by young adult men during the festive period, is more frequently hunted at this time of year than at any other. Although certain parts of these animals are used in the manufacture of items of ritual dress, their meat is always eaten as part of the day-to-day diet. Other animals which are hunted seasonally include the armadillo, which is hunted mostly in the middle of the rainy season (August – September) and the deer, which is most frequently sought at the beginning of the rainy season (May – June). The tortoise is hunted systematically only towards the end of the dry season (March – April), not so much for domestic consumption as for sale to the criollos for whom the tortoise is a traditional dish over the Easter period.

In a similar account of the animals hunted by a Panare community living in the mountains, mountain-dwelling creatures such as tapirs and monkeys and birds such as guans would feature more prominently. Correspondingly, certain plains-dwelling creatures such as deer and agouti would be less important. Indeed comparing the Colorado list with the list compiled by Dumont in a nearby plains-dwelling community, half a dozen years previously, suggests that even the diets of communities that share more or less the same natural environment show certain differences in the relative importance of the animals consumed over the course of a year. Furthermore, of course, one should bear in mind that the Colorado record only refers to one particular year and that a more long-term study might have given different results.

The Panare keep a range of domesticated animals. Every man likes to have at least one dog to take hunting with him and a pack of scrawny hounds is to be found in every Panare settlement. Some plains-dwelling communities keep donkeys and mules for transport and haulage. Cats and parrots are kept as pets. Pigs are bought as sucklings from the criollos, fattened up and sold back to the criollos when they are full grown. There are reports that some Eastern Panare communities used to keep cattle for the same purpose but they do not do so now. In addition, every Panare community has a number of chickens and other domesticated birds such as turkeys, guinea fowl and ducks. But these birds are treated more like pets than as potential sources of protein. They invariably belong to children, who treat them as playthings, chasing them around the settlement. Their eggs are largely ignored. Sometimes these birds are sold to the criollos, but only under exceptional circumstances (such as when a chicken gets killed by a dog) do the Panare themselves ever eat them.

Although gathered foods never constitute a central part of any major collective meal, they act as an important supplement to the Panare diet at certain times of year. For the Panare, who delight in sweet foods, the most important of these gathered foods is undoubtedly honey. The surrounding forest is inhabited by a diverse range of honey-producing bees and the Colorado Panare identify some fifteen different varieties. Honey is available from the beginning of the dry season (January) through to the middle of the rainy season (August – September), reaching its peak in the months of May and June. The Panare are prepared to spend an inordinate amount of time looking for honey, and during the period when honey reaches its peak collective meals frequently end with one or more large bowls of honey diluted with water. Honey collecting is an exclusively male activity and it is the men who consume most of it, since only a small proportion of the honey collected ever reaches the settlement. Most of it is consumed neat *in situ*, or mixed with water from a stream and drunk during a rest on the way home.

Of the gathered foods, honey may be the one that the Panare most enjoy; but over the course of a year the most important in terms of their contribution to the Panare diet are palm fruits. Although the Colorado Panare identified over twenty-five different varieties of edible wild fruit to me (and probably know many more), only the most important are listed in Table 6. Once again seasonality affects the supply of this food resource and hence its importance in the Panare diet. Although they are available in varying degrees over the best part of the year, kokorite and coroba palm fruits play a very important part in the diet during the months of June and July. This is a lean time of year for the Colorado Panare and often there is nothing much else to fill up with during this period. The other palm fruits listed in the Table are mainly eaten in the latter part of the rainy season (July – November). Mangoes, on the other hand, play an important part in the Panare diet during the latter part of the dry season (March – April). At this time, the Panare often spend as long as a week living beneath a clump of mango trees out on the savanna, gathering the fruit and fishing in the nearby streams. All the remaining fruits in the Table are also available during the dry season except the jobo which is only available in the latter part of the rainy season.

Grubs and insects play a very minor part in the Panare diet. Even the few they do eat are subject to seasonal availability. In the first few weeks of the rainy season, clouds of flying ants descend on the Panare settlements located on the edge of the savanna. These ants are captured by the children and their hind parts are roasted and eaten. In the rainy season proper, grubs are dug out of rotting palm trunks. They are of two types: *tamana* which are found in seje trunks and *poyo'* which are found in coroba trunks. But these sources of food are no more than incidental to the Panare diet. Only children ever go out to look for them systematically and they are eaten only as a sort of snack, never as part of a collective meal.

It is not only food that Panare derive from the natural environment. Although many of the most important tools used in subsistence activities are now bought from the criollos, the natural environment continues to provide the Panare with many items of domestic technology. The Panare also rely on the local flora to provide them with a wide range of medicinal plants, as well as the poisons used in fishing and hunting with blowpipes. Some of the most important of the plants they use for these purposes are listed in Table 7. This list represents only a fraction of the knowledge that the Panare have of wild plants. Most adult Panare men are capable of reeling off the names of over 150 different wild plants, most of which have some sort of use, or are known to be the preferred food of some sort of animal or bird. Although the great majority of these wild plants provide the Panare with neither protein nor calories, a knowledge of them is as essential to their subsistence as the flora and fauna they actually eat.

Most of the resources that the Colorado Panare exploit lie within a radius of three or four hours' walk of their permanent settlements in the heart of the valley. But throughout the year individual members or family groups make expeditions to distant resource zones. During the rainy season, expeditions of this kind are usually to the mountains in search of game, whilst during the dry season they generally involve a sortie out of the valley and across the savanna to fish in the rivers, collect mangoes or visit the criollo settlements. Generally speaking however, these expeditions rarely involve more than a day's walk before a temporary camp is established. From this camp, they may go a further half-day in search of game or wild fruit, returning to the camp at night. Roughly speaking then, a circle with a radius covered by a day-and-a-half's walk from the permanent settlements in the heart of the valley encloses almost all the natural resources that the 226 members of the Colorado valley community use to sustain themselves over a given year. But a great proportion of the area enclosed by such a circle is completely useless to them. At least half of the area enclosed is savanna from which the Panare derive nothing more than one or two game animals of minor significance. Even in the forested area enclosed by such a circle, there are parts which are known to be very poor in animals and fruits and/or unsuitable for agricultural purposes. Obviously the extent of the area exploited by any Panare community depends greatly on how rich the local environment is in the resources that the Panare use. Thus one would expect that the members of a community located in a more silvine context than Colorado would probably not have to roam so far in search of game. On the other hand, they might well have to go further than the Colorado Panare in search of large quantities of fish.

One of the most discussed issues in the literature of lowland South American societies is the question of the degree to which the movement of settlement sites is dependent on environmental factors. As far as the Panare are concerned, the presence of criollo settlements has had more effect, over the years, than has the natural environment. As mentioned in Chapter 1, the Panare have been gradually drawn out of their ancestral homeland in the upper Cuchivero by the material attractions offered by the criollos. But whilst the presence of the criollos may explain these 'macro-movements' during the course of the last century or so, the 'micro-movements', shifts of a few kilometres which each settlement makes every few years, can be affected by environmental factors.[5] Some 'micro-movements' are made when local natural resources have been exhausted; others are made just for convenience. A Panare house takes only about a fortnight of intermittent work to build and rarely lasts for more than three or four years. By then, the thatch has become so rotten that it is easier to build afresh rather than continue patching the old roof. Faced with

5. The terms 'macro-' and 'micro-movements' have been slightly adapted from their use by Chagnon (1973).

the prospect of rebuilding, the residents may decide to move their site to bring themselves a few minutes' walk closer to their gardens or to a source of palm thatch, or to get away from the accumulated debris around the old house, or merely for the sake of change itself. In short, environmental factors may influence the choice of a new site but cannot be said to determine it. Indeed no single factor, environmental or other, ever determines a micro-movement. Members of the community facing a move will weigh up the advantages of the various alternative strategies described above, taking into account not only environmental advantages and access to the criollo settlements but also social considerations related to the rules of post-marital residence. (These latter considerations will be discussed in Chapter 5.)

Furthermore, in discussing the effect of environmental factors on the settlement patterns of the Panare, or any other indigenous group, it is essential to take into account their general attitude towards exploitation of natural resources. Clearly, a group that is disposed to husband its resources in one way or another is going to be able to remain in one spot longer than one that is not. The fact that the indigenous societies of lowland South America have been able to survive for centuries without destroying the natural environment in which they live is often taken as a sign that their ecological adaptation is fundamentally 'conservationist' (see, for example, Siskind 1973 : 230-1). In one sense this may be true, but it is essential to identify what this 'conservationism' consists of. In actual fact, in some spheres, the subsistence activities of many South American societies involve a frankly prodigal use of natural resources. The Panare are a case in point. The principle that appears to underlie their appropriation of nature is that of exploiting a given resource site until a significant decline in the return given for the labour invested makes it less arduous to start anew elsewhere. As we shall see in subsequent chapters, their internal social organization imposes only the weakest constraints on the semi-nomadic settlement pattern that such an attitude to the exploitation of natural resources implies. As a result, unless a concern to maintain economic relations with the criollos or missionaries serves to make them more or less sedentary, the members of a Panare settlement group are likely to move the site of their house long before they have exploited the natural resources in the immediate vicinity to a point where they are completely incapable of recuperating. In this way, the Panare avoid the destruction of their natural environment. But it is confusing to call this attitude towards the exploitation of nature 'conservationist', since it is not an intentional conservationism, derived from a conscious perception of the need to husband natural resources, but rather a conservationism, as it were, by default.

The Panare's prodigal attitude to natural resources is evident in all spheres of their subsistence activities. When confronted with a fruit-bearing palm tree they will consider whether it requires more effort to shin up the tree to get the cluster of fruits than it would simply to cut the tree down. As often as not, they adopt the latter strategy. This practice amazes and dismays the local criollos, particularly when the Panare deal in this cavalier fashion with the mango trees out on the savanna which are regarded by the criollos as being a form of public property. I do not believe that the Panare, in actual fact, ever do chop down an entire tree, but I did see them lop off large branches when they had been unable to shake the fruit off. The same attitude is revealed in fishing activities. The Colorado Panare continue to poison different stretches of the river running through the valley until there are no more fish to be had. Although the fish in the river partially replenish themselves each year, the Panare lament that there are significantly less fish in the river than a few years ago. In hunting they continue to pursue species in the immediate vicinity of the settlements even when their numbers are drastically reduced.

In practices such as these, there is hardly any conservationist element, either in intention or in consequence However Panare agricultural activities provide an example of practices that may be considered ultimately conservationist in consequence even though they may not be conservationist in intention. The Panare cut down a new piece of forest to make a garden approximately every two years. The reasons they give for this practice are, firstly, that the general yield of the garden declines rapidly after the second year and, secondly, that the older the garden, the more weeding it requires. The botanical evidence cited by Carneiro in his classic paper on slash and burn cultivation in lowland South America suggests that one of the reasons for the decline in the yield of a garden is the competition that the cultivated plants receive from the invading weeds (Carneiro 1973 : 112). If this is in fact so, then it could be argued that a garden could be maintained for longer than the two years that is normal amongst the Panare if there were greater input of labour into weeding. This hypothetical argument is corroborated to some extent by the testimony of the local criollos, who claimed that a garden could be maintained for six or seven years, even up to twelve years, provided the regrowth were cleared. But they admitted that this was very uncommon since, even if properly weeded, the productivity always declines progressively after the first year. Moreover, the most recent studies of slash and burn agriculture in this region indicate that, depending on such factors as the initial quality of the soils and the slope of the land, to keep a garden going for such lengthy periods would, at best, serve to increase the amount of fallowing time necessary before the  area could be re-used for agricultural purposes, or, at worst, lead to a permanent deterioration in the productivity of the soils such that they could never again sustain agriculture without the aid of fertilizers (see Petriceks 1968 : 178 – 85).

To the degree that the Panare's attitude to the exploitation of natural resources encourages them to move on to a new site rather than continue to weed the old, it could be said to be 'conservationist'. But this is not from any conscious appreciation of the long-term consequences of maintaining gardens for longer than they are accustomed to do. On the contrary, I found the Panare totally uninterested in speculating on how long a garden could be kept in production provided the necessary weeding was done. Nor, consequently, were they interested in the long-term effects of doing so. Instead, they would point out that although cutting a new garden is hard work and often dangerous (because of falling trees), it is also exhilarating and far preferable to the tedious drudgery of weeding.

Although I have described the Panare's attitude to the natural environment as 'prodigal', this attitude is obviously the most rational *in an economic sense* in a situation where natural resources are infinite since the ratio of labour time invested to the amount of food produced is kept to a minimum. In the past, when the Panare had their permanent settlements in the mountains, where the natural resources on which they depended were more or less infinite, this attitude was entirely appropriate. If resources ran out in one area, it was easy enough for the Panare to move elsewhere since their houses require so little labour to build. Temporary and local shortages could be compensated for by sorties to resource habitats lying further afield. But now that Panare communities are beginning to move down to the plains, to an environment that is less rich in the natural resources they exploit, and to live there at a greater density than they used to in the mountains, this attitude to the appropriation of natural resources is beginning to produce conditions of food scarcity.

The seasonality of Panare subsistence activities has always involved alternating periods of glut and relative scarcity, but the periods of scarcity were never as severe as they can be in large plains-dwelling communities. In Colorado the strain that this change in settlement pattern is putting on the resources of the valley is most evident in its effects on the availability of animal protein. Regardless of the density of settlement, the quantity of game on the plains is never as great as the game available in the mountains. Now that there are a large number of people living on the valley floor, game has become very scarce there. The situation is further exacerbated by the fact that many Panare in the community now own shotguns, which are much more effective than traditional weapons. They try to compensate for this scarcity of animals on the plains by making sorties to the mountains, but now that the best hunting spots are a considerable distance away, fish seem to have taken over, to some extent, the place of game in the Colorado Panare diet. Living down on the plains, the Colorado Panare are closer to the best fishing resources than they were when they lived in the mountains. But as one would expect with so many people depending on the rivers to provide them with protein, the fish population in and around the valley has been depleted. Whilst many Panare may lament this fact, the criollos complain about it bitterly.

It is difficult to gauge the effect of the settlement density in Colorado on the agricultural resources of the valley. In the rainy season of 1975, some (though not all) of the settlement groups in the valley ran out of food from their old gardens before the new ones that they had cut earlier that year had come into production. This shortfall was not a result of the fact that there were no tracts of forest left to cut down and make into gardens; it was merely that some men had not cut big enough gardens the previous year. Nevertheless, even this shortfall might be interpreted as a result, albeit indirect, of the move down to the plains, since it suggests that the Panare have not yet begun to compensate for the impoverishment of other food sources by cutting larger gardens than they needed in the past. Furthermore, although the settlement density of Colorado may not yet have caused a shortage of forest suitable for swiddening, it could well do so in the future. In 1976, when a local criollo rancher threatened to take over the mouth of the valley, the Panare protested vigorously on the grounds that there was 'not much' potential swiddening forest in the valley. The rancher withdrew and through the *Instituto Agrario Nacional*, as we shall see in Chapter 7, the Panare were endowed with a legal title to the valley and some of the surrounding mountains. Whether this endowment will be sufficient to sustain the population of the valley indefinitely is impossible to say at this juncture, since I have data neither on the proportion of the endowed land that is suitable for agricultural activities, nor on mortality and natality rates in the population which would permit the identification of future demographic trends. Although the population of the valley appears to be increasing at the present time, it is difficult to forecast to what extent, if at all, this increase will be compensated for by emigration from the valley as the Panare become more acculturated and more integrated into the local criollo economy.

It is clear that the present situation of the Panare communities that have moved down to the plains requires some change in their attitude towards the exploitation of natural resources. But any such change would involve more than a simple modification of subsistence techniques. The Panare attitude to the appropriation of nature is intimately bound up with the social organization of production, distribution and consumption: hence a change in one would require a change in the other. Moreover, any change in economic relations would have repercussions on the other spheres of social life. I will return to this point from a different perspective in Chapter 8.

*Table 2. Trade Goods*

| English | Spanish | Panare | Average price per unit * |
|---|---|---|---|
| | | Self-adornment | |
| beads | *cuentas* | *hë'nan* | Bs. 150.00 per kilo |
| comb | *peine* | *manka'* | Bs. 0.50 |
| perfume | *agua oloroso* | *tahpïnto* | Bs. 1.50 a bottle |
| scissors | *tijeras* | *mera* | Bs. 4.00 |
| mirror | *espejo* | *cikirin* | Bs. 1.00 |
| belt | *correa* | *pakapihpë* | Bs. 2.00–10.00 |
| cloth | *tela* | *kamisa* | Bs. 10.00 a metre |
| clothing | *ropa* | *kamisa* | – ** |
| | | Food and drink | |
| sugar | *azucar* | *asuka* | Bs. 2.00 per kilo |
| salt | *sal* | *pamë* | Bs. 25.00 for 50 kg |
| rice | *arroz* | *aro* | Bs. 1.00 per kilo |
| bread | *pan* | *pan* | Bs. 2.00 for four rolls |
| alcohol | *aguardiente, ron* | *romo* | Bs. 15.00 a bottle |
| soft drinks | *refrescos* | *prehko* | Bs. 0.50 |
| | | Means of production | |
| machete | *machete* | *espara* | Bs. 15.00 |
| knife | *cuchillo* | *pre* | Bs. 8.00 |
| axe | *hacha* | *cistë* | Bs. 30.00 |
| hoe | *chícora* | *cikura* | Bs. 15.00 |

\* Prices refer to those in Caicara in 1976 and are only approximate. At that time, there were about seven bolivares to one pound sterling.

\*\* The Panare very rarely buy clothes. Most Panare acquire secondhand clothes as gifts from the criollos. Some young Panare men however are beginning to buy themselves new, smart clothes.

## Table 2. Trade Goods (continued)

| English | Spanish | Panare | Average price per unit* |
|---|---|---|---|
| fish hook | anzuelo | wënëtë | Bs. 2.00 for 8 |
| fishing line | hilo | wënëtëaci | Bs. 10.00 for 100 m |
| shotgun | escopeta | kapuca | Bs. 150.00–750.00 |
| shot | plomo | kapucaru | ? |
| powder | pólvora | kapucayon | Bs. 5.00 for 100 gm |
| dog | perro | kërënëpën | Bs. 20.00 |
| aluminium pot | olla | mara' | Bs. 15.00–30.00 |
| aluminium bowls | perola | mara'kin | Bs. 10.00–25.00 |
| cassava griddles | budare | to'utokehto | Bs. 50.00 |
| iron casserole | caserola | enyë | Bs. 50.00 |
| file | lima | rima | Bs. 2.00 |
| torch | linterna | rinterna | Bs. 10.00 |
| ball of cotton | pábila | tokëtë | Bs. 2.00 per ball |
| needle | aguja | kuca | Bs. 2.00 for 4 |
| bicycle | bicicleta | pataikai'mën | Bs. 400.00 (new) |

### Domestic Consumption

| | | | |
|---|---|---|---|
| mosquito net | pabellón | kamisa | Bs. 150.00 |
| blanket | cobija | kuwiha | Bs. 50.00 |
| aspirin | 'cafenol' | tu'nin | Bs. 2.00 for 8 |
| radio | radio | yuwarin | Bs. 50.00 |
| record player | picó | yuwarin | Bs. 75.00 |
| kerosene | querosén | kerosen | Bs. 5.00 for 10 lts. |

## Table 3. Cultivated Plants

| English/Spanish | Panare | Botanical | Importance |
|---|---|---|---|
| | | Roots | |
| sweet manioc | amaka | Manihot sp. | *** |
| yam | wanka | Dioscorea alata | *** |
| bitter manioc | uto'nye | Manihot sp. | ** |
| ocumo | na'ʻ | Xanthosoma sagittifolium | ** |
| sweet potato | co' | Ipomoea batata | ** |
| ocumito | tu'kwa | Xanthosoma violaceum | * |
| | | Fruits | |
| plantain | paru | Musa sp. | *** |
| topocho | pare | Musa sp. | *** |
| banana | kampure | Musa sp. | * |
| pawpaw | paya | Carica papaya | * |
| calabash | kayama | Cucurbita sp. | * |
| pineapple | onkye | Ananas comosus | — |

*Table 3. Cultivated Plants* (continued)

| English/Spanish | Panare | Botanical | Importance |
|---|---|---|---|
| | | Other Edible Plants | |
| rice | *aro* | *Oryza sativa* | *** |
| maize | *ke'nya* | *Zea mays* | ** |
| sugar cane | *karana* | *Saccarum officinarum* | ** |
| pepper | *pimi* | *Capsicum frutescens* | * |
| peanuts | *ko'nye* | *Arachis hypogaea* | — |
| | | Inedible Plants | |
| tobacco | *kowae* | *Nicotiana tabacum* | — |
| cotton | *tokëtë* | *Gossypium* sp. | — |
| curagua | *kawa'* | *Ananas erectifolius* | — |
| fish poison | *kayin* | *Tephrosia purpurea ( ?)* | — |

*Table 4. Fish and Amphibians*

| English/Spanish | Zoological Name | Panare | Importance |
|---|---|---|---|
| bocona | (?) | *amara* | *** |
| bagre rayado | *Pseudoplatystoma faciatus* | *kërrëpihpë* | ** |
| caribe (piranha) | *Serrasalmo Nattereri* | *pinye* | *** |
| picua | (?) | *tankicëkëmnë* | ** |
| payare | *Hydralicus scomberoides* | *pikua* | ** |
| coporo | (?) | *anaiko* | ** |
| (?) | (?) | *perewa* | ** |
| palometa | *Mylopus rubripinnis* | *kïïï* | ** |
| prinche | (?) | *kïrï* | * |
| mataguaro | *Crenicichla geayi* | *katawoin* | * |
| morocoto | (?) | *morokoto* | ** |
| guabina | *Hoplias malabaricus* | *wayu* | ** |
| pavón | *Cichla ocellaris* | *poom* | ** |
| curito | *Hoplesternum thoracatum* | *ankata* | ** |
| aguadulce | (?) | *are* | ** |
| sardinetas | (?) | *kiripe* | ** |
| eel | *Electrophorus electricus* | *karinya* | ** |
| caiman | *Caiman sclerops* | *onwe* | ** |
| turtle | *Podocnemis unifilis* | *arakaya* | * |

*Table 5. Game Animals*

| English/Spanish | Zoological Name | Panare | Importance |
|---|---|---|---|
| | | Land Game | |
| agouti | *Dasyprocta aguti* | *akwoin* | *** |
| tapir | *Tapirus terrestris* | *wara* | *** |
| white-lipped peccary | *Tayassu pecari* | *pinkë* | *** |

*Table 5. Game Animals* (continued)

| English/Spanish | Zoological Name | Panare | Importance |
|---|---|---|---|
| collared peccary | *Dicotyles tajacu* | *paika* | ** |
| deer | *Mazama americana* | *waiki* | ** |
| paca | *Agouti paca* | *ongoma* | ** |
| capuchin monkey | *Cebus apella* | *amsirï* | ** |
| howler monkey | *Alouatta seniculus* | *kota* | * |
| night monkey | *Aotus trivirgatus* | *makwën* | * |
| capybara | *Hydrochoerus hydrochaeris* | *ciwiri* | * |
| coati | *Nasua nasua* | *marisana* | * |
| tree anteater | *Tamandua tetradactyla* | *wënki* | * |
| armadillo | *Dasypus novemcinctus* | *kahkam* | * |
| tortoise | *Testudo tabulata* | *ya'ara* | — |

| Birds | | | |
|---|---|---|---|
| guan | *Crax alector* | *poi'* | ** |
|  | (?) | *anamae* | ** |
|  | (?) | *wai'ka* | ** |
| toucan | *Pamphastos* sp. | *cipuko* | ** |
| macaw | *Ara* sp. | *kamaya* | ** |
| parrot | *Amazonia* sp. | *nörö* | * |
| tinamou | *Crypturellus* sp. | *pö'ne* | * |
| guacharaca | *Ortalis motmot* | *tankohka* | * |
| pava rajadora | *Pipile cumanensis* | *kuyi* | * |
| (?) | (?) | *nötö* | * |

*Table 6. Edible Wild Fruits*

| English/Spanish | Botanical Name | Panare | Importance |
|---|---|---|---|
| Palms | | | |
| kokorito | *Maximiliana regia* | *wë'sae* | *** |
| coroba | *Jessenia* sp. | *kuruwa* | *** |
| yagua | *Jessenia* sp. | *kötö* | ** |
| ite (moriche) | *Mauritia* sp. | *ankayano* | ** |
| seje | *Jessenia bataua* | *kahse* | * |
| pijiguao | *Guilielma gasipaes* | *acama* | * |
| Others | | | |
| mango | *Mangifera indica* | *manko* | *** |
| charo | *Heliocostylis tomentosa* (?) | *canka* | ** |
| caruto | *Genipa* sp. | *anku'* | ** |
| merey | *Anacardium occidentale* | *mëre* | * |
| jobo | *Spondias mombim* | *mopae* | * |

## Table 7. Useful Wild Plants

| Panare | Botanical Name | Use/Preparation |
|---|---|---|
| | Poisons | |
| mankowa | Strychnos fendleri * | Curare, used for blowpipe darts. The bark is peeled off, mashed in water and boiled up to produce the poison |
| enerima | Lonchocarpus sp. (?) | A liana that grows in the serranía, used as a fish poison. |
| kayin | Tephrosia purpurea (?) | Fish poison, cultivated in the gardens but also grows wild. |
| mincawa | Piper sp. * | Fish poison, not used as frequently as the others. |
| | Medicines/Drugs | |
| kosiyo | (?) | Emetics used to 'cure' stomach |
| caimiyo | Clavija lancifolia * | upsets or pains. Kosiyo is more common. |
| kowĕnye | (?) | Emetics used in the preparation of |
| maipihpë | Sapindaceae fam. * | boys for their initiation ritual. |
| kërëkëruma | (?) | |
| enyëre | Ruellia affin. pterocaulin * | Emetic used during the course of preparation to become a shaman. |
| amarapuhemkai'mën | Anadenanthra sp. (?) | A sort of seed pod (?) said to resemble the scales of a fish and to be found on the ground in the serranía. Mixed with tobacco and the bones of two particular species of bird, it has a psychotropic effect when inhaled through the nose. |
| söwö, poihpo'pin, etc. | (?) | Ta'mento, i.e. medicines taken to bring success at hunting. The Panare take a wide range of these. |
| marana | Copaifera officinalis | An oil is extracted from the bark and is used for anointing wounds. The inner bark is also used as a basketry binding and the trunk is often used in house frames. |
| | Body Paints | |
| anku | Genipa sp. | Sp: Caruto. Unripe, it produces a juice that stains the skin black. Ripe, it is eaten. |

* identified by Dr M. Kalin de Arroyo

*Table 7. Useful Wild Plants* (continued)

| Panare | Botanical Name | Use/Preparation |
|---|---|---|
| *wace* | *Bixa orellana* | Onoto. Mixed with plantains to form a red paste, with which bodies, loincloths, hammocks, etc., are painted. Also used to flavour food. |

### Basketry

| | | |
|---|---|---|
| *wë'sae* | *Maximiliana regia* | Kokorito. Palm leaves most commonly used to weave carrying and storage baskets. Fruit is eaten. |
| *manankye* | *Ischnosiphon obliquiformis* * | Itiriti. Used in the manufacture of manioc sieves, presses and *wapas*, decorative baskets sold to the criollos. |
| *mahco* | *Myrcia* sp. * | Used to produce a black varnish to paint elements of *wapas* with. |
| *kehco* | *Byrsonima crassifolia* * | Used to produce a red varnish. |

### Musical Instruments

| | | |
|---|---|---|
| *areare* | *Olyra* sp. * | Bamboo-like grass from which panpipes are made. |
| *kosanka* | *Cecropia* sp. | Larger bamboo-like plant from which the *aramëlaimë*, long twin flutes, are made. |

* *Identified by Dr Mary Kalin de Arroyo*

# CHAPTER THREE

# The Economic System

Having provided the necessary background information in the first two chapters, I am now in a position to enter into a more analytical account of the internal organization of Panare society. I choose to begin with a discussion of their economic system, largely as a matter of convenience: I certainly do not do so because I consider the general structure of Panare society to be entirely determined by economic factors. Rather I conceive of the economic system as standing between the ecological system in which the Panare live, on the one hand, and their system of social and political relations on the other. The economic system both determines and is determined by their relationship with the natural environment. Similarly, the social and political organization of Panare society both determines and is determined by their system of economic relations.

In the concluding section of the last chapter, I discussed the Panare's attitude toward the exploitation of natural resources, describing it as both 'prodigal' and, under traditional circumstances, entirely rational. It must be considered an intrinsic aspect of their ecological adaptation, since it gives rise to a pattern of extensive resource exploitation rather than the intensive exploitation of the resources at any one site. Yet this attitude is not some free-floating idea that the Panare happen to hold for entirely fortuitous reasons. Nor can it be explained simply as a device whereby, without their conscious knowledge, they are maintained in some sort of equilibrium with available resources. Rather it is the product of a given social milieu, an integral part of which are a set of economic relations structured in a particular way. My purpose in this chapter will be to describe the principles underlying these economic relations, discuss how they work together as a system and show how they fit with the Panare's attitude towards the exploitation of natural resources. Then, in subsequent chapters, I will go on to discuss how this system of economic relations articulates with other domains of Panare society.

The most fundamental guiding principle of Panare economic life is the division of subsistence duties according to sex. In the activities taking place beyond the immediate vicinity of the settlement, it is the men who play the most active role. Hunting and fishing are primarily the responsibility of men: although women may join in expeditions to cook for the hunters when they return to camp at night and may participate in the collection of fish after a creek has been poisoned, in both these activities their role is clearly secondary to that of the men. Women play a more active role in agriculture and in gathering. But it is the men who cut and fire the gardens and who are primarily responsible for clearing the debris afterwards. Men do the heavy work when the planting begins in a new garden: it is they who dig the holes in which banana stumps are planted and turn over the circular mounds of earth for the planting of manioc cuttings. Women plant the other, less important root crops (yams, sweet potato, etc.) and the seed crops (maize, rice, fruits, etc.) around the perimeter of the garden. Men also take charge of the planting of sugar cane gardens. Weeding is the responsibility of both sexes but most of the harvesting is done by women. Men harvest only certain crops systematically: rice, because it has to be cropped as soon as it is ready in November before it rots or is blown down by the winds of the *serainpe* (December–January); tobacco, because they are very fond of it, and sugar cane for the beer consumed at dances because at this time the women are usually busy preparing the beer itself. The gathering of wild fruits is both a male and female activity but the collection of honey is exclusively male since it frequently involves felling honey-bearing trees with an axe, a task that women are not thought capable of doing. Finally, the gathering of plants used in the manufacture of domestic artifacts or from which poisons or medicines are made is also almost exclusively a male activity.

But although the men play the most active part in the subsistence activities taking place outside the settlement, it is the women who do most of the work within it. Entering a Panare settlement, one is struck by the contrast between the men lounging in their hammocks and the women carrying water and hewing wood, preparing and cooking the food, tending children and keeping the floor of the house and the surrounding area free of debris. If the men do anything within the settlement, it is usually basketry, either for sale to the criollos or for domestic use. In communities where the blowpipe is still in regular use, the men will often be seen preparing darts from the splinters of the trunk of a palm tree and, very occasionally, preparing the curare with which these darts will be painted. In north-western Panare territory, where commercial basketry plays an important part in the economy, some men dedicate a great deal of time to this activity. Elsewhere I have estimated that, taking the year as a whole, the adult

Panare men of Colorado spend an average of between one and two days a week engaged in commercial basketry. But although basketry can be time-consuming, it is not a particularly strenuous activity: the collection of the raw material requires a special expedition to the mountains, but most of the preparation of these materials and the actual weaving are performed on the days when the men are taking a rest from their normal subsistence activities. These times would otherwise be used only for resting and chatting. Moreover when a man does work on commercial baskets on a rest day, he will intersperse bouts of basket work with long periods of relaxation in his hammock (Henley and Müller, 1978: 51 *et seq.*).

Women also manufacture certain articles of domestic use. In the communities where pottery is still used, that is in those of the southeastern sector of Panare territory, the women produce a course black ware in a standard shape of varying dimensions. In all Panare communities, women spend a great deal of time spinning cotton and weaving hammocks and loincloths from it. They also twine human hair to make the gaiters that both men and women wear around their calves. During the latter period of the rainy season, they are busy preparing balls of body paint by mixing onoto with a mash of cooked bananas.

The productive roles of men and women are complementary, and between them an adult man and an adult woman are capable of carrying out the great majority of day-to-day productive activities. Consequently a man and his wife (or wives) constitute a largely self-sufficient unit of production. So does the combination of a widow and an unmarried adult son. In theory, so would the combination of a widower and an unmarried adult daughter but in actual practice combinations of this type are very rare. Individuals who do not have an adult partner of the opposite sex are obliged to tack themselves on to the conjugal family of a sibling or an offspring. In most cases, the members of these various permutations on the basic self-sufficient unit of production will hang their hammocks around one of the hearths distributed along the perimeter of a Panare communal house. These hearths are maintained by the women of the unit and act as a sort of centre of gravity for it. Only in the case of a unit consisting of a widow or divorcée and her unmarried adult sons are the hammocks of the members of the unit separated from one another. In this case the unmarried men's hammocks are hung in the centre of the house whilst those of their mother and their sisters will be located a few yards away at the perimeter of the house. Even so, the unmarried sons of such a production unit gravitate to their mother's hearth if they want anything of her, so it is convenient to refer to this and all the other social variations on the basic unit of production as a 'hearth group' (see Silverwood-Cope 1972).

Although the work roles of men and women are complementary, the rhythms of male and female work are quite different. Men's work, being more closely linked to the production of raw materials and hence to the seasonality of subsistence resources, is more variable and episodic than that of women. At certain times of year, notably during the first months of the rainy season, the men of a settlement are extremely busy preparing and planting new gardens. But during the dry season, men can fulfil their duty to provide meat without much effort because large quantities of fish are readily available in the rivers. Moreover, there is not much weeding to be done in the gardens. At this time of year, therefore, the male members of the settlement are free to spend many of their days loafing about in their hammocks, drinking one of a number of forms of slightly intoxicating beer. Women's work is not subject to these dramatic seasonal fluctuations. Furthermore, much of the work they do in the settlement is less intensive than that of the men. As they go about their domestic chores, there are moments when women can sit in their hammocks and chat with one another about the day's events. But in Panare society too, a woman's work is never done. Even in the dry season, when food is generally easier to come by and their menfolk lounge about drinking beer, the women are usually busy preparing it. In short, although a woman's work is generally less intensive than a man's, it is more routinised, more time-consuming and more tedious. A man may leave on a hunting expedition at dawn and return at dusk exhausted, having spent the whole day in pursuit of game without a mouthful of food to sustain him. But the next day, and possibly the day after that as well, he will remain in his hammock or engage in a little basketwork and nothing more. A woman on the other hand, even if she has been on a strenuous expedition to the mountains, will be up and about the next day, working as ever at her domestic chores.

The fact that the rhythms of male and female productive roles are quite different makes it difficult to compare them directly; even so, it is still generally true to say that, overall, women have a harder working life than men in Panare society. This is never more apparent than in the situation where a load has to be carried. If both men and women are present, it is invariably the women who do the carrying. On one occasion, I joined a collective expedition to the mountains to pick over the old garden sites there. We left at dawn and were back in the settlement roughly twelve hours later. On the return journey, which took up about a third of this time, the women were laden with heavy back-packs of bananas weighing at least 25 kg each. As they

Plate 7. A group of men from Tiro Loco and their sons, about to disappear into the forest to hunt down a herd of peccary whose tracks had been spotted earlier in the day.

inched their way down the steep slopes of the mountainside, they used sticks to prevent themselves from falling. Although the men were very ready to offer advice on how to negotiate difficult stretches, it apparently never occurred to them to relieve the women of their loads. Although some of the men were carrying pieces of game that they had shot during the expedition, or basketry materials, these weighed far less than the loads the women were carrying. Yet, next day, although it was the women who had had the most exhausting trip to the mountains, the men lay in their hammocks complaining about their weariness, whilst the women went out to pick palm fruits. The rationale for this practice of giving women any load to be carried is that the men should always have their hands free, in case a game animal should cross their path on the way home. But even when a man has no weapons with which to kill an animal, or has no intention of using those that he does have, he will usually walk home freely whilst his wife plods along behind, carrying her load and often a suckling child as well.

After the sexual division of labour, the next most important principle underlying the social organization of production is the absence of property rights over natural resources. The Panare have a strong sense of private property in so far as items of personal use are concerned. Even within the conjugal family, the property rights of individuals are respected. I found that a man would not sell me the baskets he had woven for his wife without consulting her. Nor would he sell me a hammock or a loincloth without discussing the price with her, explaining as he did so that it was she who would have to weave a replacement. Between the Panare themselves however, the question of ownership over these sorts of items rarely arises: every hearth group produces all items of indigenous manufacture, so there is never any reason for the exchange of such items. Moreover the number of items of personal property that an individual Panare is likely to have is very small and mostly consists of tools, hammocks and articles of dress.

In the past, when a person died his few personal possessions were either destroyed or went with him to the grave. But now that the Panare have begun to acquire industrial goods worth several hundred *bolívares* and which are not easily replaced, they do not always destroy or bury the deceased's possession. A case in point involved the shotgun of a man who died shortly before I arrived in the settlement where I stayed throughout most of my period in the field. Shotguns are one of the most expensive items that a Panare man ever owns, and at that time a government moratorium on hunting and the sale of hunting arms and ammunition made them particularly hard to come by. The man's sons were loath to part with the shotgun and it remained in the communal house. But this disturbed one of his widows who felt that so long as the gun remained within the house, her husband's spirit would not be free to go to the place of the dead. Instead, it would remain hovering around the house. This she considered to be very dangerous, it being widely believed that the dead often return to their house to seek out a member of their family to take with them. The widow therefore insisted that the shotgun be disposed of. After some discussion, the eldest son finally agreed on a compromise whereby the gun was not destroyed but was sold back to the criollos from whom it had been bought many years before instead.

In the communities where the Panare derive a substantial income from commercial basketry, most hearth groups have a full complement of the basic tools used in subsistence activities—principally, axes, *chícoras* and machetes. In addition, some men, particularly young men, use the income derived from the sale of baskets to acquire a number of 'luxury' goods: bicycles, record players, radios, perfumes, etc. Given that most hearth groups have a full complement of basic subsistence tools, very little borrowing goes on between them. This is not quite so true when it comes to blowpipes and shotguns, both of which are now in short supply. Panare men will borrow these from one another on occasion, but prefer not to do so, owing, apparently, to their strong sense of private ownership of items of personal use.

Apart from rights over instruments of labour, no individual has any permanent or alienable property rights over the means of production. No stretch of river or forest is regarded as the exclusive preserve of a given group or individual. A man can cut a garden wherever he thinks the land is suitable or hunt wherever there is game. Once he has cut a garden, the product belongs to him and to the other members of his hearth group. But this right is no more than a right of usufruct. When a garden is abandoned as the banana production begins to decline, the owner's rights over the product begin to become tenuous. Although the fruits of the garden are said to remain his in perpetuity, no serious objections are raised if others enter an old garden and pick off anything they can find there. When a man dies whilst his gardens are still actively producing, their product reverts to his wife (or wives) and children.[1]

In the absence of any individual ownership of the means of production (other than tools), no individual depends on another for access to them. Furthermore, only a limited number of subsistence activities absolutely require collaboration between two or more individuals. When two men are opening gardens side by side, they usually collaborate with one another for the sake of convenience since a tree felled in one plot will usually bring down a number of others adjacent to it, including trees within the limits of the neighbouring plot. Similarly, when the gardens are fired, the flames will pass from one to another easily. But once the gardens have been fired, each man, along with his wife and children, works his own plot. A straight line of bananas or the trunk of a fallen tree serves to demarcate one plot from another.

Men also collaborate in certain forms of hunting and fishing. Some animals, notably peccary and tapir, are better hunted by a group than alone. When such collective hunts are successful, the prize is divided amongst all the participants, regardless of whether they have been in at the kill or not. These divisions are made in a somewhat haphazard way and not much importance is set by them since most of the meat will be consumed collectively. As we shall see, this collective pattern of distribution and consumption levels out any differences in the volume of food that individual men bring back to the settlement. There is a similar apparent lack of justice about the way in which the product of

1. Although there is no necessary homology between language and social attitudes, it is interesting to note that the structure of the Panare language does not lend itself to statements indicating possession of any feature of the natural environment (cf. Müller 1974).

Plate 8. (left). Men poisoning fish with the aid of *enerima* in a river running through the Colorado valley. It is the height of the dry season, and the river is very low. Behind them, their harpoons, up to 3m in length, stick up out of the water.

Plate 9. (right). A man digs a hole for a plantain root in his recently cleared garden. He uses a *chicora*, a metal adze head obtained through trade with the criollos.

a fish poisoning expedition is shared. When a stream is to be poisoned, almost all the members of a settlement group will participate, including the women and the children. Somebody has to go to the mountains or to the gardens to collect the fish poison beforehand. But no special rights are accorded over the product to the men who go to collect the poison. On the contrary, the men who provide the poison are very likely to get less than their fair share of the catch, for whilst they are busy preparing the poison and immersing it in the water upstream, the others will be stationing themselves at the choice vantage points downstream. But here too, this seemingly unjust form of appropriating the product is compensated for by the system of distribution and consumption.

Within the area of the settlement, the only collective male activities are the construction of the communal house and the preparation of the beer canoe and other paraphernalia used in dances. Although all the male members of a settlement usually take part in the construction of the house, there is no absolute obligation to do so. It was quite noticeable that some men were more active in this task than others. But once the house is completed, all members of the group have a right to live in it regardless of the extent of their participation in its construction. Although the house may then be referred to as the 'house of *x*', *x* being the senior man of the settlement, this term is merely one of reference and implies no exclusive right over it. There are no circumstances in which he can alienate the house nor, on his authority alone, deny any other Panare the right to live in it. The same observations apply to the preparation of beer canoes; most or all or the men in the settlement participate in the production of these items and on completion they are regarded as articles of collective property. But, although these collective enterprises form a crucial part of Panare economic life at certain periods, they account for only a minor part of the labour an individual man expends on productive activities over the course of a year.

Women's work is generally more collaborative than men's. Within the settlement, sisters and/or mothers and daughters often share a common cooking hut, and within these they may help one another in the preparation of food and the tending of children. Women never leave the settlement alone, so, should their husbands be absent, they will go accompanied by a mother, daughter or sister. But, as in the case of men, very few of the women's activities absolutely require cooperation.

Although every individual has the same duties as every other person of the same sex, the amount of time that an individual spends working varies with age as well as with idiosyncratic factors of individual preference and ability. Furthermore, the way in which individuals allocate the time they spend working on subsistence tasks varies in the same way. This is readily apparent when one lives in a Panare settlement; but I tried to get a more exact measure of this effect by keeping a work diary. In attempting to do so, I came up against insuperable difficulties that made any form of precise quantification impossible. It is worth citing some of these difficulties because, in themselves, they highlight certain features of the Panare work pattern.

On a day that he has decided to work, a man usually leaves the settlement at dawn or shortly afterwards. Unless it begins to rain or the sun gets too hot for comfort, he will normally return about mid-afternoon and, having bathed in the stream nearby, he will retire to his hammock. When he leaves the settlement he will have a more or less clear idea of what he will do since this will influence the kind of weapon or tool that he takes, as well as, of course, the direction in which he sets off. But should some other opportunity present itself, he may well abandon his original plan. Thus a honey- or fruit-collecting expedition might turn into a hunting trip should tracks be spotted and the man have his shotgun with him. Alternatively a man might get bored with weeding his garden and decide to set off instead in search of some medicinal plant. If a stream runs by the edge of his garden, a man may take his hook and line and try his luck with that for a while. If the fish are biting, his plans to weed his sugar cane will be abandoned.

The only way in which one could keep an exact account of what an individual did with the time that he was absent from the settlement was to go with him. This meant I was able to keep track of only one man at a time outside the settlement. It was even difficult to keep track of what the Panare were up to within the settlement. The Panare are prone to begin working at all times of day and night. Men would get up at 3 a.m. in order to start work on weaving baskets by the light of a kerosene lamp. At this hour, baskets are easier to weave because the air is damp and the basket elements are more supple. During the period when cassava bread is an important part of the diet (mostly the dry season), the women of the settlement would sometimes spend the whole night taking turns on the manioc grater. To record all these activities would have required constant vigilance day and night.

Faced with these difficulties, I contented myself with writing down what each of the men of the settlement spent most of their time doing on each day. I tried to keep track of women's work also but there were many lacunae in my record. I kept this work diary systematically over three thirty-day periods: May–June 1975 (early rainy season); November–December 1975 (late rainy season) and February–March (high dry season). Even this modest project had its difficulties, as throughout the year one or more of the hearth groups of a Panare settlement are likely to be absent on an expedition to a distant resource zone or on a visit elsewhere. Although an expedition to the mountains in search of game might last several days or even weeks, only part of this time would actually be spent hunting. Similarly, although the immediate motive for a visit to another settlement or to the criollos may be purely 'social', such visits would usually have some economic aspect as well. Thus a visit to another settlement would often take place at a time when a particular wild fruit or a certain animal was known to be available in the vicinity. An expedition to the criollos, although often the occasion for cadging food or drinking a spot of rum, normally also involved some sort of economic exchange.

Only the most minute account of such expeditions would allow one to separate the time spent in economic activities from that spent on what could be termed 'non-economic' behaviour. I usually found it impossible to get anything more than a loose account of how the members of an expedition had spent their time. Moreover, the distinction that I had in mind between economic and non-economic behaviour was quite alien to my informants. Although the Panare never confuse work with relaxation, they have no set times for working and neither the interest nor the means to compute the time dedicated to it. During the dry season, expeditions are very frequent; and this makes keeping a systematic work diary impossible because the inhabitants of a settlement are in a constant state of flux. In fact at one point in March 1976, in the middle of the dry season, there were more visitors than hosts in the settlement in which I was living.

But even though the data that I collected were not as systematic as I had hoped, they were quite sufficient to discern a number of general trends. A man does not become a fully productive member of the settlement until he is married, that is, when he is in his early twenties. Until then, a male adolescent leads a carefree life, doing as little work as possible. He may work in his parents' gardens occasionally and participate in collective hunts and fishing expeditions. But most of his time will be spent in the settlement, either just loafing or making baskets for sale to the criollos. When these are ready, he will go off on an expedition to Caicara and buy all kinds of 'luxury' goods with the money he makes. He will remain in Caicara until the money runs out and then return to start making baskets again. The parents of such young men take an indulgent attitude to this sort of behaviour and assume that they will in the nature of things become more responsible as they grow older.

Even young married men are prone to go running off on visits to other Panare settlements or to the criollo towns, but gradually, as their families begin to grow, they become more diligent. By the time he reaches about twenty-five, a man is usually a fully productive member of his settlement group and he will remain so, increasing in skill and competence until he is about forty-five. By this time, he will probably have adult sons and sons-in-law living in his settlement and will therefore play a slightly less energetic role in subsistence activities. Even so, most senior men continue to pull their weight in the productive activities of the settlement until old age brings on physical incapacity.

Unless otherwise stated, in the following generalizations about the work pattern of men, I will be referring to that of mature men at full productive capacity. The first period in which I kept a work diary, the early part of the rainy season, is the busiest time of the year for men. During this period, I found that mature men spent on average between one day in three and one day in four in the settlement. It is very rare for a man, unless he is on a hunting or fishing expedition to a distant resource habitat, to spend two or more consecutive days doing the same thing. The days that he spends outside the settlement will alternate between strenuous and less strenuous subsistence activities. After a hard day working in the gardens for example, the next day is likely to be spent collecting palm fruits or searching for honey, neither of which require a great deal of effort. If the day after that is not spent in the settlement, it will probably be spent hunting, which although not quite as intensive as gardening is usually more exhausting on account of the large distances that have to be covered. Mature men rarely do absolutely nothing on the days that they rest from sub-sistence tasks. If they do not use these days for basket-weaving, they may well go on a visit to the criollos or to another Panare settlement. If a man feels tired on the day after one of these excursions, he may take that day off from subsistence activities as well.

In the second period in which I kept a work diary, the late part of the rainy season, the ratio of days spent in subsistence activities to days spent within the settlement or on 'social' visits was about the same as in the first period. But despite this overall similarity, there were a number of significant differences in the day-to-day work pattern. The mature men of the settlement spent fewer days in their gardens and a correspondingly greater number of days fishing (mainly with hook and line because the water level in the rivers had only just started to fall). Furthermore, the subsistence tasks of this period of the rainy season were generally less strenuous than those of the earlier period. Then, agricultural work often consisted of clearing debris from fired gardens and planting banana roots and sugar cane. At the end of the rainy season however, men's garden work consisted mainly of weeding, cutting rice and tending tobacco. Although the first two of these activities are time-consuming and tedious, they are far less strenuous than preparing the ground for planting. Although the amount of time dedicated to hunting remained more or less the same in the two periods, fishing began to take over from hunting in the later period as the most important source of animal protein. Fishing is a less physically demanding activity than hunting and has the added advantage that it frequently takes place in the immediate vicinity of the settlement. Finally, the working days in the later period were generally shorter than in the early period of the rainy season. It was often the case during the later period that men would return at midday and spend the remainder of the day relaxing or working on baskets. Alternatively they might spend the best part of the day in the settlement and then go out for a couple of hours towards dusk, hoping to catch the game birds which are an important part of the diet at this time of year, as they came back to roost.

The diary I kept during the height of the dry season indicates that men do even less work at this time than they do in the latter part of the rainy season. Fish are in plentiful supply at this time of year and the gardens planted at the beginning of the previous rainy season are beginning to come into full production. Consequently, subsistence needs are easily met and the ratio of days spent on subsistence activities to the days spent inside the settlement or on 'social' visits fell from three or four to one to between two and three to one. In fact, much of the work that men do at this time of year is directed not towards meeting immediate subsistence needs but to storing up a hoard of smoked meat to be consumed during dry season dances. Men very rarely visit their gardens at this time of year unless, of course, they have decided to cut a new one. But the cutting of a new garden, which takes between one and two weeks of intermittent work depending on its size and the density of the undergrowth, is merely an interlude in an otherwise easy time of year for Panare men.

Within the limits of these overall seasonal variations, the way in which time is allocated varies from individual to individual. I have already mentioned that adolescents and young adults dedicate a disproportionate amount of their time to producing baskets for sale to the criollos. But even within the cohort of mature men, the way in which time is allocated seems to depend on personal factors of preference and ability. Garden work is generally regarded as the most tedious form of labour but some men are more diligent at it than others. Likewise, some appear to be better hunters than others and consequently spend more time on it. I even noticed a tendency towards specialization in the variety of animals hunted: some men were 'experts' at killing deer, others more frequently came home with agouti. To a certain extent this informal specialization is dependent on the weapons a man has. If a man has a shotgun, he is more likely to go after larger game; if he only has a blowpipe he will be able to kill only small game and birds. A man who has neither, rather than be continually borrowing someone else's weapons, will prefer to fish with hook and line, which are comparatively cheap and easy to acquire.

Very little attempt is made to plan and coordinate the work of the men of a settlement group. On an individual level, a man may plan ahead for periods as great as a year: if he intends to put his son through the initiation ceremonies one dry season, he will plant an extra large garden of sugar cane the previous rainy season so as to be able to provide a good quantity of beer at the dance. But on a day-to-day basis, an individual will only plan his working days in the loosest way, weighing up the immediate food needs of the settlement against his personal interests and inclinations. For example, it was not infrequent at a men's collective meal at which there had been very little meat, for it to be generally agreed that the next day should be spent in hunting and fishing. But there would always be individuals who stayed at home the next day, either because they had a commercial basket they wanted to finish off, or because they were feeling tired, or simply because they could not be bothered to do anything else. Others would leave the settlement intent on working in their garden, leaving the problem of the meat deficiency to be solved by others.

As we shall see in Chapter 5, there are no strong political authorities in Panare society that might direct the economic activities of others. Consequently, whether or not subsistence needs are met very much depends on the sense of responsibility that individuals feel towards the settlement group in which they live. Although the Panare see no particular merit in hard work *per se*, there is a form of moral prestige to be gained from sharing out large amounts of food. Yet there are always some individuals who are more responsive to the group's needs than others and these are invariably the more mature members of the group. This is particularly the case when something has to be produced for the group as a whole, from which the producer cannot hope to get any direct personal benefit. For example, during the dry season when cassava bread is important in the diet, the women of a settlement need a manioc press and a number of sieves with which to process the manioc mash. These rarely last more than one season so that every year a new set has to be made. It is never the young men, with the most time on their hands, who make these items of collective property: they are too busy making commercial baskets to exchange for record-players and bicycles. Instead, this task is invariably left to the older men of the settlement.

The working pattern of women varies much less from season to season than does that of men. Throughout the year, women's work conforms to the general pattern of one day in the settlement, the next day out. Women never dedicate the whole day to lounging as the men do, although they may relax for short periods during the course of a day spent in the settlement. Furthermore, the labour intensity of women varies less according to age than does the labour of the male members of the settlement. Working life starts much earlier for a girl than for a boy. Even little girls of four or five can be seen helping their mothers in domestic chores whilst their brothers run freely about the settlement. The young girl's involvement in her mother's duties gradually increases until she is about 15 by which time she will have become nubile. After marriage she takes on all the responsibilities of an adult woman. The life of a young married woman is very laborious and it is only when her own daughters approach puberty and begin to take some of her domestic chores that her lot seems to improve. But even a mature woman with adult daughters spends more time working than her male counterpart.

In summary then, the hearth group forms a more or less self-sufficient unit of production even though the members of such a unit will collaborate with others on occasion. But in the sphere of distribution and consumption the reverse is the case: whilst some proportion of the product is consumed within the hearth group, the greater part is distributed and consumed collectively by all the members of the settlement group.

In describing the relations of distribution and consumption, I will be referring almost exclusively to the distribution and consumption of food. Each of the hearth groups provisions itself with tools and other items of technology, whether these be of indigenous manufacture or derived from trade with the criollos. The only exceptions to this general rule that I observed involved cases of married sons providing widowed mothers with trade goods. In these instances, the widows had no other means of acquiring such goods, for like all women in Panare society, they did not trade directly with the criollos, whilst their unmarried sons, who formed the male part of their hearth groups, were either too young or too preoccupied with provisioning themselves with trade goods to worry about their mothers' needs.

The typical daily routine of food distribution and consumption is as follows: the individuals who have spent the day outside the settlement usually return by mid-afternoon, the women usually somewhat earlier than the men. Whilst the men retire to their hammocks, the women start to prepare the cooking fires. Each adult woman has her own hearth on which she prepares the food brought back by herself and the other members of her hearth group. Once the food is prepared, the male members of her hearth group may come to her hearth and sample a portion of the meal. If there is a lot of food, these private meals can be quite substantial. But generally speaking, whatever the volume of the day's product, the food consumed privately is usually less than the amount surrendered for collective consumption.

In the case of men, collective consumption takes the form of a meal which is usually eaten just before sunset. The men who have produced something that day, or whose hearth group women have done so, contribute bowls of food. These are usually placed in a group on the ground, meat bowls in the centre, vegetable foods at the edge, just outside the door of the principal house in the settlement. All the men of the settlement have a right to partake of this food, regardless of their contribution on that day or any other. There is no clear principle of hierarchy as to who eats which of the foods provided, although I noted that the younger men tended to refrain from being the first to pick out the choice pieces of meat or the largest fish. When male visitors are present, they are invited to eat their fill first, accompanied only by the most senior men of the settlement, whilst the remainder of the men wait on the sidelines. It is generally regarded as bad manners to show oneself to be eager to eat and mature men always show great restraint around the food bowls, even when they are very hungry. In times of great scarcity, senior men will eat very little or even nothing at all, eyeing the younger men superciliously should they show themselves too keen to get at the food. Anyone can initiate a men's collective meal by placing his contribution on the ground and calling the others to eat. But no one will do this until all the men of the group are present, even if this means waiting until long after dark for a man known to have gone on a long hunting trip.

Women never participate in the collective meals of men. Although women often have their own collective meals, in or around the cook huts, these are less frequent and less formal affairs than those of the men. Instead, a certain amount of food sharing goes on amongst the women as they are preparing the meals. Since the cooking hearths of a mother and her married daughters are often located next to one another within a single cook hut, it is easy for them to pass one another samples of the food they are preparing.

Generally speaking, the distribution of food beyond the range of the hearth group and the process of collective consumption take place simultaneously at the collective meal. But there are one or two exceptions to this general pattern. The most common is the gift of raw meat that a daughter sometimes makes to her mother. As part of his bride service obligation, a man is supposed to provision his mother-in-law with meat but he always does so *via* his wife. Any game that he brings into the settlement is handed over to his wife who gives part of this, if she thinks fit, to her mother. The mother will then prepare the meat on her own hearth and when it is cooked, give part of it to her husband (the producer's father-in-law) to contribute to the man's collective meal or even to eat privately by her hearth. The other exception to the general pattern of simultaneous distribution and consumption involves the distribution of garden produce. Should the woman of one hearth group be short of food to prepare, the woman of another may invite her to come and harvest from her garden. There are no strings attached to such an invitation; the invited woman takes what she likes back to the settlement, and prepares and distributes it in the normal manner, as if it were her own produce. Arrangements of this kind often involve mothers and their married daughters but (unlike the gift of meat described above which forms a recognized part of bride service) it could just as well be the mother who invites her daughter as *vice versa*. In fact, there are no restrictions on who invites whom: in my settlement, one particular man used to allow his widowed mother to harvest food from his garden because his unmarried brothers did not support her properly; in another case, the wife of a newcomer to the Colorado valley was allowed to harvest her sister's garden until her husband had got his own garden established.

On most days, there is one main male collective meal at dusk. During the day each individual hearth group fends for itself. But this normal pattern does not hold during periods of glut, nor in periods of scarcity. During periods of glut, there are sometimes two or three collective meals a day, while during periods of scarcity there are sometimes no collective meals at all. During these latter periods, each hearth group keeps its food to itself, consuming what it has in surreptitious private meals. The Panare's attitude to these private meals during periods of scarcity is somewhat uneasy because they conflict with the general principle underlying food sharing in Panare society: no-one should go hungry when someone else has food in the house. There are various simple devices by which an individual can remove such private meals from the public stage: he can eat in the relative privacy of his wife's cook hut or, if he prefers to eat in the communal house, he can make show of the fact that he is engaging in a private meal by the simple means of turning his back on the others present as he eats. But although these conventional procedures are usually respected, they do not, of course, prevent others from knowing that someone has food at a time when others do not. Too many private meals at a time when food is scarce can lead to the circulation of remarks about the stinginess of those who engage in them. In order to escape from this tense situation, some hearth groups may break off from the settlement and retire to a temporary house in the forest or in the mountains. On the other hand, a man who throws open his private meals to the public, particularly at a time when food is scarce, is regarded as *ayape*, a term used to denote anyone who is considered to be good in a general moral sense, a condition which for the Panare is measured to a large extent by how generous one is with the food one has produced.

This food-sharing principle militates against long-term accumulation of food on the part of any individual hearth group. Climatic factors make storage difficult for the Panare but by no means impossible. Smoked meat can be kept for several weeks, whilst rice can be stored for over a year. Maize can be dried and hung in the rafters of the house where it will keep for at least a year. In some Panare settlements I have seen smoked balls of mashed manioc and other roots which last for several weeks. Even cassava bread will keep for a few weeks. All these foods taste better when eaten fresh but. it is the principle of sharing rather than straightforward considerations of tastiness that militates against accumulation. Accumulation of meat is only *socially* feasible at times when there is a surplus. This surplus has to be large, larger indeed than the amount that could be consumed in a couple of days. In the rainy season, this is quite impossible. On one occasion in the rainy season of 1975, a group of men from the settlement in which I was living brought back a tapir and a number of monkeys and game birds from a hunting expedition to the mountains. This hoard of food lasted the twenty-three adults and nineteen children of the settlement no more than a couple of days. It was consumed at the rate of two or three collective meals a day until it was all gone, whereupon the settlement returned to the customary spartan diet of the rainy season. It is only the glut of fish that is available in the dry season that allows any significant accumulation of smoked meat. At this time, the more diligent hearth groups store away baskets of smoked fish in the rafters of the house. There is no pressure on them to surrender these to collective consumption during the dry season itself because further supplies of fish are easily acquired. But by the end of May, when the fishing season is over and the rainy season has set in, the pressure on those with smoked fish begins. In Colorado, although everyone knew that lean times lay ahead, these stores of smoked fish were rapidly consumed in substantial collective meals so that by the middle of June there was nothing left.

Accumulation of garden produce is somewhat easier. Although there are periods in the year when the gardens produce comparatively little, the supply of garden produce is not subject to quite the same cycle of glut and scarcity that is an inherent feature of the meat supply. Throughout the year, most Panare gardens have a little something in them, and if they do not, it is more the consequence of the failure to plant a big enough garden than the effect of the seasons themselves. But garden produce is not as highly regarded as meat, and in some senses the Panare do not really regard it as food at all. On more than one occasion, I was informed that there was no food in the house only to be simultaneously offered a bowl of boiled manioc. Nevertheless, once the dearth of the rainy season has truly set in, the baskets of rice that some hearth groups have managed to store away, begin to attract the attention of the other members of the settlement and their owners feel obliged to share them out.

A discussion of the Panare economic system is not complete without reference to the dances they hold almost every dry season. In this chapter, I will confine myself exclusively to the economic aspects of these dances, whilst in Chapter 5 I will discuss certain of their social aspects. They fall into three basic categories: dances described as *tëwënmën*, literally 'for nothing' dances, that is, dances held just for the fun of it; *pahpëto*, held following a death and, finally, a whole series of ceremonies spread out over the dry season, involving three major dances and a number of minor dances and ceremonies as well. The central feature of the last major dance in this series is the initiation of boys, whilst the other two major dances involve the celebration of the Panare's subsistence activities. Throughout this series of events, these two themes are ceremonially interwoven with one another. All three categories of dance require the preparation of large quantities of beer and in case of the series of ceremonies culminating in male initiation, large quantities of smoked meat and cassava bread as well. To produce the necessary food and drink requires a great deal of labour, not to mention the time needed to prepare the beer canoe and all the other ritual and musical paraphernalia that are an essential feature of any Panare dance.

A dance always has a *tihcen*, a male sponsor or 'owner' who provides the bulk of the sugar cane and garden produce used in the preparation of the beer. In the case of a *pahpëto*, the death dance, the *tihcen* will be a member of the conjugal family of the deceased; whilst in the series leading to male initiation, the *tihcen* will be the father(s) of the boy(s) to be initiated. In a *tëwënmën*, a 'for nothing' dance, the *tihcen* can be anyone who has a large surplus of sugar cane. But in all cases, the *tihcen's* supply is always supplemented by other members of his settlement who are free to make whatever contribution they think fit.

A few days before a dance, the men of the settlement begin bringing sugar cane from the gardens to the settlement where it is passed through a crude wooden press. The juice that is extracted is handed over to the women who prepare the beer by mixing it with bananas and burnt cassava bread. Although most of the members of the settlement will participate in the preparations for a dance, it is the women who do most of the work.

The men of the *tihcen's* settlement also pool their resources to provide the food for the series of dances leading to male initiation. Prior to the first of these, the men go on extended hunting and fishing trips. Part of the meat that is brought back is consumed during the first major dance of the series, the *murankinto*. The remainder is set aside and wrapped in banana leaves. Over the next few weeks this store of meat, known as the *kaimo'*, is supplemented by further supplies and during the second dance of the initiation series, the *kaimoyonkonto*, it is hoisted into the rafters of the house during a special ceremony. There the *kaimo'* must remain until the final dance in the series, the *katayinto,* when, on the day following the dressing of the initiands with their loincloths and items of ritual paraphernalia, it is taken down and distributed amongst all the people present. On no account must the *kaimo'* be touched before then because this could have a harmful effect on the initiands. The Panare stick rigorously to this principle even if there should be a temporary hiatus in their normal food supply.

The paraphernalia used in these dances is also the product of collective effort. A great deal of labour is expended in producing this gear. The provision of the beer canoe itself is no mean task. A large ceiba tree is selected, chopped down and hollowed out. The size of these canoes varies considerably from settlement to settlement. The one used in the settlement in which I was living in the dry season of 1976 was about 3m long and 1m deep, although I have seen them both larger and smaller. This hollowed trunk is then rolled and hauled back to the settlement. Clearly the labour involved in this task very much depends on how far the tree is from the settlement, but in the case just mentioned it took twelve men about two days of work each. All the men of the settlement, plus one or two outsiders, lent a hand, though some worked intermittently whilst others worked more or less throughout.

Plate 10.   The discarded stock of sugar cane from which the juice for the beer consumed during a season of initiation ceremonies was extracted.

But the beer canoe is only the first of the items of paraphernalia to be prepared. All the gear that the initiands will wear has to be made for the occasion. Prior to initiation a boy wears nothing but a hair belt and one or two minor adornments. During the initiation ceremony, he dons a large number of articles of apparel, the most important of which are his loincloth, his bead armbands and the *amsïrïyën*, a necklace of capuchin monkey teeth, from which a cluster of toucan pelts hang down the back of the wearer. Apart from the beads for the armbands, which are acquired by the initiand's father from the criollos, the other items are all produced through collective effort. The loincloth is woven by the women of the initiand's settlement, his mother and sisters playing the most active part. It is then passed to the men to be decorated. Although the female members of the initiand's family take part in the weaving of the loincloth, his father and brothers and other close relatives are expressly prohibited from taking a hand in the decoration of the loincloth. The loincloth is painted with a number of conventional designs by the remaining male members of the initiand's settlement during an all-day drinking session. The painting proceeds extremely slowly because every step in the design is the subject of rambling aesthetic discussions. The men who are not involved in the painting of the loincloth (and who are not members of the initiand's immediate family) sit about making other adornments for the initiand: his crown of plaited palm leaves and macaw feathers, his ear and nose adornments, the cotton bandoliers which young adult men wear and, most importantly, the *amsïrïyën*. The members of the settlement start collecting materials for the latter several months beforehand. They have to start early because a good *amsïrïyën* requires the canines of at least 15 capuchin monkeys and the pelts of 25 toucans. These animals are not hunted solely for the materials they provide for the *amsïrïyën*: for several weeks prior to the dancing period, their meat forms a regular part of collective meals. Even so, a considerable amount of time is spent stockpiling the necessary materials for the initiand's *amsïrïyën*, not to speak of the effort required to drill holes in the monkey teeth and weave the cotton band by which the cluster of pelts are attached to the necklace. Not surprisingly therefore, the Panare are loath to part with these objects and compute their market value at Bs.500 (then about £70).

The principles underlying the participation of the members of a settlement group in the preparation of the material means for a dance are the same as those of everyday economic life. Although the *tihcen* may adopt a supervisory role over the preparations, he has no power to command the labour of others. He does not appeal to any principle of past indebtedness in order to get the other members of the settlement to participate, nor does he promise future payment for any contribution they might make. Similarly although the *tihcen's* wife may supervise the preparation of the beer, she has no coercive power over the other women of the settlement. No formal work parties are ever organized, either amongst the women or amongst the men. All the members of the settlement are free to contribute to the preparations as they see fit but since everyone enjoys a big dance, all the members of the settlement, albeit in varying degrees, are normally willing to throw in their lot with the *tihcen*. As a result, the preparations for a dance, which are spread over a number of weeks, usually involve a degree of collective effort in the sphere of production that is rarely encountered in day-to-day subsistence activities. In a purely economic sense therefore, a dance serves to bind the members of a settlement group to one another in a way that normal economic life does not.

In Western Panare territory, each settlement holds the series of dances culminating in male initiation every two or three years. Death dances are somewhat less frequent but at least one *tewënmën*, that is, a dance purely for the sake of amusement, takes place every dry season.[2] In any dry season therefore, but particularly during a dry season in which male initiation takes place, a large proportion of the labour time of the members of a settlement group is directed towards the preparation of the material means for dances. The prospect of a series of dances therefore serves to intensify dry season economic activities, since the members of the settlement group continue to meet their immediate subsistence needs whilst at the same time building up a surplus for the dances. But most of this surplus is consumed within a few days of the end of the series of dances. The members of the *tihcen's* settlement are helped in disposing of it by the *panakon*, i.e. visiting Panare from other settlements who are present at most dances and whose attendance at the *katayinto*, the dance in which the initiands don their loincloths, is vital because they have certain important ritual functions to fulfil during the course of it. The *panakon* usually arrive a couple of days before the ceremony and sometimes linger on a few days afterwards. Throughout this period they are provisioned with food and drink by the host settlement. In addition, on the day after the initiation ceremony, when the store of smoked meat is taken down from the rafters and shared out, each visiting family receives a portion equal to that received by the families of the host settlement. So by the

---

2. The dances held in the communities of the south-eastern sector of Panare territory are somewhat different from those held in the north-western sector. Informants' accounts suggest that dances involving the consumption of large amounts of food and drink are less frequent in the south-eastern sector.

time the *panakon* eventually leave, the host settlement has usually given away or consumed most of its food supply.

In economic terms, the position of the host settlement group *vis-à-vis* the *panakon* is the same as the position of the most active producers relative to the other, less productive, members of a settlement group on a day-to-day basis. The principle of generosity in food distribution leads the *tihcen* and his fellow settlement members to divest themselves of their smoked meat and piles of cassava bread even though they know that the rainy season and the period of scarcity will follow shortly. Once they have recuperated from their hangovers, the members of the host settlement hurriedly set about cutting their gardens and pulling the last of the fish out of the dried-up rivers and streams before the onset of the rains. As they do so, at least they can console themselves with the thought that, the following year, it could be their turn to be *panakon*.

To conclude the chapter, I shall consider Panare economic organization as a system of interrelated parts. Perhaps the most striking feature of the system is the contrast between the atomistic nature of production, each hearth group producing more or less independently and largely according to its own wishes, and the predominantly collective nature of distribution and consumption. Although apparently at odds, these two aspects of Panare economic life in fact complement one another. The productive autonomy of the hearth group is clearly well suited to the dispersed nature of the resource zones in Panare territory: at any time of year, but particularly during the dry season, one is likely to find one or more hearth groups absent from the settlements where they are normally resident, either on a visit to relatives who have more food than they or on a sortie by themselves to a distant resource zone. Yet even though a hearth group can, in theory, sustain itself in economic isolation for long periods of time, there is one major economic advantage (there are clearly social advantages as well) to be gained from living in association with other such groups: namely, that the collective nature of distribution and consumption compensates for short-term variation in the work pattern of the members of the individual hearth groups. If a man is ill, or tired from a long expedition the previous day, he will still be able to eat at the evening collective meal. Alternatively if a man has spent the day weeding his garden, he will still be able to eat meat just so long as one of his co-residents has been hunting or fishing that day. If a man's wife has not been to fetch carbohydrates from the gardens, it is very likely that someone else's will have, so that there will always be vegetables to accompany the meat of the collective meal. The same applies to the female members of the settlement but in an inverse way: if a woman's husband has not brought home meat on a given day, she will receive it from the women whose husbands have done so.

But if this system is to work properly, the principle of food-sharing must be respected: from each according to his immediate food-supply, to each according to his hunger. In other words, the food-sharing principle plays an important ideological role in Panare society, being a condition essential to the operation—under normal circumstances—of the economic infrastructure of the residential group. Food sharing compensates not only for short-term variations in the work pattern of the members of the group but also for gross differences in labour intensity. At one end of the spectrum, it means the old people are provided for in their declining years, whilst at the other end, it means that the young men can live off the system whilst they enjoy themselves. The food-sharing ideology also effectively militates against any significant accumulation on the part of individual hearth groups: there is no point in building up a large stock of food because one only has to give it away when food gets scarce. It is possible to build up a limited supply of rice or smoked fish in times of plenty, especially if one makes a large contribution to the collective food pool anyway, but gross differences in food resources are not compatible with Panare social values. Instead it is better to produce as much as one thinks fit and hope that others will compensate for one's own shortcomings.

By militating against accumulation, the food-sharing ideology has a number of general economic consequences. Firstly, it means that male labour resources are not used to capacity. Not only do young men spend a relatively small part of their time engaged in supporting themselves, but even the most active male producers of a Panare settlement work less hard than they might do. In the early period of the rainy season, Panare men work hard, if not as hard as the local criollo peasants. But during the latter half of the rainy season and during the dry season, the Panare men have an easy time. These periods of relative plenty could be used for cutting larger gardens or building up a stock of smoked meat. But the Panare prefer to use them for relaxing, drinking and dancing. Here one should bear in mind that the Panare economic system employs female labour more intensively than male: that is, the female members of a settlement are working closer to capacity than the male. Therefore any increase in the productivity of the men would eventually be limited not by their own working capacity, but by the capacity of the women of the settlement to process the raw product the men generate. Even so, if accumulation were socially feasible, there could be some increase in male productivity before the ceiling imposed by female labour capacity were reached. However, under traditional conditions there is no compelling reason why the men should work any harder since, contrary to the conception popular amongst many criollos, the Panare as a whole are well-nourished. In fact it has only been in recent years, since they moved closer than ever before to the criollo settlements, that they have suffered any serious shortages of food.

The second consequence of the absence of accumulation is that a Panare settlement is vulnerable to any seasonal fluctuations in the food supply. Although the food-sharing ideology serves to level differences in productivity between the various constituent hearth groups of a settlement on a short-term basis, it merely reinforces and even accentuates the seasonal fluctuations in the subsistence resources by inhibiting storage in times of plenty in order to meet the needs of times of scarcity. I earlier described how, at the beginning of the rainy season of 1975, the members of the settlement in which I was living were rapidly consuming their store of smoked fish even though they knew that lean times lay ahead. More systematic planning could have permitted a more even pattern of consumption over the early months of the rainy season – but would have conflicted with the food-sharing ideology. Yet here again, this effect is not of great significance under traditional conditions. For once the dry season supply of fish comes to an end, the members of communities still isolated from the criollos turn to hunting instead. The food supply may not necessarily be as plentiful as in the dry season, but it is nevertheless quite adequate. In the vicinity of the criollo settlements however, the wild animal population has been severely diminished and the Panare groups living there frequently go hungry at the beginning of the rainy season as a result. Under these new circumstances, the fact it is not possible to store up food during the dry season can have serious consequences.

In summary then, the Panare economic system as a whole is antithetical to the planned use of resources. In the sphere of production, each hearth group works as a more or less independent entity. In the sphere of distribution and consumption, the food-sharing ideology militates against the careful husbanding of the food supply. There is nothing integral to the structure of the economic organization that serves to regulate and coordinate the productive efforts of independent hearth groups. Thus the system of economic relations also provides no social mechanism for regulating the way in which the settlement group as a whole appropriates the natural environment. Nor, as we shall see in subsequent chapters, does the kinship system or the political system, such as it is, provide any such mechanism. This lack of planning and coordination in the use of labour resources and the Panare's 'prodigal' attitude towards the use of natural resources go hand in hand, complementing and reinforcing one another.

The fact that the economic system is antithetical to the planned use of resources makes it particularly vulnerable to the environmental effects of the changes taking place in the Panare settlement pattern described in Chapter 1. As the Panare gravitate towards criollo settlements or missions, they tend to live at greater local densities than they did previously, in clusters of two or more independent settlement groups, no more than a few minutes' walk from one another. Under these circumstances, in the absence of any means of laying an exclusive claim to any part of the natural environment before it is actually exploited, the members of a settlement group located close to another are tempted to exploit resources before they reach their seasonal maxima. For example, a man confronted with a cluster of palm fruits that are not quite ripe knows that if he leaves them for another day, he may well come back to find that someone else has cut them down in the interim. If this other person is a member of his own settlement group, he will benefit indirectly by means of the system of collective distribution and consumption. But if that person belongs to another settlement group, he will have lost the fruits entirely. Therefore, even though the fruits may not be quite ripe, a man in this situation is likely to chop them down anyway. In this way, the absence of any social mechanism for coordinating the productive activities of independent settlement groups serves to exacerbate the strain that the increase in settlement density puts on local natural resources.

But there is another, and more critical, way in which the change that is taking place in the settlement pattern puts a strain on the internal economic organization of the Panare. As I have tried to show in the course of this chapter, the collective system of distribution and consumption, which holds the settlement group together as an economic entity, depends on the willingness of individual hearth groups to surrender the greater part of the food that they have produced independently to the common pool. This they are willing to do under normal circumstances since there are certain obvious advantages to be gained from participation in the system of collective consumption and, moreover, such participation is strongly reinforced ideologically. Yet, under conditions of food scarcity, there is a tendency for this collective system to break down, as each hearth group reverts to feeding itself. As a result, the settlement group becomes nothing more than a conglomeration of economically independent entities held together only by kinship ties and the physical constraints of the communal house. These may be insufficient to hold the group together and some hearth groups may move off elsewhere.

The point to emphasize here, on account of its relevance to the latter part of the book, in which the Panare's relations with the criollos are discussed, is that conditions of food scarcity are more common, and more intense, amongst the settlement groups that have changed their location in recent years in order to be closer to the criollos. In effect then, this change of settlement pattern serves to undermine the collective system of distribution and consumption of food which in day-to-day life is one of the most important of the social mechanisms maintaining the social solidarity of the Panare settlement group.

# CHAPTER FOUR

# Marriage and Kinship

Day-to-day life within a Panare settlement rests upon a continuing series of exchanges of food between the hearth groups of which it is composed. In the last chapter, I described the advantages of a purely economic kind which, under normal circumstances, individual hearth groups stand to gain from this pooling of resources. However, it is more than economic self-interest that persuades individuals to contribute the greater part of their daily produce to the collective meals. For, in addition to economic ties, the hearth groups that share a settlement site are bound together by multiple and mutually re-inforcing ties both of consanguinity and affinity. In effect, hearth groups are no more than conjugal families in an economic guise: the economic exchanges that take place between them on a daily basis replicate the marital exchanges that brought them into existence in the first place. It is with the factors influencing the pattern of these marital exchanges that I will be principally concerned in this chapter.

At the simplest level, Panare marital exchanges are governed by a rule that enjoins a man to marry the daughter of a woman whom he classifies as a relative prior to marriage. Thus the marriage rule cannot be understood, nor even expressed, in isolation from the kinship terminology.[1] In purely formal terms, the Panare terminology falls into a general class of terminologies that has been identified under various labels in the literature: bifurcate-merging,

---

1 The terms presented in this chapter are those used in the Western Panare region. In Eastern Panare communities, I found that some Western Panare terms were simply not recognized, although I did not stay long enough to establish the differences between the terminologies of the two regions with precision. In Southern Panare communities, there is a greater elaboration of terms used exclusively in address than amongst the Western Panare, as well as significant differences in the reference terminology and in the marriage rule. But here again, my data have not been sufficiently cross-checked for me to feel confident about publishing them here. However, when I feel that the Southern Panare material could throw light on the Western Panare data, I will mention it in footnotes. Recently, Villalón has published an interesting account of Panare social organization, including a discussion of Western Panare kinship data. However I must say that I think she has not fully understood the material, partly on account of the formalistic theoretical perspective from which she has approached it (Villalón 1978).

Plate 11.   A young woman from Western Panare territory with her children. She wears a rag around her waist on account of the presence of the photographer (photograph by Jean-Paul Simonin).

Dravidian, symmetric, two-line etc. (Murdock 1949 : 141 ; L. Dumont 1953, and 1971 : 114 – 15 ; Rivière 1977). As in the Panare case, such terminologies are often associated with a positive rule of marriage which identifies, amongst others, the bilateral cross-cousin, genealogically defined, as a potential spouse. Marriage systems of this kind are found all over the Guianas and in most other parts of tropical forest Amazonia. They have also been described in several other areas of the world, notably in South India and Australia. This global distribution would appear to invite an explanation for such systems of a similarly universalistic character. But to formulate a hypothesis along these lines would require a lengthy comparative discussion far beyond the scope of a case study such as this. I am therefore obliged to follow the example of the Panare themselves and accept, for the time being at least, the rules governing marriage and the classification of relatives as a given feature of their social existence. However, at the end of this chapter, once I have examined the Panare kinship system in detail, I will briefly consider how it is related to their economic system and ecological adaption.

In the absence of any form of kinship-based corporate groups in Panare society, an individual classifies his kin primarily by means of a set of terms identifying their deemed personal relationship to himself rather than as members of a group standing in some sort of marital exchange relationship to his own. These terms are those shown in Figures 3a and 3b, for male and female Ego respectively, and are of the type commonly known in the anthropological literature as 'reference' terms, used to refer to an individual in his absence and contrasted with 'address terms', used in his presence.[2] However, it is useful in this case (and I suspect in many others as well), to distinguish between terms of the type shown in Figure 3, which involve the ascription to Alter of a given kinship status relative to that of Ego, and terms which are simply used to identify a third person in the course of a conversation. Where it is necessary to make the distinction, I shall refer to the former as 'ascriptive' reference terms and the

2. 'Ego' refers here to the hypothetical individual who acts as the centre of reference in the discussion of kinship relationships, whilst 'Alter' refers to individuals to whom Ego is related. In addition, the following conventional abbreviations are used: F = father; M = mother; B = brother; Z = sister; S = son; D =daughter; H = husband; W = wife; gF = grandfather; gM = grandmother. G+1 and G+2 stand for 'one generation above' and 'two generations above' Ego respectively; G−1 and G−2 stand for 'one generation below' and 'two generations below' Ego respectively; whilst G.O means 'of the same generation' as Ego.

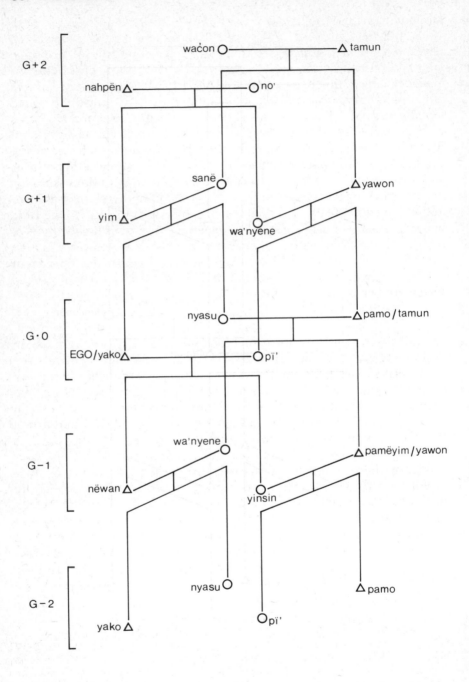

Figure 3a.    Male ascriptive reference terminology.

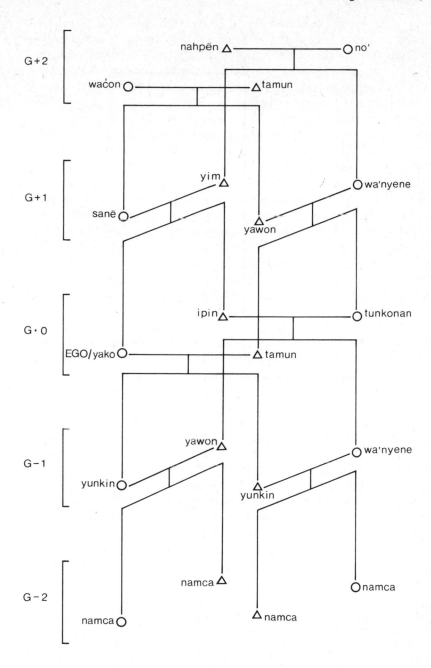

Figure 3b.    Female ascriptive reference terminology.

latter as 'descriptive' reference terms. Although the latter terms may also carry connotations of the relative kinship status of speaker and person referred to, the terms employed are not necessarily kinship terms in the strict sense, since personal names, teknonyms, pronominal forms, as well as nicknames and criollo names, may be used instead, as I shall describe below. First, though, I shall discuss the ascriptive reference terms and then the address terms that the Panare use. This discussion may seem rather lengthy: its justification lies in the over-riding importance of these terms in the ordering of the Panare social universe.

Within the ascriptive reference system, a man uses fifteen terms that exclusively and specifically denote categories of kin whilst a woman uses only ten. None of these terms carry an exclusively affinal connotation in the sense that they are used exclusively to refer to actual affines in post-marital circumstances. Nor are there any terms not shown here that are used for this purpose. Two of the terms shown in Figure 3b, corresponding to female Ego, are not exclusively kinship terms. *Yunkin,* used by female Ego to refer to her children and those of same sex siblings, both 'real' and classificatory, would be most accurately glossed as 'my offspring', whilst the term *namca* used to refer to members of G−2, simply means 'infant'. When it is necessary to be specific about her relationship to a member of G−2, a woman explains it from the latter's point of view, indicating whether she is his or her *no'* (paternal grandmother) or his or her *wacon* (maternal grand-mother).

It is important to point out that Figures 3a and 3b are not meant to be a demonstration of Panare kinship terms applied to a genealogy in the real world but rather a model of the principles that govern the application of these terms.[3] The most important of these principles is that same sex siblings are classified as equivalent elements within the system and are contrasted with opposite sex siblings. This principle is clearly expressed in the three medial generations. Thus male Ego, for example, distinguishes between brothers and sisters in his own generation, extending this distinction into the next generation by classifying his brothers' children by the same terms as he classifies his own and distinguishing them from his sisters' children. Similarly, in

3. The diagrams in Figure 3 were originally inspired by a series of such diagrams presented by Alan Campbell at a conference in the University of East Anglia in April 1979. I prefer this form of presentation to the two-dimensional 'box' diagram employed in the most sophisticated analyses of Guianese kinship systems (see Rivière 1969 and Kaplan 1975, but L. Dumont 1953 for the origin of this technique) because to my mind the latter requires one to present kin terms as if there were some lineal descent principle underlying them.

the generation above himself, Ego classifies all his father's same sex siblings along with his father and his mother's same sex siblings along with his mother, in each case contrasting these relatives with his parents' opposite sex siblings. Furthermore, since within the logic of the system, his parents' same sex siblings are equivalent to his parents, it is entirely consistent that Ego should consider their children equivalent to his parents' children and call these 'parallel' cousins by the same terms as he uses for his 'real' siblings. These siblings, both 'real' and classificatory, he contrasts with his parents' opposite sex siblings' children, i.e. with his 'cross' cousins. Similar principles govern the way that female Ego applies terms to her relatives in these three medial generations.[4]

By means of these simple principles, this system of categories can be extended to include a wide range of relatives. It is easy to see why : Ego uses sibling terms to refer to his parallel cousins since they are the offspring of his parents' same sex siblings. However those whom his parents call by same sex sibling terms will include not only their 'real' siblings but also all their parallel cousins as well, i.e. all the offspring of Ego's grandparents' same sex siblings. But in this generation too, the grandparents' same sex siblings will include not only their 'real' siblings but also their parallel cousins. And so on, as far as people's interest or memory will stretch. In every generation, siblings and parallel cousins are contrasted with cross cousins and their parallel cousins. In practice, the system can be extended to include the totality of an individual's social universe.

The factor that ensures the reproduction of this terminological system from one generation to the next is the rules governing marriage. The Panare give explicit recognition to a rule that enjoins an individual to marry a *wa'nyenkin,* the child of a *wa'nyene.* In the three medial generations, this category of relative includes the FZD for male Ego (FZS for female Ego), i.e. the patrilateral cross cousin. But, if the marriage rule has been systematically followed in previous generations, male Ego's FZ, his *wa'nyene,* will be married to his MB or to someone whom Ego calls by the same term, *yawon.* In effect then, the rule of marriage with a *wa'nyenkin* identifies both the matrilateral and patrilateral cross cousins as marriageable. In fact, a potential spouse will normally be simultaneously Ego's matrilateral and his patrilateral cross cousin, i.e. a bilateral cross cousin, if not in the strict genealogical sense, then at least in a classificatory sense. Although the

4. In order to avoid tedious repetition, I will generally discuss Panare terminology from the perspective of male Ego only. Only when there are significant differences in the way that men and women apply kin terms will I discuss the terminology from the perspective of female Ego also.

Panare phrase the marriage rule with reference to the *wa'nyene,* they also recognise the effects of the rule and say that if one calls a man *yawon,* 'it means you can marry his daughter'. Should an incorrect marriage occur, the immediate relatives of the couple accommodate their personal kinship terminologies, classifying their new affines as if the marriage had been correct.

In short, as far as the three medial generations are concerned, the Panare have a conventional system of the kind usually, if somewhat unsatisfactorily, known in the literature as a system of 'prescriptive bilateral cross cousin marriage'. But the Panare system is of particular interest because there is more to it than this. For the Panare system allows one to marry not only members of one's own generation but also certain members of the generations two above and two below one's own. This practice is a neat way of reconciling social reality to the fact that in a polygynous society such as this, it is quite possible for an individual to be fifty years or more younger than his eldest sibling and therefore of the same age or even younger than the latter's grand-child. Moreover, it is a matter of simple arithmetic that under a system that permits Ego to marry members of generations other than his own, there will be a greater number of potential spouses within any given area than there will be under a system that restricts marriage to members of Ego's own generation. In other words, a system in which marriage is possible between members of alternate generations as well as between members of the same generation permits a higher degree of local endogamy than a straightforward system of bilateral cross cousin marriage. At the same time though, marriage between members of alternate generations, such as the Panare system permits, does not give rise to as many structural ambiguities as does avuncular marriage (a form of marriage between members of adjacent generations) which, further east in the Guianas, appears to be the principal means whereby Amerindian groups augment the degree of endogamy that is possible within their marriage systems (see Thomas 1973: 159–63; Kloos 1971: 134–7; but particularly Rivière 1969).

The Panare system is not without its problems however. The explicit marriage rule states that one should marry a *wa'nyenkin,* but, in fact, not all *wa'nyenkin* are marriageable. Such is the case when the *wa'nyenkin* is, from male Ego's point of view, a 'real' son's daughter. This situation arises quite frequently since the term *wa'nyene* covers not only the FZ of Ego, but also his ZD, genealogically defined (as well as all the ZD's classificatory siblings, of course). Given that Ego's son, as an opposite sex cross cousin, is an eligible spouse for Ego's ZD, it often results that this type of *wa'nyene* is mother of Ego's 'real' son's children. A son's children are referred to by the same terms as those for siblings and are not considered marriageable.[5] However, when Ego's ZD is married to a classificatory son, and preferably a fairly distant one, then the ZDD is a perfectly legitimate spouse for male Ego. I will suggest some reasons why this should be below; here, I merely want to emphasize that whereas a 'real' son's daughter is not regarded as marriageable by a male Ego, a 'real' daughter's daughter certainly is. Indeed from the diagram in Figure 3a one can see that a daughter's children are referred to by the same terms as cross cousins by male Ego. This enables one to understand why male Ego's ZS should be referred to as *pamëyim*, which literally translated means 'father of my *pamo*' : since male Ego's ZS is a *wa'nyenkin* to Ego's daughter, he may well be married to the latter and therefore father of Ego's DS who falls into the category of *pamo* for Ego. In other words, a *pamëyim* is the G−1 equivalent of a *yawon* in G+1 : in both cases these relatives are actual or potential fathers-in-law and simultaneously, as a result of the rules permitting marriage between members of alternate generations, actual or potential sons-in-law to one another. In the case of female Ego, the equivalence of these two types of relative is even more clearly expressed in the ascriptive reference terminology, since she uses the term *yawon* to refer to both her BS and her MB (and, as usual, all their respective siblings, 'real' and classificatory). It would appear that the teknonymous usage in the case of male Ego is due to the fact that, normally speaking, the ZS will be younger than Ego, and that therefore to apply the term *yawon* to him, with its connotations of slightly superior status, would be inappropriate. In cases where a ZS is older than Ego, Ego is more likely to classify him simply as *yawon*. In female Ego's case also, when her brother's children are a good deal younger than herself, she will use the term *wa'nëpun*, which carries fewer formal connotations than the terms *yawon* and *wa'nyene*, to refer to both her BS and her BD, without distinction of sex.

It is important to draw attention at this stage to a highly distinctive feature of the Panare terminology: namely, that whereas in G−1, the individuals denoted by the terms *yawon* and *wa'nyene* are siblings to one another, in G+1 they are actual or potential spouses to one another. This distribution of terms has a number of important practical effects. Most immediately, it means that the ascriptive reference terms used between actual or potential affines of the same sex are entirely

5. Intriguingly, the Southern Panare terminology may be more consistent in this particular detail since I was told that a man calls his ZD *'sanë'*, i.e. by the same term as he uses for his mother and her same sex siblings, whilst his SD, who will normally be a 'real' or classificatory daughter of his ZD, he calls *nyasu*, sister, just as male Ego does in Western Panare territory.

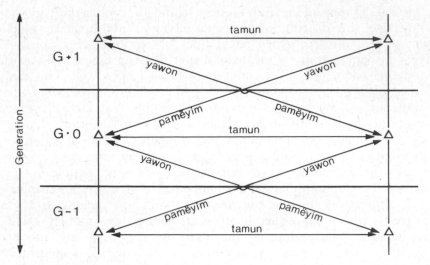

Figure 4a. Reciprocal male affinal terms

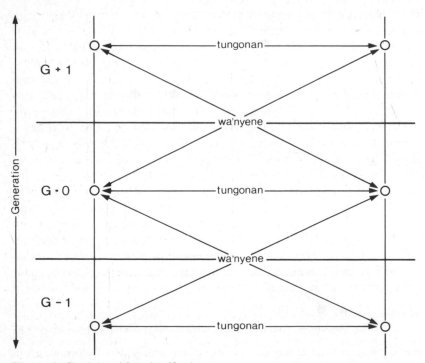

Figure 4b. Reciprocal female affinal terms

reciprocal, as one can see from Figures 4a and 4b. From a more global perspective, this distribution of terms serves to inhibit the development of two discrete genealogical lines or sections. This point is easiest to demonstrate by means of a specific case. Figure 5 involves two of the oldest men of the communities that I knew well. The man marked (2) is a very old man, probably in his eighties, from the community of Portachuelo. This man has married his 'real' DD. The man marked (1) is presently in his sixties and lives in Colorado. Under normal circumstances, it would be very difficult to work out a Panare genealogical tree extending over four generations because of the Panare's lack of interest in the deceased. It was only possible in this case because the man marked (1) happened to be a very good informant. Although (1) is somewhat younger than (2), he belongs to G+1 relative to (2), being a classificatory brother of (2)'s mother. (The classificatory relationship is indicated by a dotted line in the diagram.) When he was a young man, (1) married (2)'s daughter. This was a perfectly legitimate form of marriage since (2) is (1)'s classificatory sister's son, that is, his *yawon*. At a later date, (1) gave (2) his daughter, (3), as a second wife. In this way, (2) came to marry

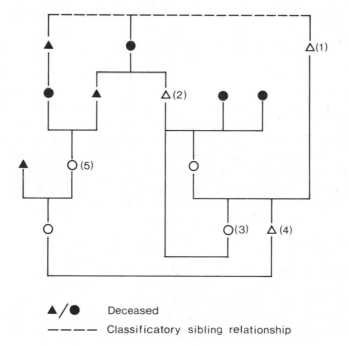

▲/●    Deceased

— — — —    Classificatory sibling relationship

Figure 5.   The blurring of the marriageable/non-marriageable distinction through intergenerational marriage

his daughter's daughter. (1) has a number of other offspring, including the son marked (4) on the figure. This man married the daughter of the woman marked (5). By one means of reckoning, (5) is a classificatory sister of (4)'s mother since they are daughters of men who were full brothers. On this basis, (5) would be *sanë* to (4) and her daughter would be *nyasu* and not marriageable. But by another route, it is perfectly legitimate for (4) to marry the daughter of (5). By this alternative route, (5)'s mother is a parallel cousin of (4) since their fathers were classificatory brothers to one another. Thus (5)'s mother is a classificatory sister to (4), and her daughter, (5), is a *wa'nyene*. Since the marriage rule enjoins an individual to marry the child of a *wa'nyene*, (4)'s marriage to (5)'s daughter is entirely in conformity with the rule.

In short, as this case clearly shows, it is entirely possible within the Panare marriage system for a given female Alter to be simultaneously a classificatory sister and a potential spouse for Ego without any incorrect marriages having taken place to produce terminological ambiguities. In a two-line or two-section system, strictly defined, such a confusion of marriageable and non-marriageable categories of kin would not occur except in the instance of some marital irregularity. This feature of the Panare system may seem somewhat extraordinary at first sight but the distribution of terms which gives rise to it is entirely in conformity with the simple principles underlying the system outlined above; most specifically, it conforms with the fundamental distinction made between siblings of opposite sexes and their respective children. Moreover, the Panare system is not unique in this regard. Their Carib-speaking neighbours to the east, the Ye'kuana, also permit marriages between members of alternate generations, although their system is slightly more restrictive in the sense that all 'real' grandchildren are ruled out as potential spouses for Ego, whereas amongst the Panare it is only 'real' opposite sex children's children that are prohibited. However, apart from these restrictions, in theory at least, any two members of alternate generations are potential spouses amongst the Ye'kuana, regardless of the intermediate links between them. Thus one would not expect a system involving two discrete genealogical lines to develop amongst them either (Arvelo-Jiménez 1971 : 151–4, 158, 170).

It is this possibility of marriage between members of alternate generations that explains another distinctive feature of the Panare terminology: namely, the distinction of four categories in G+2, two for each sex. Given that a man can marry his DD, male Ego's maternal gF is a potential ZH, just as his male cross cousin is. This common identity is demonstrated by the fact that both types of relative can be referred to as *tamun*. But, although a 'real' MF is always called *tamun*, a classificatory MF or cross cousin may just as well be called *pamo*. I found the precise significance of this distinction hard to ascertain. '*Tamun*', I was told, 'is a sister's husband.' However, *tamun* also means, simply, husband, i.e. a woman's spouse. Furthermore, despite the 'native' definition, I found that the term *tamun* could be used by male Ego of all those classed as *pamo*, whether or not they were married to a 'real' sister, and whether or not they were married at all. Both terms can be used, on occasion, as terms of address. My general impression was that the term *tamun* carries connotations of greater intimacy, of closer social ties than *pamo*; I noticed that it was used particularly frequently, as an address term, during dances, when everyone is normally in an expansive mood. But whatever the exact nuance of the semantic distinction between the two, it is clear that, in terms of the overall logic of the ascriptive reference system, the terms *tamun* and *pamo* are directly equivalent, grouping together certain members of alternate generations G−2, G.0 and G+2 and contrasting them with those in the generations G−1 and G+1 denoted by the *paměyim/yawon* set. This is clearly visible from the vertical axis at the extreme right of Figure 3a.

But the identity of alternate generations goes further than this. Bearing in mind that the MF is equivalent to Ego's male cross cousin, one would anticipate that his MFZ would be a potential spouse for Ego just as his male cross cousin's sister is. Now under normal circumstances, Ego's MFZ will be Ego's FF's actual or potential spouse, that is, Ego's FM or *no'*. By the same logic, one would expect Ego's MFW to be the same as his male cross cousin's wife to Ego, i.e. a 'real' or classificatory sister. Ego's MFW is, of course, his MM or *wacon*. Finally, one would expect Ego's *nahpën* or FF to be equivalent to a brother to Ego since they share the condition of potential spouse for Ego's *no'*. However, in practice I found that, for the most part, Panare men generally rejected the idea of marrying a 'real' grandmother on the grounds that she would be 'too old and ugly' (even though, as we shall see, they are prepared to marry women who are much older than themselves). Nevertheless, for male Ego, a 'real' FM is *yipipe*, like a wife, and in theory at least, he is prohibited from talking to her, just as he is prohibited from talking to his potential spouses in G.0 and G−2 (mainly his female cross cousins and his DDs). On the other hand, no such prohibition holds for Ego's MM, on the grounds that she is *nyasupe*, like a sister, whilst her 'real' or classificatory brother, Ego's FF, is as one would expect *yakope*, like a brother. Generally speaking though, grandparental terms are not extended to Alters other than 'real' grandparents. Many Panare have only the most tenuous knowledge of their grandparents' siblings and found questions about them difficult to answer. Although some informants accepted the idea that the 'real' siblings of grandparents who were close in age to the latter should be called by the same terms as grandparents, most preferred to classify them by some other route, via relatives in G+1. However, given that, in any case, either Ego's mother will be a *wa'nyene* and/or his father a *yawon* or *paméyim* to his grandparents' siblings, Ego will fall into the category of potential spouse for the latter. In effect then, it would appear that, apart from the rejection of 'real' grandmothers on the grounds of relative age, all women of G+2 are eligible spouses for male Ego, whilst for female Ego, apart from the prohibition on the 'real' FF (the same as the prohibition on the 'real' SD for male Ego, discussed above), all men of G+2 are eligible husbands.[6]

There is one final term that appears in Figure 3 that must be discussed: *tunkonan,* used by female Ego to refer to her same sex cross cousin. This term appears in brackets because it is both more and less than a kinship term. In general usage, *tunkonan* means 'another of a different kind', and is contrasted with *piyaka*, 'another of the same kind'. In the context of kinship terminology, the referents of the category for male Ego are all those whom he refers to by the terms *tamun* and *no'*, *pamo* and *pi"* (thereby including, amongst others, his MF, FM, cross cousins of both sexes and his daughters' children, genealogically defined). All the rest of his relatives are *piyaka,* including actual or potential affines of adjacent generations. The referents of these terms for female Ego are somewhat different. For her, the category *tunkonan* includes all those whom she may refer to as *tamun* (including her MF, her male cross cousin and her SS genealogically defined) and her female cross cousin for whom she has no more specific term. All the rest of her relatives are *piyaka*. In order to be entirely homologous with the distinction between *tunkonan* and *piyaka* made by male Ego, a woman would also have to include her *no'* and her SD in the category of *tunkonan*. But informants were quite adamant that these relatives were *piyaka* for a woman, citing as evidence that she addressed them by means of a term (either a personal name or a

6. In Southern Panare territory, the identification of the FM, female cross cousin and DD appears to be more explicit since it is said that all three are to be classed as *no'*. Moreover, the marriage rule proscribes an individual falling into this category. On the other hand, Jean-Paul Dumont, in his second book (1978 : 83, 111), claims that in Western Panare territory, marriage with a MM is not only theoretically possible, but actually practised, whilst marriage with a FM is prohibited. Having checked the matter several times in the field (the last time being in March 1981, after having read Dumont's book), I conclude that Dumont is just plain wrong on this point.

kinship term), whereas people who fall into the category *tunkonan* should either not be addressed at all (if they are potential spouses) or should be addressed merely by means of the simple pronoun, *amën*, 'you'.

The terms *piyaka* and *tunkonan* are often used as a sort of shorthand for indicating whether someone is marriageable or not for a given Alter. In reply to a question about whether a particular woman were a potential spouse for a third party, an informant would often remark, *'Cika, i'yakae kë'*, 'no, she's his *piyaka*'. Similarly, the term *tunkonan* might be used to designate a potential spouse, particularly by women, since actually to say, 'He's my *tamun'*, always seemed to cause embarrassed giggles. The substitution of *piyaka* and *tunkonan* was especially common when the referents were very young, as if there were something rather absurd about using sibling or potential spouse terms for children still crawling around on their hands and knees (although, as the case illustrated in Figure 5 showed, marriage with a 'real' daughter's daughter is far from being a merely theoretical possibility). Nevertheless, even though the terms *tunkonan* and *piyaka* can be used to distinguish between marriageable and non-marriageable categories of kin, it is quite clear that they do not denote discrete classes of 'kin' and 'affines' who could be conceived of, in any way, as groups engaged in marital exchanges with one another.[7]

As in the case of ascriptive reference terms, the terms that the Panare use in address obey, in theory, a number of simple principles, though in actual practice these principles may not always be followed to the letter. All siblings, 'real' and classificatory, and the children of those of the same sex as Ego, plus Ego's own children, are all addressed by their personal name. The children of opposite sex siblings are all also addressed by their personal name but with the addition of the suffix –*can*. If male Ego is speaking to a ZS who is considerably younger than himself, however, he may use the reference term *pamëyim*, in address, instead. Parents and their respective same sex siblings are all addressed by ascriptive reference terms, although in a case where Alter is of the same age as Ego, the latter may well use a personal name instead. Parents' opposite sex siblings, just as opposite sex siblings' children, are addressed by personal names with the suffix –*can*, thus demonstrating once again the identity of these two generations in the Panare kinship system. (Furthermore, imperatives take a slightly different form when they are directed to those whom one would address using the formula of personal name plus –*can*. These imperatives appear to be slightly more 'polite' than normal forms.)

7. For reference purposes, a list giving definitions of all the kinship terms discussed in the foregoing paragraphs is presented in Appendix 3.

The identification of the alternate generations G−2, G.0 and G+2 can also be seen in the use of address terms. As already noted, opposite sex cross cousins, as potential spouses, are not addressed at all, since to do so is considered tantamount to a sexual proposition. The situation with same sex cross cousins is somewhat more ambiguous. Normally these Alters are addressed as *amën*, 'you', but I often heard the terms *tamun* and *pamo* being used as address terms as well. Amongst women, despite what informants said when they were defining the term *tunkonan*, female cross cousins would frequently address one another by personal name. This usage appears to be similar to the male use of the term *tamun:* in both cases, social distance is minimized by substituting an address term for the simple pronoun *amën*.

In theory, similar principles regulate the use of address terms with members of generations two above and two below Ego. It is said that a man should not address his FM but this prohibition is frequently broken, particularly if Ego is very young. More commonly observed, probably for being less onerous, is the prohibition on using personal names for MF. Other grandparents are addressed by male Ego using ascriptive reference terms. Female Ego, on the other hand, addresses all grandparents by these terms with the exception of the MF whom she should not speak to at all since he is a potential spouse. As far as G−2 is concerned, same sex children's children are addressed by personal names, or if very young, by the term *namca*, 'infant', whilst opposite sex children's children, once they leave early childhood, are addressed according to the same principles as same generation potential spouses and their siblings.

Finally, it is worth mentioning the terms used for descriptive reference only. For this purpose, a speaker will normally use the same terms as he would use to address the individual referred to. Someone whom the speaker should not address at all, he will refer to as *më* or *manë*, which in this context simply mean 'you-know-who!'. Both male and female Ego use this formula to refer to their actual spouses as well. Also, there appears to be a partial tabu on referring to actual affines in adjacent generations by personal name. I noticed that, whenever possible, people would refer to relatives of this kind by using the term *mëcan*, rather than the conventional address formula of personal name plus the suffix.

Clearly, this system of descriptive reference can only work if the listener has a good knowledge of the speaker's personal genealogy. But given the high degree of endogamy in Panare society, this condition is normally fulfilled. In fact, most of the individuals that a person comes across in day-to-day life will share a number of close relatives with himself. Only when two individuals from distant communities meet is this condition not likely to be fulfilled, and then their conversation will normally start with an exploration of genealogies in order to establish their mutual kinship status as soon as possible, since this will affect even the grammatical forms they utilize as they speak to one another. Thus, under normal circumstances, when a speaker refers in a purely descriptive context to someone by a personal name, the listener will probably know whom he is referring to since the latter must be either a sibling, a child, or at a pinch, a grandchild of the speaker. This will reduce the ambiguity considerably but not necessarily entirely since, as noted above, the Panare have only six adult male names and four adult female names. There is, however, a much longer list of children's names, so that teknonyms often serve to identify an individual where a personal names does not. If even a teknonym does not suffice, an individual's Spanish name, or a nickname, may be used to make the identification exact. Teknonyms may also be used as address terms, when there is a possibility of ambiguity or as yet another means by which men who are *tamun* to one another can avoid the bald use of the pronoun *amën*. Finally, teknonyms are also used by both men and women to refer to their spouses once they have children.

Having identified the rules governing the classification of relatives and examined some of their structural effects, we are now in a position to examine the way in which these linguistic categories are manipulated in the formation of groups on the ground. In so doing, I will be referring primarily to genealogical and other ethnographic material collected in the Colorado valley. As I have already noted, this valley had a population of 226, distributed amongst ten independent settlements. The population of the valley represents 13.2 per cent of the total estimated Panare population. The distribution of this population by age and sex was shown in Figure 1.

In Panare society, marriages are arranged by the members of the conjugal families of the prospective bride and groom. Should a young man decide that he wants to marry a particular woman, he will turn to his father to make the necessary arrangements. If there is no suitable spouse within the young man's locality, it is the responsibilty of the father to seek out his more distant classificatory sisters to see if they have daughters of a suitable age for his son to marry. If a man has no father, then his mother or an elder sibling should approach the parents of the prospective bride. The parents of the bride may consult other members of their residential group but ultimately the decision whether to accept or reject a proposal of marriage lies with them and their daughter. Should they reject the proposal, it is said that the young man should never ask again. If the proposal is accepted, and the prospective partners live in the same settlement group, the groom merely relocates his hammock next to that of the bride. If they live in different settlement groups, the groom usually moves into the house of his parents-in-law. In some cases that I witnessed, there appeared to be an initial trial period during which time the man was said to be the woman's husband 'only a little bit'. If the girl has already reached puberty, the prospective groom may have sexual access to her during this time, but if not, he is obliged to wait until after her first menses. If the arrangement is found to be satisfactory, the trial union will be consolidated by the normal passage of time. If not, it can be broken off by either party. At no stage, however, is marriage the subject of any form of ceremony or public ritual.

No doubt a multiplicity of personal reasons motivate individual Panare to get married. But whatever these may be, the Colorado material suggests that most men marry women of an approved category. At the time of my fieldwork in the Colorado valley, there were fifty-four unions, of which both partners were living, or of which only one partner had died during a period of no more than two years prior to my arrival.[8] Only two of these unions were regarded as in some way incorrect. One of these, illustrated in Figure 6, involved a man who had married the daughter of a woman who was a co-wife and classificatory sister of his own mother. Even though the man's wife's genitor was not his father, this marriage was regarded as highly improper since, in Panare terms, he had married his sanëyakonkin, i.e., his mother's sister's child. Sanëyakonkin are piyaka and should not marry. The other union that was generally regarded as incorrect is illustrated in Figure 7. It involved a man, marked (1) in the diagram, who had married the daughter of a classificatory sister, marked (2). Being a woman of an adjacent generation who was neither a mother nor a daughter, this man's wife, marked (3), should have been a wa'nyene to him. According to the marriage rule, one should marry the child of a wa'nyene but not the wa'nyene herself.

There are no explicit sanctions against incorrect marriages in Panare society. When pressed, some informants said that those who married incorrectly would die. But I did not feel that this response was the expression of a deeply-held belief. In Panare society, most incorrect behaviour is sanctioned by this amorphous threat of death. Of the two incorrect marriages in Colorado, only the case involving

8. For present purposes, the number of unions represented by polygynous marriages will correspond to the number of women involved. Thus a marriage involving two women will be computed as two unions, one involving three as three unions etc. The incidence of polygyny will be discussed below.

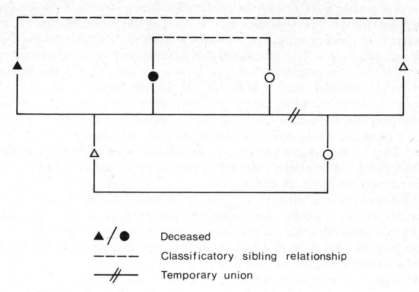

▲/●     Deceased

----     Classificatory sibling relationship

—//—     Temporary union

Figure 6. The marriage of *sanëyakonkin*

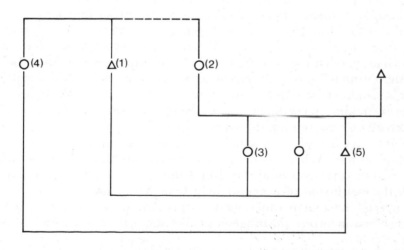

----     Classificatory sibling relationship

Figure 7. Tëna's incorrect marriage and its sequel

marriage between *sanëyakonkin* was seriously stigmatized. When the Evangelical mission station was set up in the valley in 1972, this couple was the first to establish itself beside the mission. They lived alone in front of the mission for three years until 1975, when two settlement groups also established themselves there. One of these two groups included the mother of the wife of the incorrect union as well as classificatory siblings of both the husband and the wife. Predictably therefore, the isolated couple became part of this settlement group, participating in communal meals and subsistence activities.

In practice, the high degree of conformity with the marriage rules in Panare society is explained by the flexibility of those rules rather than by the sanctions against breaking with them. More specifically, the rules permitting marriage between individuals of alternate generations make it comparatively easy for a man to find a wife of an approved category within his own locality. In the first place, if a man can choose a wife from the members of alternate generations as well as his own, he has a wider range of individuals to choose from. Secondly, as I showed by means of the diagram in Figure 5, the rules governing marriage between members of alternate generations lead to the breakdown of the distinction between marriageable and non-marriageable categories of relations. It is difficult to stipulate exactly to what degree the rules can be manipulated without provoking expressions of disapproval but comparison of Figures 5 and 6 gives one some idea of where the line of demarcation between permissible and impermissible manipulation lies. In the case illustrated in Figure 5, the man marked (4) married a woman who by one means of reckoning was the daughter of a classificatory sister of his mother, and therefore *piyaka,* but who by another means was the daughter of a *wa'nyene,* that is, a potential spouse. Figure 6 refers to the case of marriage between a man and his mother's co-wife's daughter by a genitor other than his own father. In both cases, the men involved married a *sanëyakonkin,* that is, a child of a classificatory sister of their mother, but whilst the former marriage was regarded as legitimate, the latter was not. The reason probably lies in the fact that in one case the mothers of the spouses were once married to the same man whilst in the other case they were not. Furthermore, although it may have been possible for the man of the marriage regarded as incorrect to show by one means or another that his wife's genitor were a classificatory brother of his mother, that is, a *yawon,* to himself, by a more direct route, his wife's genitor was a classificatory brother of his father.

In effect then, the susceptibility of the kinship terminology to manipulation is compatible with a high degree of local endogamy since it enables an individual to re-define as marriageable a local woman whom by one means of reckoning might be considered *piyaka*. The Panare are quite explicit in stating their preference for local marriage. It is said that marriage with members of distant communities is bad because it separates one from one's *piyaka*. In this context, the term *piyaka* is used not in the restricted sense denoting non-marriageable relations but in the more general sense denoting those like one's self, that is, those whom one knows and has grown up with. As we shall see in the next chapter, the members of each settlement group generally have a derogatory opinion of most other settlement groups and the greater the physical distance separating the groups and the fewer the demonstrable relationship ties between them, the more negative their attitude to one another. This negative attitude towards outsiders complements and reinforces the Panare's stated preference for marrying locally. However the Panare marry locally, not so much on account of their attitude to outsiders, as because of the positive value they attribute to staying close to one's family and peer group.

Despite the flexibility of the rules governing marriage, periodic local shortages of marriageable women do occur. This can be attributed in part to the practice of sororal polygyny. In the sample of fifty-four unions in the Colorado valley, fourteen are accounted for by seven polygynous marriages involving two co-wives and a further three by one case of a man with three wives. There is no *de jure* limit to the number of wives that a man may have during the course of his life or at any one time. But in Colorado, there was no case of a man who was maintaining more than two wives at the time of my stay there.[9] The reason for this is entirely practical: to maintain even two wives is regarded as 'a lot of work' by Panare men. Of the eight polygynous marriages in Colorado only four were still fully functional. In two cases, the husband had recently died; in two other cases, including the case of the marriage involving three unions, all but one wife had been divorced, or, as the Panare put it, 'thrown away'. At the time of my fieldwork, neither the widows nor the 'thrown away' wives had re-married and the economic support they had previously been given by their husbands was being provided by their sons or sons-in-law. In summary then, seventeen out of the fifty-four extant unions in the

9. In no part of Panare territory did I come across a man supporting more than two wives at a time. Wilbert (1961 : 34) reports a case from an Eastern Panare community of a man married to four sisters but does not stipulate whether the husband actually supported all four of them. In the same source, Wilbert provides a photograph of an Eastern Panare man together with his three wives and their children. All the children in the photograph are young suggesting that all three unions were still active.

Colorado valley, that is approximately 30 per cent, were one of a series of unions in a polygynous marriage. Put another way: of the forty-five married men in the valley, eight − almost 20 per cent − had more than one living wife.

Combined with demographic fluctuations in the male : female ratio within the various age cohorts of the population (see Figure 1), one would anticipate that the practice of polygyny would result in periodic local shortages of marriageable women of the approved categories. The Colorado material suggests that when such shortages do occur, some Panare men prefer to marry much older women or wait for an immature woman to reach puberty rather than marry outside their locality. At the time of my fieldwork in Colorado, there were three men living with their prospective parents-in-law, waiting for their future wives to reach maturity. One of these cases deserves special mention. It involved a man whose first wife, an elder sister of his immature prospective wife, had died prematurely. Under these circumstances, the Panare recognize that a widower has a claim on a younger sister of his deceased wife, if there is one. In this particular case, the man in question had been waiting at least three years for his first wife's younger sister to reach maturity. At the other end of the scale, there were four cases in Colorado of men who had married women who were older than themselves by fifteen years or more. Three of these unions involved widows who had offspring of the same age or older than their present husbands. The most remarkable case involved a man of approximately twenty-two years of age married to a woman of at least forty-five. The woman concerned had one son of approximately thirty years of age, almost a decade older than her husband.[10]

It is difficult to give any statistical measure of the degree of local endogamy in Panare society on account of the impermanence and fluidity of Panare settlement groups. A number of individuals in the older segment of the Colorado population have spouses who originally came from outside the valley. This is as one would expect, given that when these individuals were young adults, the number of people in the valley was considerably less and the probability of finding a spouse of an approved category within the valley correspondingly smaller. However, as a result of the increase in population of the valley which has taken place in the course of the last few decades, the young men now in their twenties have a better chance of finding a woman of an approved category within the Colorado community. Indeed, of the

10. The procedure by which the ages of individuals in the Colorado population was estimated is explained in detail in Appendix 2.

twenty-six unions in the valley involving men under thirty years of age, only three involve individuals who were born or grew up outside the valley. In short, the statistical evidence from Colorado suggests that the great majority of Panare men marry women of an approved category living within their own locality. In other words, the rules governing the classification of relations and marriage and the preference for local endogamy, both of which are explicitly recognized by the Panare, play a large part in determining the empirical pattern of Panare marriages. But the statistical evidence from Colorado suggests that the empirical pattern of marriage is also influenced by a concern on the part of the Panare to marry someone from a conjugal family to which their own conjugal family is already connected by earlier marriages. This principle apparently underlying the pattern of Panare marriages I shall refer to as the principle of 'serial affinity'. Given the rules of the Panare kinship system, there are three main ways in which serial affinity can be achieved: by a series of marriages between members of two sibling sets, by 'real' cross cousin marriage, and by the marriage of a man with his daughter's daughter. The first of these means of achieving serial affinity involves the repetition of affinal ties between two conjugal families within a single generation, the second involves the extension of these affinal ties from one generation to the next and the third, the extension of affinal ties from one generation through a second to a third.

One can identify two distinct forms of serial affinity within a single generation. If the male members of a particular sibling set marry a number of women of another, all the resultant unions can be said to replicate the alliance established between the two conjugal families involved by the first of the series of unions. In a case of sororal polygyny, one man replicates his own first union with each subsequent marriage. When two or more brothers marry women who are sisters to one another, each marriage replicates the other(s). The principle of *replication* underlying a series of marriages between a set of brothers and a set of sisters can be distinguished from the principle of *reciprocation* underlying a series of marriages in which the sons of two conjugal families marry each other's sisters. Clearly the two principles are not mutually exclusive. A set of male siblings marrying a group of sisters are replicating each others' marriages but if their wives' brothers marry their sisters, reciprocation can be said to have taken place also. However replication can take place without reciprocation and *vice versa*.

Figure 8 is designed to illustrate the importance of both these forms of serial affinity within a single generation in the marital exchanges that have taken place in the Colorado community. The numbers along

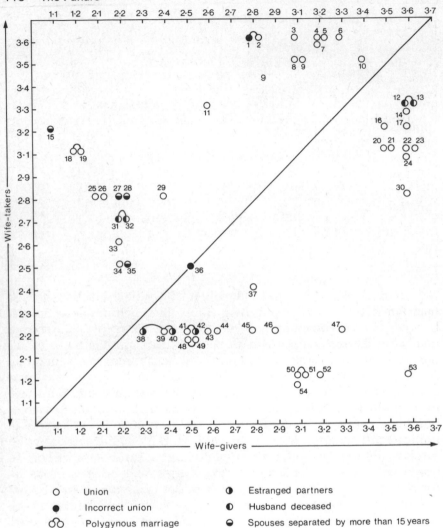

Figure 8. Marriage alliances in the Colorado valley

each axis of the diagram refer to all the conjugal families that have participated in marital exchanges so as to produce the extant unions in the Colorado valley. Each conjugal family appears both in the vertical axis as a wife-taker and in the horizontal axis as a wife-giver. By reading the diagram horizontally, one can see where the sons in each conjugal family found wives. When a number of circles are clustered around a single point in the diagram, this indicates that replication of previous unions has taken place. For example, the marital alliance between conjugal families 2.2 and 2.5 is replicated four times by unions 41, 42, 48 and 49. By reading the diagram vertically, one can see to whom the parents in each conjugal family gave a daughter. By comparing horizontal and vertical readings, one can see whether a particular union or series of unions involved any reciprocation. For example, reading horizontally, one sees that the sons of conjugal family 1.2 took three daughters from the conjugal family 3.1 (unions 50, 51 and 54). Reading vertically, one sees that the conjugal family 1.2 gave two women to the sons of the conjugal family 3.1 (unions 18, 19). Thus some degree of reciprocation is involved in this series of marriages between two sibling sets, even though there is not a one-to-one correspondence in the number of women exchanged. In contrast, unions 52 and 53, involving two other sons of conjugal family 1.2, do not involve any form of reciprocation. This can be verified by reading the diagram vertically which reveals that conjugal family 1.2 gave women to neither of the families that contributed women to the unions 52 and 53.

Two of the extant unions in Colorado have been excluded from the diagram. These unions involve two of the oldest couples in the valley. In order to assess whether these two marriages form part of a series of marital exchanges, it would have been necessary to collect information about the marriages of the siblings of the four old people involved. All of these siblings were either already dead or lived in distant communities and I found it impossible to gather the necessary data. For the opposite reason, two unions involving people who live in the neighbouring community of Portachuelo have been included. The core of the community at Portachuelo is made up of individuals who used to live in Colorado and a number of individuals in each community have primary kin in the other. In order to set some Colorado unions in the context of a series of exchanges between two conjugal families, it has been necessary to include unions 26 and 29, both of which involve sons of conjugal family 2.8.

If all the marital alliances between the conjugal families represented in the diagram had involved reciprocation, the two sides of the diagram would have been symmetrical. Although the symmetry is not perfect, the distribution of circles on each side is clearly far from random. This indicates that many, though not all, alliances in Colorado involve some degree of reciprocation. The frequency of replication in the intermarriages of sibling sets is indicated by the clusters of circles around a number of given points in the diagram. In addition to these clusters around particular points, there is an evident clustering effect in the diagram as a whole. This is a function of the way in which conjugal families have been ordered along the two axes. This ranking procedure obeys two principles. Firstly, the families have been loosely ordered according to the generation of the parents in each family. This ordering can only be loose since the generation of some couples is ambiguous on account of prior incorrect marriages between members of adjacent generations. Secondly, when one or other of the parents of a given conjugal family is a same sex sibling of one of the parents of another, the two conjugal families concerned are ranked alongside one another. It is this ranking principle that results in the overall clustering effect. To show how this works, I shall turn to specific examples. The husbands of conjugal families 3.5 and 3.6 each have two wives. The wives of the two families are sisters to one another. These two conjugal families have therefore been ranked side by side. The husband in conjugal family 3.1 is a brother to all of the wives of families 3.5 and 3.6. Five of his sons have married their father's sister's daughters, that is, their patrilateral cross cousins, thereby producing unions 20–4. The father in conjugal family 3.2 is a brother of the father in conjugal family 3.1 and therefore also a brother to the wives in conjugal families 3.5 and 3.6. Two of his sons have also married their patrilateral cross cousins thereby producing unions 16 and 17. The father in conjugal family 3.3 is a close parallel cousin of the fathers in 3.1 and 3.2. Two of his sons have also married women from family 3.6, i.e. their classificatory patrilateral cross cousins. One of these sons, now dead, married two women from family 3.6, corresponding to unions 12 and 13 in the diagram; the other son is the husband in union 14. In summary then, this series of patrilateral cross cousin marriages has produced the cluster of circles at the right-hand margin of the diagram involving ten unions (12–14, 16, 17, 20–4). If one looks at these alliances from the opposite perspective, with 3.1, 3.2 and 3.3 as wife-givers and 3.5 and 3.6 as wife-takers, one encounters a similar series of marriages. In the diagram, this is represented by the cluster of circles just below the upper margin, involving seven unions (3–9).

In short, the graphic properties of the diagram indicate that serial affinity involving the intermarriage of sibling sets is an important principle in Panare marriage practice as represented by the Colorado sample. This interpretation of the graphic features of the diagram is corroborated by a summary statistical account of the relevant data. One union, 36 in the diagram implies no form of alliance since it involved the marriage of *sanëyakonkin*, the offspring of co-wives. This union, as I have already remarked, was thought to be unambiguously wrong by the Panare. The remaining fifty-three unions are accounted for by twenty-two alliances between pairs of conjugal families. Half of the unions in the sample are accounted for by the alliances between six conjugal families.

However, in order to substantiate the importance of this form of serial affinity in determining the pattern of Panare marriage it is necessary to refer, not only to statistical evidence, but also to the Panare's view of the matter. Yet whilst in the field it did not occur to me to look at Panare marriages as a series of exchanges between conjugal families, and consequently I did not seek in any systematic way to elicit explicit statements as to the importance or otherwise of marrying where one's brother or sister had or of exchanging sisters with other men. I shall therefore rest my statistical argument on two interesting cases of deviant behaviour.

The first case involves the only incident of physical violence that I came across amongst the Panare. The generally pacific nature of the Panare makes the present case all the more extraordinary. The incident took place in the community of Chaviripa in the dry season of 1976. An elderly man and his unmarried sons set about the former's son-in-law with poles, beating him up badly and breaking his nose. When I visited the settlement several days after the event, the man who had been attacked was to be found sitting in his house, situated some hundred metres from the communal house, nursing his wounds. The fact that his house was located so far from the house of his affines suggested that the feud was of long standing, but the immediate cause, as it was explained to me, was the the man had failed to give his brothers-in-law a sister in exchange for the wife that he had taken a number of years before. In his defence, the man claimed that he had no sister to give. I never discovered the rights and wrongs of the case but whatever these may have been, the case indicates that the principle of reciprocation in marital alliances is clearly recognized by the Panare.

The second case illustrates the importance of the principle of replicating siblings' marriages as a means of consolidating links between conjugal families. It involves the series of marital exchanges illustrated in Figure 7. It was not long after I began to investigate marriage patterns in the Colorado valley that I discovered that the marriage of a man called Tëna, who corresponds to the symbol marked (1) in Figure 7, was generally regarded as wrong. It was said that he intended to rectify his incorrect marriage by taking a second wife. Naïvely, I assumed that he would compensate for his first marriage by marrying correctly. In this way, the terminological system would be set on an even keel again. But the fate of the system was clearly of no concern to Tëna for when he did marry a second time, just before I left Colorado, he married the sister of his first wife.

But in contrast to his first marriage, the second marriage was generally regarded as perfectly legitimate. By virtue of his first marriage, Tëna's first wife's mother had become his *wa'nyene* even though she was neither an FZ nor a ZD. Thus in marrying his first wife's sister, he was marrying his *wa'nyenkin*, the approved category of spouse. Furthermore, between the time of his first and the time of his second marriage, a sister of Tëna, marked (4) in Figure 7, had been married by a brother of his wife, marked (5). This union was not considered to be incorrect, presumably because it was seen as following on from the earlier marriage of Tëna and constituted a form of reciprocation for the marriage of Tëna to (5)'s sister. When Tëna married for a second time, he further consolidated and legitimated the alliance he had initiated with his first marriage.

If the intermarriage of sibling sets serves as a means of repeating affinal ties between conjugal families within one generation, 'real' cross cousin marriage serves as a means of extending those marital alliances from one generation to the next. Figure 9 is designed to show how this works. In the diagram, (1), the son of the conjugal family enclosed within the circle marked (A), has married (4) the daughter of the conjugal family marked (B). The woman marked (2), the sister of (1), has married (3), the brother of (4). All four individuals have married their cross cousins since the parents of (1) and (2) are the opposite sex siblings of the parents of (3) and (4). By their marriages, the individuals marked (1)–(4) bring into being two new conjugal families (C) and (D). Thus individuals (1)–(4) each belong to two conjugal families, their families of birth (A and B) and their families of marriage (C and D). When the children of the conjugal families (C) and (D) marry one another, they marry their cross cousins and, in so doing, reiterate the alliance established between conjugal families (C) and (D) by the marriage of their parents, whilst at the same time bringing into existence two new conjugal families, (E) and (F). If the children of these families marry their cross cousins, the alliance will be reiterated once again. And so on, in theory, *ad infinitum*. However it is clear that this means of achieving serial affinity will always be vulnerable to demographic fluctuations affecting the availability of cross cousins. For example, in the hypothetical case illustrated in Figure 9, it could have resulted that all the offspring of individuals (1)–(4) were of the same sex. Under these circumstances, the offspring would be obliged to look to other conjugal families to provide them with spouses. Alternatively considerations of age can lead to a breakdown in a series of such marital exchanges. If a man wishes to get married immediately, he may look to another conjugal family, if his 'real' cross cousin is not yet mature or is too old for his liking.

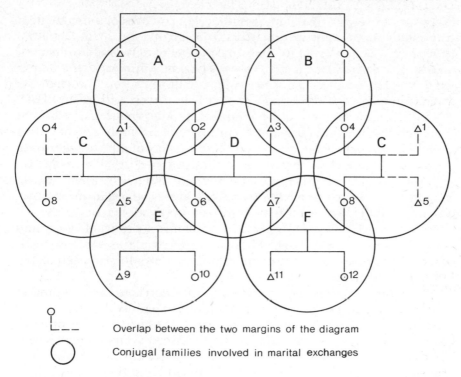

Overlap between the two margins of the diagram

Conjugal families involved in marital exchanges

Figure 9. Serial affinity across generations

On the basis of these considerations as to the effects of demographic fluctuations, one can posit that 'real' cross cousin marriages will only be frequent in a given segment of the population when one generation within that segment contains at least one large group of siblings, more or less equally distributed between the sexes, each of whom also has several offspring of his or her own. Under these circumstances, each of the offspring will have a comparatively large number of 'real' cross cousins amongst whom to find a suitable spouse. This condition for frequent 'real' cross cousin marriage can be defined in vertical genealogical terms as follows: 'real' cross cousin marriage will only be frequent in a given segment of the population if that segment contains at least one local cognatic descent line of three generations' depth, in which there are a large number of members in the second and third generations, more or less equally distributed between the sexes.

For present purposes, any case of marriage between the offspring of two individuals of opposite sexes who share at least one parent in common will be regarded as a case of 'real' cross cousin marriage. By this definition, a marriage between the children of two individuals of opposite sexes who are offspring of different co-wives of the same man constitutes an example of 'real' cross cousin marriage. In the Colorado sample, out of a total of fifty-four unions, there are twelve documented cases of unions between 'real' cross cousins, approximately 22 per cent of the sample. Of these twelve unions, seven involved the marriage of men with their FZD and five of men with their MBD. (None of these unions formed part of a polygynous marriage.) If further genealogical information relating to individuals who had died or who lived outside the community had been available, it might have been possible to show that some of these cases of 'real' cross cousin marriage also continued cases of 'real' bilateral cross cousin marriage. All were classificatory bilateral cross cousins to one another as they should have been. All twelve cases involved men under the age of thirty. Since only twenty-six of the unions in the whole Colorado sample involve men under thirty years of age, the cases of 'real' cross cousin marriage represent approximately 46 per cent of the unions involving men in the 15–29 age cohort.

This concentration of 'real' cross cousin marriage in the youngest adult male cohort of the population can be explained by two factors, one to do with the way in which the data were collected, the other to do with a particular aspect of the data themselves. Firstly, insufficient data were available to establish the exact genealogical relationship between some of the men over thirty years old and their wives. If this information had been available, it might have been possible to identify a number of cases of 'real' cross cousin marriage involving the men of the more senior age cohorts. However, even if all the dubious cases had in fact been cases of 'real' cross cousin marriage, the incidence of such marriages in the 30–44 and 45–59 cohorts would still have been less than in the 15–29 age cohort.

The concentration of 'real' cross cousin marriages in the youngest adult male cohort is primarily due to the fact that many of the men of this cohort are members of the third generation of a local cognatic descent line fulfilling the conditions for frequent cross cousin marriage stated above. This line is descended from a man called Puka who died about ten years ago. By three different wives, this man had nineteen children who reached adulthood, ten of them male and nine female. The oldest of Puka's offspring is approximately fifty-five years of age and the youngest about twenty. All of his offspring except the youngest have married. So far they have produced eighty-one children of their own, forty male and forty-one female. Five of these grand-children of Puka, and one of his sons, live outside the valley and are therefore not included in the sample. The remaining seventy-six grandchildren are equally divided between males and females and represent roughly a third of the total population of the valley. Consequently, as these grandchildren reach the age of maturity, they have a good chance of finding a 'real' cross cousin available to them as a spouse within the valley. To date, of the thirty-nine grandchildren of Puka in the valley who have married, twenty-two have married another grandchild of Puka. These eleven unions account for all but one of the total cases of 'real' cross cousin marriage in the Colorado population.

If the intermarriage of sibling sets is a means of repeating affinal ties within a single generation, and 'real' cross cousin marriage a means of extending affinal ties from one generation to the next, the marriage of a man with his DD (or a woman with her MF) is a means of extending a marital alliance into a third generation. One can demonstrate how this works by returning to Figure 9 again. If the man marked (1) in the diagram took his DD as a wife, necessarily as a second wife, he would be marrying the woman marked (12) in the diagram. By this means he would be repeating the affinal ties between his conjugal family of marriage, (C), and conjugal family (F), the conjugal family brought into being by the marriage of his son-in-law, (7) in the diagram, to his daughter, (8). At the same time, Ego's second marriage could be conceived of as a repetition of the alliance established between families (C) and (D) by the exchange of offspring in the generation below Ego and, in Ego's own generation, by his own first marriage and that of his sister to (3), a man who is simultaneously Ego's wife's brother, sister's husband and daughter's father-in-law.

Although marriage with a DD is regarded as a highly desirable form of marriage by Panare men, for obvious reasons to do with the longevity of a man such marriages are comparatively rare. Nonetheless, the genealogical material that I collected in Colorado and neighbouring communities contained two examples of marriage with a DD. The first case was illustrated in Figure 5: in this case (1) married the daughter of (2) and at a later stage reciprocated by giving (2) his own daughter as a wife. The second case is illustrated in Figure 10. This marriage had not actually taken place when I left Colorado but was rumoured to be on the point of doing so. In this latter case, the principle of reciprocation in the exchange of women is even more pronounced than in the first case. In this case, it was said that if the man marked (1) took his DD as a second wife, his son-in-law, marked (2), would be given another daughter of (1) as a second wife. This latter marriage would have involved the repetition of affinal ties in a horizontal sense as well since two of (2)'s prospective second wife's brothers are married to his sisters.

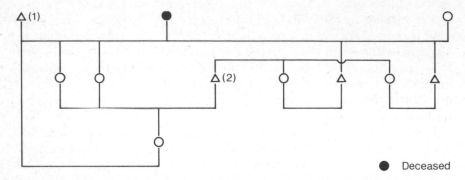

Figure 10. Reciprocal exchange between men of adjacent generations

As this last case shows very clearly, the rule that permits marriage with a DD (or of female Ego with her MF) can be conceived of as a means by which men of adjacent generations can establish and/or perpetuate an alliance by exchanging their daughters with one another. The same line of analysis can be used, in a negative sense, to suggest the reason why the other logically possible form of marriage between a man and an offspring's child, marriage with a SD – or, from the perspective of female Ego, marriage with FF – is precluded if the son in question is a 'real' son. It is easy to see from Figure 9 that such a marriage would in no way permit an alliance to be formed or perpetuated between two conjugal families. If the man marked (1) were interested in marrying his SD, marked (10), he would not be able to exchange a daughter with the prospective bride's father since his daughter (8) would be the latter's sister.[11]

Although I did not encounter any example of an alliance established on this basis in the Colorado valley, there is yet another way in which serial affinity between conjugal families can in theory be achieved, given the rules of the Panare kinship system. In discussing marriage with members of G+2 above, I pointed out that although Panare men reject the idea of marrying 'real' grandmothers, male Ego

11. Villalón (1978 : 28) reports a case from Southern Panare territory of a man married to a SD. Although she states that the union lasted only a short period, she clearly believes it to have been in conformity with the rules of the system. All that I can say is that the data that I collected in Southern Panare territory flatly contradict this point of view. My own data indicate that the men of this region refer to the DD as *no'*, the same term that they use for the female cross-cousin genealogically defined, and for FM. Individuals denoted by this term they consider marriageable and the marriage rule is phrased with reference to it. In contrast, the SD is called *nyasu*, the same term that is used for a 'real' sister and female parallel cousins, and she is not considered marriageable.

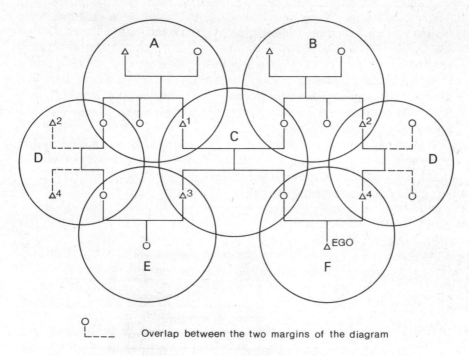

O
L___   Overlap between the two margins of the diagram

Figure 11. Serial affinity in the marriage of male Ego with a woman of G+2

nevertheless represents a potential spouse for his grandparents' female siblings since either his mother will be a *wa'nyene* to them or his father will be their *yawon*. In effect then, this makes both his paternal gFZ and his maternal gFZ potential spouses for male Ego. However, by means of Figure 11, it is possible to show that, in theory, marriage to one type of grandparental sibling serves to reiterate previous alliances whereas marriage to the other does not. If Ego, in the youngest generation in the figure, married his maternal gFZ, he would reiterate the alliance established between his father (4) and his MF (1) when the former married the latter's daughter. This alliance was itself a reiteration of the one established between Ego's MF and his FF (2) when they exchanged sisters in the previous generation. In terms of alliances between conjugal families, Ego's marriage to his maternal gFZ can be seen as an alliance between his maternal gF's family of birth (A), and the family created by his father's marriage (F), mediated by common alliances with families (C) and (D). This alliance relationship could also involve reciprocation since, if Ego had a sister, she would be the DD of his maternal gF and hence a potential spouse. Thus Ego might be in a position to exchange sisters with his maternal gF. In contrast, Ego's link with his paternal gF involves no alliance relationship: Ego's relationship to his father is obviously one of filiation rather than alliance, as is Ego's father's relationship to Ego's FF. Furthermore, the marriage of Ego to his paternal gFZ cannot involve reciprocation since Ego's Z is a 'real' SD to Ego's paternal gF and therefore *piyaka,* not marriageable. In short, there are grounds for positing that a preference for serial affinity would favour maternal over paternal gFZ marriage. In contrast to the case of SD marriage discussed above, this preference does not here entail an outright prohibition on paternal gFZ marriage. But, on theoretical grounds, one would expect it to be less common than marriage with a maternal gFZ. As matter of hard empirical fact, though, both types of alliance appear to be extremely rare.

Whatever the empirical possibilities of this last type of inter-generation alliance, it is clear from the evidence that I have presented in this chapter that the Panare rules of kinship and marriage provide several different channels through which marital alliances within a confined circle of related individuals may be repeated, not only within one generation but from one generation to the next. In all kinship systems that prescribe marriage with a category of relative that includes the bilateral cross cousin, genealogically defined, it is possible for an alliance established in one generation through the exchange of sisters to be extended into the next through the exchange of daughters. But in the Panare system, such alliances can be extended one generation further: for, given the institution of DD marriage, it is not only men of the same generation who can exchange their daughters but men of adjacent generations also.

In this chapter I have attempted to explain the pattern of marriages in the Colorado valley in terms of three principal determinants: the rules governing the classification of relatives and marriage, a preference for local endogamy and a preference for serial affinity. In passing, I have referred to the manner in which fortuitous demographic factors can influence the operation of these determinants. In most marriages in Colorado, these three determinants reinforce one another: most men have married local women of an approved category whose conjugal families had previous marital ties with their own. However on account of demographic fluctuations, it is not always possible for a man to repeat former alliances. Alternatively, he may not want, for personal reasons, to marry the particular woman that marriage rule or the principle of repeating former alliances might require him to. But under these circumstances, the Colorado material suggests that most Panare men continue to conform to the rules when seeking a wife. As we have seen, if there is no young woman of the appropriate category at the time they wish to get married, some men are prepared to marry much older women or to wait for an immature girl to reach puberty. Other men are not prepared to do either of these things and marry out of the community instead. Other men again, rather than marry out of the valley prefer to manipulate the rules so as to re-define as marriageable a woman they previously would have classed as *piyaka*. In the Colorado sample, there are only two men who broke completely with the rules when they married their wives and, as we have seen, in one of these cases the repetition of the alliance formed by marriage served to legitimize it in the eyes of the community. This case could be seen as an example of respect for the principle of serial affinity overriding respect for the rules that normally regulate the classification of relatives. In short, although the three determinants that I have defined reinforce one another in most marriages in Colorado, a wide variety of circumstances can set them at odds. Under these circumstances, all sorts of personal and idiosyncratic factors influence which of the three determinants is overridden by the others.

The genealogies collected in other Panare communities suggest that the high degree of endogamy recorded in the Colorado valley is typical of Panare communities in general. However, it should be noted that Colorado is atypical of Panare communities in two important respects. Firstly, Colorado is the largest of all Panare communities and the density of settlement in the valley is abnormally high. Given that the larger the population of his community, the greater is the chance that an individual has of finding a spouse of the appropriate age and category within it, one would anticipate that the degree of local endogamy is higher in Colorado than it is in other communities. The second atypical feature of the Colorado community is the presence of Puka's descent line which accounts for approximately 40 per cent of the total population of the community. There are similar local cognatic descent lines in the genealogies I collected in neighbouring communities and elsewhere, but none of these is quite as numerous as that of Puka. Furthermore, even when one does come across such lines, the members of the third generation (the first generation in which the members of a descent line can legitimately marry one another in Panare society) are usually dispersed over a number of different communities. Under these circumstances, the repetition of previous alliances through 'real' cross cousin marriage would be in conflict with the stated preferences for local endogamy more frequently than it is in Colorado. One would anticipate therefore that the incidence of 'real' cross cousin marriage would not be as high in other Panare communites as it is in Colorado. Even so, despite these atypical features of the Colorado community, I believe that the three determinants of Panare marriage patterns that I have identified on the basis of the data from Colorado can be generalized so as to apply to Panare communities in general. For throughout the genealogical material I collected, there is a marked tendency for marriages to conform with the rules, to be locally endogamous and to repeat former marital alliances between conjugal families.

The role of the conjugal family as the basic social unit involved in marital alliances exactly matches its role within the economic system as the basic social unit engaged in the exchange of food on a day-to-day basis within the settlement. In effect, the conjugal family is the basic unit both of production and reproduction within Panare society. There would appear, then, to be a direct structural relationship between these two domains of Panare social organization: the system of relations of kinship and marriage both determines and is determined by the system of economic relations. Moreover, one can also discern an indirect structural relationship—indirect in the sense that it is mediated by the system of economic relations—between the kinship system and the ecological adaptation of the Panare. As we saw in Chapter 3, the productive autonomy of the conjugal family within the system of economic relations represents an aspect of the Panare's adjustment to the dispersed character of the resources that they exploit. This autonomy permits individual conjugal families, as independent hearth groups, to break off from the main settlement group to exploit distant resource zones or, more generally, to move around Panare territory in response to fluctuations in the local food supply. The atomistic relations of production with which the autonomy of the hearth group is associated are incompatible with careful conservation, either of human labour resources or natural resources, and as such are entirely consonant with the Panare's 'prodigal', although completely rational, attitude towards the exploitation of the environment. As described in Chapter 2, the practical result of this attitude is a pattern of extensive resource exploitation over a large area, which in turn gives rise to a scattered settlement pattern and low population density. However these demographic conditions pose few problems of a social kind to the Panare on account of their system of kinship and marriage. Given the high degree of endogamy that it permits, most individuals are able to find spouses within a very reduced circle of close relatives. As a result, despite the small size of the communities, very few people ever have to leave the immediate geographical area in which they grew up to get married. In the absence of any superordinate kinship-based institutions, the social composition of Panare communities remains fluid: the autonomy of the conjugal families of which they are composed remains high. They are always free to break off, as hearth groups, to exploit the natural resources as they are available. It is in these several ways that the system of kinship and marriage, the economic system and the form of the Panare's ecological adaption are related one to another. Between them, these domains of Panare social organization account for the reproduction of the material infrastructure of the society. In the following chapter, we shall see how they are related to the developmental stages of the settlement group and a number of the more superstructural features of Panare social life.

# CHAPTER FIVE

# Social Solidarity

The Panare settlement group is always in a state of flux. Throughout the year, as we have seen, the structure of economic relations allows individual conjugal families to take off on sorties to distant resource zones. Yet it is rarely from economic necessity pure and simple that they do so: frequently just as important a consideration is a desire to get away from the somewhat enclosed social environment of the settlement. Several men in the settlement group in which I was living had built themselves small houses by the side of their gardens, at an hour or two's walk from the main settlement site and they would take off there with their wives and children for periods of several days in a row. They used these occasions to work intensively in their gardens but they also appreciated being alone with their families for a while. Women were generally not as keen on these solo expeditions as the men. One particular man, named To'se, maintained a garden and a small house way up in the mountains and he would take his family up there for weeks, sometimes months, at a stretch. He was somewhat marginal, genealogically speaking, to the settlement group and, moreover, was rather reserved personally. His wife however, rather more closely related to the group than he, and considerably more sociable, did not relish these trips at all and would complain to the other women of the settlement whenever he announced that he wanted her to pack her things together so as to be ready to leave for the mountains.

These short-term fluctuations, corresponding to the re-shuffling of the settlement group that takes place over a given year, can be contrasted with the long-term fluctuations that take place over the course of several years. After about three or four years, as the thatch on a collective house begins to rot and the rubbish around the edge of the settlement builds up to intolerable levels, the inhabitants start to discuss where they should build a new house. This is always a democratic process in which both men and women are involved. One or two years may elapse before the plan is actually put into effect: houses are usually built at the end of the dry season at the time when gardens are cut, and if the rains come early or the dry season ceremonies go on too long, the plan to build a new house may well be abandoned and the old one patched up instead. But, with one exception, I came across no traditional house that had been occupied for more than seven or eight years. The exception was a medium-sized house of the conical variety, close to the abandoned airstrip at Cuchiverito, which had once also been the site of a small criollo settlement. One of the inhabitants of this house claimed that it had been standing for fifteen years. The Panare are never very accurate when it comes to assessing the passage of time numerically, but certainly this house looked old, for the roof was full of holes and the interior walls were caked jet-black with the soot of years of smoke that had percolated upwards from family hearths.

The recent history of the group in which I spent most of my time in Colorado serves as a good illustration of the fluidity of the typical Panare settlement group. Around the year 1970 there were two groups whose principle settlement sites were located in the forested mountains overlooking the Colorado valley within an hour's walk of one another. The senior man in one of these groups, Tëna, was married to two sisters of the senior man in the other, Nahtë. Nahtë also had two wives, though neither of them was full sister to Tëna. Nevertheless, the two men called each other *tamun*, indicating the closeness of their relationship. This relationship was consolidated by the marriage of two of Tëna's sons to daughters of Nahtë and the marriage of a son of Nahtë to a daughter of Tëna. When the two men built new houses on the edge of the savanna in the valley in 1973, shortly after the arrival of the missionaries, they built them side by side. Each man lived with his wives, unmarried children, married daughters and in-married sons-in-law. The inhabitants of the two houses on the savanna formed a single settlement group, sharing collective meals and collaborating in collective subsistence activities. Thus the two groups that had formed more or less independent residential units in the mountains had now become one. Tëna however continued to maintain his house in the mountains, keeping one of his wives up there and the other on the savanna.

In the dry season 1974–5, Tëna was killed by a falling tree whilst collecting honey in the forest near his house in the mountains. Both his houses were vacated and the one in the mountains was burnt down. There was talk of burning down the one on the savanna also but in the end it was left standing. This was partly due to the fact that I moved into it a few months after his death. In the middle of the rainy season, whilst I was absent from the field, his house was re-occupied, not by Tëna's family but by Nahtë, one of his wives, a daughter married to a man from another settlement group and one of his own sons who had returned with his wife from his mother-in-law's settlement. Nahtë's house was occupied by Tëna's sons, his widows and one of Nahtë's wives and their children. Not long afterwards, one of Tëna's widows went to live in the settlement group of a prospective son-in-law, taking her unmarried children with her.

The following dry season, 1975–6, the remaining inhabitants of both houses moved into an open-air camp in a stretch of nearby forest. As in-married sons-in-law often do, Nahtë's son-in-law moved out to live with his mother in a different part of the valley. A son of Nahtë married to this son-in-law's sister moved in. In moving into their open-air camp, Nahtë's group established itself close to that of one of his brothers and the latter's wife, their offspring and a number of daughters- and sons-in-law. During this period of the dry season, both groups acted as a single settlement group, sharing in collective meals and collaborating in collective subsistence activities. Meanwhile, yet another group had moved into Nahtë's settlement and the surrounding pockets of forest in order to prepare for the initiation ceremonies that were due to take place there. In other words, in the dry season 1975–6, Nahtë's group, slightly modified by the departure of a son-in-law and the arrival of a son, moved out of its settlement site and fused with the settlement group of his brother, whilst Nahtë's settlement site and the surrounding area was occupied by a group from another part of the valley.

At the beginning of the rainy season of 1976, Nahtë and his group established a new settlement site about 250m away from the two old houses. His son who had moved in for the dry season returned to his mother-in-law's house. The son-in-law who had moved out returned to Nahtë's group. All the remaining members of Nahtë's group moved in under a single roof except for one of his sons, married to a daughter of Tëna. This man, together with the husband of a sister of Nahtë, who had previously been living nearby, built a house alongside that of his father. The genealogical connection between the two men who would live in the smaller house was remote and they said that they had decided to live together simply because they like each other.[1]

Major changes in the social composition of a Panare settlement group usually coincide with a change in settlement site, but minor changes are taking place all the time. There are always conjugal families coming and going between the settlement groups within any given area of Panare territory. In view of this fluidity, it is impossible to define any clear-cut stages in the development of a Panare settle-

1. This last case neatly demonstrates the limitations of any attempt to account for the social composition of a settlement group purely on structural grounds in a society such as this, in which there are no strict rules of post-marital residence.

ment group; but one can distinguish three ideal types of group on the basis of social composition:

(i) a group consisting of a man, his wife or wives, and his children. The senior man of a group of this type will normally be over thirty-five years of age and have adult children who can pull their own weight in subsistence tasks.

(ii) a group composed of a senior man, normally over forty-five, his wife or wives, his unmarried children and his married daughters and sons-in-law. The senior man's own adult sons will normally have moved out to do bride service elsewhere, although one or two may be living patrilocally, having already fulfilled their bride-service obligations.

(iii) a group consisting of a core of married brothers and sisters or, depending on how one wants to look at it, a core of men who are brothers-in-law to one another. The members of this core will normally be between twenty and forty years of age and most of them will have several children. Their parents may also live with them if they are old, divorced or widowed.

These three ideal types may represent sequential stages in the development of particular settlement groups, The first type consisting of a single man and his family could turn into the second type with the marriage of his children. Following his death or in his old age, the second type could become the third, if his sons who had married returned to live in the same residential group as their sisters. But few Panare settlement groups go through three such well-defined stages. Each of the three types can give way to either of the other two. For example, a son-in-law living in a residential group of the second type may decide to break off from his father-in-law's group and set up on his own with his conjugal family of marriage. Subsequently he may decide to throw in his lot with some of his brothers and brothers-in-law, thereby bringing about a residential group of the third type. Even later, this settlement group may break up and the man may set himself up on his own again but this time in a group of the second type, that is, with one or two newly-acquired sons-in-law of his own. In short, instead of passing through a series of well-defined stages of development, Panare settlements are in a state of continual oscillation between various forms of association between conjugal families. But most Panare settlement groups at any given time are cognatic in social composition, approximating to the characteristics of either the second or the third ideal type.

The fluidity of the Panare settlement group is indirectly a function of ecological and economic factors. But more immediately relevant is the nature of the Panare kinship system and, more specifically, the fact that they do not recognize descent groups. The absence of descent groups is consonant with a relatively lax set of rules governing post-marital residence and other bride-service obligations, and it is the laxity of these rules that, in its turn, provides the immediate reason why individual conjugal families move about so much. Even so, despite this freedom, most conjugal families are simultaneously bound by a number of strong ties of kinship to the other members of the settlement groups to which they are attached. In fact, any settlement group can be conceived of as an uneasy compromise between the centrifugal effects of the conjugal family's social and economic autonomy and the centripetal effects of its members' responsibilities to their relatives, both consanguineal and affinal. In the chapter dealing with the economic system, I identified the economic advantages to be gained from living in a settlement group, the principal one being that it cushions the individual conjugal family against short-term fluctuations in the food supply. But the Panare themselves would point to the social benefits to be gained from living in a settlement: it enables one to stay in daily contact with one's closest relatives, or as the Panare would put it, with one's *piyaka* (defined in this context in the broadest sense). This concern to remain close to one's *piyaka* requires no profound sociological explanation: the Panare's idea of a state of well-being is one in which one is close to those to whom one is attached by multiple bonds of an emotional, genealogical and economic character. As I noted in Chapter 4, the Panare will recur to this concern to remain close to their *piyaka* when explaining their preference for local marriage. Nevertheless, from a sociological point of view, there are four sets of dyadic interpersonal relations that are particularly important, in the sense that by crossing the boundaries of independent conjugal families they serve to counterbalance their autonomy and thereby maintain the cohesion of the settlement group. These dyadic relationships are: the relationship between mother and daughter, the relationship between siblings, the relationship between a man and his mother-in-law and the relationship between *tamun,* i.e. between men who have married one another's sisters.

Although it may be a man's duty to provide his mother-in-law with meat that obliges him to go to live in her settlement, it is the ties between his mother-in-law and his wife that serve to prevent him from leaving, even when he is deemed to have fulfilled his bride-service obligations. Since a woman will generally try to resist any attempt by her husband to move out and set up an independent household, a compromise is often struck whereby the man builds himself a house, just large enough for himself and his conjugal family, that is only a few minutes walk away from his parents-in-law's settlement. A house at this distance is sufficiently far away to act as an independent social and economic entity but sufficiently close for the wife to remain in daily social contact with her mother if she wishes. Many settlement groups corresponding to type (i) described above originate under these conditions.

This bond between mother and daughter is far stronger than the bond between daughter and father or between a son and either of his parents. A girl begins to help her mother in her domestic chores from the time she is about four or five years old. She remains in close daily contact with her mother until she is married, working with her during the day, sleeping around her hearth at night. After marriage, she leaves her mother's hearth only to set up her own hearth alongside it. A boy, on the other hand, has no such close collaborative relationship with either of his parents. In contrast to a girl, who is socialized primarily through the daily contact she has with her mother, the socialization of a boy is more of a collective matter. Although a man will occasionally take his son on a hunting or fishing trip a boy learns most of what he needs to know in the way of technical skills by tagging along on collective ventures. This collective interest in male socialization is expressed in the elaborate series of male initiation ceremonies that take place every few years during the dry season: in comparison the rites connected with female initiation are negligible.[2] A boy also leaves his parents' hearth much earlier than a girl. When he is about ten, he begins to hang his hammock alongside those of the other bachelors in the centre of the communal house. After marriage, he may well leave his parents' settlement group altogether. Men who marry out often return however on visits to their parents' settlement. The purpose of these visits, as the Panare invariably express it, is to visit their mothers. This way of putting it, as well as the way in which they interact with their respective parents, underlines the fact that the bond between mother and son is more intimate than the bond between father and son. Even so, the bond between mother and son is still less intimate than the bond between mother and daughter.

The social bond between siblings derives simply from the fact that they belong to the same conjugal family of birth and therefore grow up together. Even after they are married and thereby form independent conjugal families of their own, same-sex siblings will often continue to live in the same settlement as one another. Sisters remain living

2. In Western Panare territory, there is a minor ceremony connected with female puberty, attended by women only. In Southern Panare territory also there appears to be a ceremony marking the arrival of female puberty. But to the best of my knowledge, this Southern Panare ceremony does not form part of a large public dance either, being a private affair involving only the girl concerned and her immediate family.

together in their parents' settlement and continue to collaborate with one another, and with their mother, in daily subsistence tasks. Due to the practice of sororal polygyny, sisters may well be married to the same man. Brothers, for their part, are frequently married to women who are sisters to one another and therefore live in the same settlement. This co-residence of same-sex siblings can continue until middle age which is the time of life when men tend to set up independent settlement groups of the first ideal type defined above, consisting of their conjugal family of marriage only. This leads to the separation of same-sex siblings as each goes off to live with their respective spouse(s).

In contrast to same-sex siblings, opposite-sex siblings lead separate lives from a very early age, even though they live in the same settlement. The sexual division within Panare society appears to be inculcated very early since even the youngest children tend to play exclusively with children of the same sex. As they grow into adolescence, the lives of brothers and sisters remain separate as the boys move their hammocks to the centre of the house and begin to participate in the life of the men of the settlement whilst girls remain attached to their mothers and the family hearth. In adulthood however, after they have married, the social division between opposite-sex siblings appears to diminish. It is clear from the way they interact, most notably during the dances but also in daily life, that they appreciate one another's company. Their relationship is in no way marked by the restraint that normally characterizes relations between men and women of the same age. By setting up a settlement of the third ideal type defined above, the members of a mixed-sex sibling set are able to extend the relationship into which they were born into late adult life.

Although a man may spend many years living in his mother-in-law's settlement, he generally avoids any direct dealings with her. He rarely talks to her directly and may even avoid looking at her. He will take even more care to avoid dealings with his wife's sisters, particularly if they are unmarried since then they are potential wives. All social contact with his female affines is mediated through his wife. The meat he brings into the settlement is first given to her, she then gives part of it to her mother and, if there is a considerable quantity, she may give some to her married sisters as well. Apart from this obligation to provide meat, the new son-in-law has relatively few specific bride-service duties. Through negotiation via his wife he may permit his mother-in-law to plant part of the area that he has cleared for a garden, whilst if she is short of food he may allow her to harvest from a garden that is already producing a crop. But a son-in-law is under no specific obligation to carry out agricultural work for his affines. (In fact, when I asked a Panare man if he was expected to clear a garden for his mother-in-law, he looked genuinely shocked and asked, in an amazed tone, if people expected that sort of thing where I came from.)

Although there is a certain degree of restraint in the dealings between a man and his father-in-law, this is not markedly greater than the restraint exercised by a young man when interacting with any senior figure, including even his own father. A son-in-law is in no sense the economic or political vassal of his father-in-law; his bride-service obligations, such as they are, are to his mother-in-law rather than his father-in-law. Hence there is no reason for a senior man to attempt to establish his authority over his son-in-law by means of extreme formality in his social dealings with him.

Far more significant than the father- to son-in-law relationship, from the point of view of the links it creates between the conjugal families within a settlement group, is the relationship between *tamun*, the men who have married one another's sisters. Relations between *tamun* who have grown up together are as informal and intimate as the relations between full brothers. If a man has married into an alien settlement group, his relations with his wife's brothers may be somewhat restrained but this is due to the fact that he is an outsider rather than to the fact that he is their sister's husband. But since many Panare settlement groups are, in effect, bilateral kindreds, a boy is likely to spend at least part of his childhood living in the same settlement as the boys who will later become his *tamun*. As children, future *tamun* play together; in adolescence, they go on youthful escapades together; in adulthood, they exchange sisters in marriage. If they continue to live together after their respective marriages, this close bond can be extended into middle age. By this time, a man will usually have nubile offspring of his own, and he can further reinforce his relationship with his *tamun* by arranging for his offspring to marry his *tamun's* offspring.

It makes perfect sense therefore for a man to call his brother-in-law *tamun*, for this is the term also used to refer to a woman's spouse. In both cases, Ego's *tamun* is someone to whom he or she is related by years of co-residence, by marriage, and usually by genealogy as well. As such, the *tamun* relationship is extremely important to Panare men. '*Tamun*', they say, 'should be *ayape* (that is good or generous) to one another.' It is this bond just as much as the ties between siblings and between parents and children that serves to unite the members of a settlement group into a social whole. Many, if not most, Panare settlements contain a group of young adult men who are *tamun* to one another and who provide the bulk of the male contribution to the collective food pool of the settlement. The ideal that *tamun* should be generous to one another therefore serves to reinforce the food-sharing principle without which the system of collective distribution and consumption would break down. Thus there is a kind of ideological match between the practice of sister exchange between *tamun* and the ideal of mutual material generosity that consolidates their common membership of the same settlement group.

There appears to be no equivalent amongst women of the male *tamun* relationship. Women have no specific relationship term to apply to their brothers' wives and refer to them simply as *tunkonan*. If they live together, they may address one another by personal name. But women do not stress the importance of the sister-in-law relationship. Even when sisters-in-law find themselves living in the same settlement, they do not have as much to do with one another as *tamun* do. This is often reflected in the physical layout of the settlement. In addition to the collective residential house, a cognatic settlement group will often have two or more independent cooking huts, each of which is used by a group of sisters and their mother. In the settlements in which I was living, there were two such huts, of approximately the same size, which stood right next door to one another and which were built at the same time. Each hut was built by a son-in-law of the senior woman who used it. (i.e. the husband of one of the other women who used it). Interestingly, the two men involved were *tamun* to one another since they had married one another's sisters. In other words, each of the two men, working independently but at the same time, built a hut for the other's mother and sisters. This case suggests that when a man continues to live in the same settlement as his conjugal family of birth after his marriage, his obligations to his mother-in-law and wife over-ride his obligations to his own mother and his sisters.

But with the exception of women's cooking huts, the spatial layout of most settlement sites reflects the undifferentiated cognatic character of the group that inhabits them. Within the principal house of the settlement, married couples and their children, and widows or divorcées and their children occupy the space adjacent to the walls of the house. Male adolescents sleep in the centre of the house. Generally speaking, it is impossible to distinguish between the two sides of the house on the basis of the affinal status the members of the group hold relative to one another. Along the walls of the house, the hearths tended by the wives of men who are *tamun* to one another are interdigitated, whilst in the centre of the house, adolescent *tamun* sleep side by side. Figure 12 shows the spatial layout of the household of Nahtë to whom I referred in the case history given earlier in this chapter.

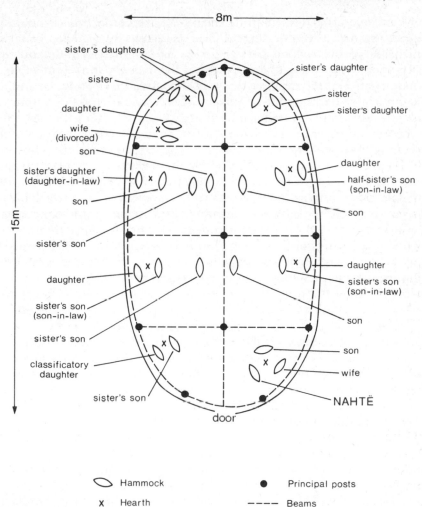

Figure 12. Nahtë's household (June 1975)

The figure shows the layout of his household at the beginning of the rainy season of 1975, a few months after his *tamun* Tëna had been killed. The position of Nahtë's hammock is indicated by the ellipse in the bottom right-hand corner of the diagram. The position of the hammocks of all the other members of the household who were old enough to sleep by themselves, and the genealogical relationship of their occupants to Nahtë, are also indicated in Figure 12. Considered as a whole, it is apparent that no clear distinction can be drawn between the two sides of the house, since both sides contain both sons and sister's sons, and daughters and sister's daughters of Nahtë.

Far more important than distinctions based on actual or potential affinal status, in the organization of everyday life within the settlement, is the distinction between men and women. This distinction pervades every sphere of Panare social life: it is the most fundamental distinction underlying the rules of the kinship system; economic activities are organized around a radical sexual division of labour; in ritual, men and women have quite distinct roles. But although male and female roles are mutually exclusive in most domains of social life, their complementarity is manifest in the petty details of day-to-day life within the settlement. The provision of meat may be a primarily male activity but a man claims to have no idea how to cook the meat he has killed. Furthermore, a meal is considered a proper meal only if it contains both meat and carbohydrates in one form or another: whilst men provide the meat, women provide the carbohydrates. A woman does most of the cartage required in daily life but depends on her husband to weave the baskets she uses to do so. She weaves his hammock and his loincloth but depends on her husband to set up the loom she uses and to make the spindle on which she spins the cotton. Women maintain the hearths that are the focal point of family life but it is men who build the collective house and the cooking huts. Examples of this kind could be extended almost indefinitely.

It is the men who dominate Panare society, although they also have certain responsibilities to the women. Even so, women are usually consulted about the aspects of social life in which they are recognized to have special expertise. For example, women are generally more knowledgeable about the details of the kinship network than their husbands. Thus a man who is supposed to find a spouse for his son will rely on his wife for information about relatives in distant communities. Furthermore, when a man makes a proposal of marriage on behalf of his son, both the mother and the father of the girl are involved in the decision as to whether or not to accept it. Similarly, although it is a man who, as *tihcen,* decides to put on a dance, he requires the consent and collaboration of his wife since it is she who organizes the preparation of the large quantities of sugar-cane beer that are an essential feature of any dance. By virtue of the important part they play in providing the material means for the dance, women determine when it will actually take place. Whenever I asked a *tihcen* what day a prospective dance would begin, he would invariably refer me to his wife for information. In short, from day to day, a man consults his wife about all sorts of minor details of social life; but although women are consulted on most decisions, it is the men who put them into effect.

Male authority is most clearly expressed within the collective context of the settlement site. There men order their wives about imperiously, and ostentatiously refrain from helping in domestic chores. An anecdote illustrates the point: one evening whilst the men were eating their collective meal, a barbecue on which the day's catch of fish was smoking collapsed, and the fish fell into the fire. The men were much closer to the fire than the women, who were round the other side of the house eating their meal. But rather than do something about the disaster, the men merely called on the women to do so instead. A moment later a woman rushed over to the fire and threw water on it. Throughout the episode the men went on chuckling about the incident, apparently impervious to the prospect of the day's catch going up in smoke. Incidents of a similar kind occur frequently within the settlement site. But when a man and his wife are on their own, they are less reserved and they collaborate more on domestic chores. When a couple are working together in the garden for example, they laugh and joke with one another and exchange gossip. Such familiarity is unusual within the settlement. There men and women spend most of their time in contact with members of their own sex and relations between couples are comparatively restrained.

The radical distinction between male and female roles means that a man has very little contact with his wife prior to marriage, even if they should live in the same settlement group. In everyday life, a man never addresses a potential spouse: to do so is said to be *te'yapanset*, that is, it causes embarrassment. The social divide separating a man and his potential spouse was made apparent to me when I was mapping out the sleeping arrangements in Nahtë's household illustrated in Figure 12. My informant, an adolescent son of Nahtë, was prepared to tell me the name of the occupants of most of the hammocks lining the walls of the house, but claimed not to know the names of the occupants of four hammocks located no more than two or three yards from his own. When I pressed him, he gave me four female child's names in an off-hand way. It later transpired that he had lived in the same settlement group as these girls for a number of years but felt uncomfortable about naming them since they were *wa'nyenkin*, potential spouses. The first direct contact that future spouses have with one another usually takes place during dances. Towards the end of a dance, when everyone has drunk a good deal of sugar-cane beer, the protocol of everyday life is relaxed. Married couples dance side by side whilst the unmarried men take the opportunity to get to know potential spouses in the darker recesses of the house or in some secluded spot outside. A young man may even persuade a potential spouse to dance by his side in full public view around the centre post of the collective house.

Yet, although men may dominate women in Panare society, no man has any significant political power over another. Even when judged by the standards of lowland South American societies, the Panare are remarkable for their almost complete lack of formal political institutions. This lack can be partly attributed to the economic organization of Panare society. The organization of subsistence activities requires no well-developed managerial roles, whilst the absence of any system of individual property rights over the means of production (other than over tools, of which most hearth groups have a full complement) means that no man can control another on account of the latter's dependence on him to meet his subsistence needs. Furthermore, the social pressures inhibiting accumulation prevent extraordinary productive individuals from using the distribution of their product as a means of establishing political control. All these economic features inhibiting the development of leadership roles invested with coercive power are shared by the Panare with most other lowland South American societies. But in the Panare case, the development of leadership roles is further inhibited by the absence of *de jure* corporate groups based on non-economic criteria. In Panare society, one cannot acquire a political following simply by virtue of becoming the most senior man of a lineage; the absence of discrete corporate groups of kin and affines militates against the development of political factions based on kinship networks. Since there are no age grades or age sets, these cannot be manipulated by politically ambitious individuals for the purposes of gaining more general political control.

Nor does the social organization of Panare society favour the development of a political authority to act as an arbiter in disputes, for the simple reason that the causes of dissension are few. Nobody can appropriate natural resources to the exclusion of others, and the economic system inhibits the development of significant differences in personal wealth. Thus there are few grounds for dispute over material resources.[3] Nor is there any cause for dispute over potential spouses. Despite the practice of polygyny and the preference for local endogamy, the rules governing the classification of relations are sufficiently flexible for most men to find a wife of the approved category locally, if not of their own generation, then in a generation two above or two below. The absence of a strict rule of post-marital residence,

3. As the Panare acquire an increasing number of industrial goods, this is beginning to change. Unlike food resources, these industrial goods are not distributed collectively. As incipient differences in personal wealth begin to manifest themselves, incidents involving the theft of industrial goods are beginning to become more frequent. But the Panare have no social machinery for dealing with this new phenomenon and when something is stolen no effort is made to get it back, even when the identity of the thief is known.

combined with the economic autonomy of the hearth group, means that people who do not get on together are not obliged to live together. Although disputes do occur, they are extremely rare and are usually resolved not by any form of arbitration, but by the simple expedient of one of the parties leaving the settlement, along with the other members of his hearh group. No great sacrifice is involved if a hearth group decides to move: if its members decide to live by themselves, not much effort is required to build a house; if they want to join another settlement, it is easy enough for them to do so because, due to the cognatic composition of most Panare settlement groups, the senior man of the hearth group is almost bound to have either a *tamun*, a sibling, a parent or an offspring living elsewhere into whose settlement he will be able to move without any sort of formal negotiation.

In actual fact, the Panare have no word to designate the role of 'chief', although in many settlements there is a senior man who has acquired a degree of pre-eminence, either on account of his age and experience, or because most of the members of the settlement are either his offspring or spouses of his offspring. But the position of such a headman is no more than *primus inter pares* and no special privileges accrue to him. His authority is very weak and never extends beyond the bounds of his own settlement. He will play a prominent part in certain critical decisions affecting the whole settlement, such as where a new house will be built and how big it will be, but he has no power to oblige others to do anything they do not wish to do. Even when such men have a large number of offspring, they do not try to arrange their marriages so as to build up their own settlement groups and hence enhance their political authority. Due to the fluidity in the social composition of the settlement, the individuals over whom a headman exercises this very limited authority are constantly changing, and there is very little he can do to prevent them from leaving his settlement and setting up elsewhere. The local criollos will refer to such a headman as *capitán* because he often acts as a sort of informal ambassador for the settlement in its dealings with the outside world. The criollos imagine that a *capitán* holds sway over the other members of his settlement, but this view of his position is more a reflection of the criollos' own hierarchical society than an accurate representation of the realities of Panare society.

Although the Panare have no word to identify the headman of a settlement, they do designate men who are thought to be especially knowledgeable about ceremonial, music and supernatural matters by a special term, *i'yan*. But this term denotes *an individual condition rather than a social role*. The *capitán* of a settlement group need not necessarily be an *i'yan* although many of them are. Conversely, one can be an *i'yan* without being the *capitán*. In fact, there can be one, several or no *i'yan* in a particular settlement depending on the circumstances. Moreover, the number of *i'yan* said to live in any settlement is very much a matter of personal opinion: some men regarded as great *i'yan* by some Panare are regarded as charlatans by others.[4]

To become an *i'yan* one is supposed to undergo a period of training, which principally consists of taking large quantities of a psychotropic drug, *amadapuhĕmkai'mĕn*, and various forms of medicinal drink (see Table 7). In addition, a novitiate is supposed to deprive himself of all food except cassava bread, refrain from talking to others and to walk through the forest all day equipped only with a knife. It is said that many young men start to train to become *i'yan* but that most give it up on account of the physical rigours involved. Although it is usually only men who attempt to become *i'yan*, some informants said that women could in theory become *i'yan* by learning from their husbands. During his period of training, a novitiate may consult an experienced *i'yan* but he receives no formal instruction. Nobody tells the novitiate when he has achieved the condition of *i'yan*, but it is said that he himself will know because he will be able to wander about the sky like a bird. He will also have in his control one or more invisible jaguars which he can cause to materialize at will. The degree of power that an *i'yan* has is expressed in the number of invisible jaguars that he has at his command. An extremely powerful *i'yan* will have three jaguars under his control whilst some past *i'yan* are said to have had as many as four, although this is regarded as well-nigh incredible. An *i'yan's* jaguars are potentially very dangerous to the *i'yan* himself since they can turn upon him and kill him. A cautionary tale is told of the *i'yan* of the community of Manare who had three jaguars in his control which were

4. Dumont (1978 : 38) states that, 'The Creoles assume that there must be one and only one headman per Panare local group. Projecting their conception of coercive power onto the Panare, they always wish to deal with the *capitán*. In fact, although the Panare do make a distinction between shaman (*tukuraxtey*) and headman (*iyan*), the political authority of a headman is legitimized by a religious sanction: his shamanistic initiation. As a result, there are local groups in which there is no headman, that is, groups where nobody has gone through the shamanistic initiation. Conversely, there are groups in which more than one man is potentially qualified to be headman without actually being so.'

Although I entirely concur with Dumont about the relationship between being an *i'yan* and possessing shamanic knowledge, I think he is wrong when he suggests that the term *i'yan* denotes the specific social role of headman. I also have my doubts about the term *tukuraxtey*. I do not fully recognize this word, but suspect that it means 'the one who cures' or something similar, being derived from the verb *kuraxtĕnye*, to heal or cure, a corruption of the Spanish verb *curar* which has become fully integrated into the Panare language. If so, it would be an appropriate term to apply to an *i'yan*, one of whose skills is to use his knowledge of the supernatural to cure the sick.

reputed to be so tame that they would lie down beneath his hammock at night. But one day, for no apparent reason, they turned upon their master and killed him.

The *i'yan's* jaguars do not appear to act as his agents in carrying out any particular task. Instead they seem to be merely a symbolic expression of the ambiguous nature of the *i'yan's* power. This ambiguity derives from the fact that the *i'yan* can use his power both for good and for ill. On the negative side, an *i'yan* is said to be able to kill people at a great distance by means of a special stone known as *pamëkai'mën* (literally, 'the thing like salt' and therefore probably quartz); alternatively, he can assume an invisible form, take to the air and visit other Panare settlements to carry out his malignant purposes in person. Once he is close to his victim, he can kill him by blowing invisible darts into his body or simply by 'biting' him. If the victim has been foolish enough to leave items of personal detritus around, the *i'yan* can attack these instead. The Panare believe that everyone has a store of *inyëto,* a sort of 'soul power' normally located within one's chest and at various other points of the body. But this *inyëto* can also be left in items of personal detritus (or in images such as photographs and tape-recordings). Even when a person's *inyëto* is disembodied in this way, it is believed to be still connected to its owner, and for this reason an attack on personal detritus can be just as serious as a direct attack on the individual himself.

When *i'yan* assume this invisible form for the purpose of carrying out evil designs, they are referred to as *mahtikëdi.* It is only the *i'yan* of distant communites or members of other indigenous groups such as the Guahibo and the Piaroa who are thought to become *mahtikëdi.* The Panare generally regard the *i'yan* of their own and neighbouring settlements as benign, at least in so far as they themselves are concerned. But *mahtikëdi* are not the only invisible entities to which the Panare believe themselves to be vulnerable. The Panare of Colorado also have numerous but somewhat badly articulated and mutually contradictory ideas about a host of other such beings. One of the few consistent features of this corpus of beliefs about supernatural entities is that all of them, without exception, are regarded as hostile. The most important appear to be loosely grouped into four categories:

    i) *wöri* — these entities seem to be very similar to *mahtikëdi,* except that they are said to 'hunt' their victims with lances rather than slay them with invisible blowgun darts.

    ii) *kwocam* — the spirits of dead Panare. At the time of the dance following a death, the *kwocam* are thought to hang around the vicinity of the settlement, thirsting for sugar-cane beer. Since they are believed to be lonely in the place of the dead without the other members of their family, this is regarded as a very dangerous time by living Panare because they fear that a dead member of their family may attack them in order to carry them off, back to the place of the dead. For this reason, the Panare try to avoid leaving the settlement until the dance is over.

iii) *në'na* — the term *në'na* is used of all entities that are in some sense active: living human beings of all kinds, animals, all supernatural entities including the dead. This term also includes therefore the *i'yan's* jaguars and two other invisible zoomorphic entities which the *i'yan* is thought to be capable of seeing when under the influence of *amarapuhëmkai'mën*. These are the *matëpoimë*, an invisible giant anteater with huge eyes said to be capable of 'burning' people, and the *kowarekai'në*, resembling a very small horse, which has a grey coat and scurries rapidly along the ground.

iv) *amana* — in a category all of its own, this entity is half-human and half animal and can manifest itself in the form of a boa constrictor. Not all boa constrictors are incarnations of *amana*, but even those that are not are referred to by the same name. Like *mahtikëdi*, *amana* can cause illness by blowing objects which appear to be blowgun darts (*waimo'*) but in reality are only 'like blowgun darts' (*waimo'kaimën*) into the bodies of their victims. Some Panare groups, but not all, believe that *amana* is the master of certain natural resources which must not therefore be exploited. All Panare groups refer to the rainbow as *amanataci*, literally the 'breath of *amana*'.[5]

An *i'yan* is supposed to be able to 'see' all these invisible entities, though some can only be 'seen' with the aid of *amarapuhëmkai'mën*. Indeed the possession of *amarapuhëmkai'mën* appears to be an essential condition of *i'yan*-ship. A number of men said that they used to be *i'yan* but were so no longer because they no longer kept a supply of the drug.

5. In his first book, Dumont claims that the Panare believe the world to have been created by a 'were anaconda' known as *Manataci'*, also responsible for maintaining the world in its present state. Dumont says that the Panare believe that this entity manifests itself in the form of the rainbow, also known by the term *'Manataci'*. Hence the title of his book: *Under the Rainbow* (Dumont 1976 : 14–15). But Dumont's discussion of this entity involves a number of errors. Firstly, the term *'Manataci'*, or more correctly *amanataci*, is used to designate the rainbow and not the entity itself. The rainbow is said to be the breath (*taci*) of *amana*, not *amana* itself. Secondly, *amana* manifests itself, not as an anaconda, as Dumont claims, but as the boa constrictor. Thirdly, although *amana* is said to be the 'master' of certain natural resources and therefore might be said to play a part in maintaining the present state of the world, in my experience no informant ever attributed the creation of the world to this entity. If the creation of the world was attributed to any entity, it was generally attributed to *marioka*, the first Panare to emerge from the mountain at the headwaters of the Cuchivero at the beginning of time.

An *i'yan* can use his powers for good by protecting the members of his settlement against the effects of the supernatural entities. He can suck out the invisible darts blown by *mahtikëdi* and *amana*. He can banish the *kwocam* to the land of the dead during the course of the death dance. In the communities where *amana* is thought to be the master of certain natural resources he can identify which these are.[6] In addition to these supernatural skills, an *i'yan* is expected to know all the songs that should be sung during the ceremonies connected with death and with male initiation. Yet unlike the shamans of some indigenous societies of lowland South America, the Panare *i'yan* derives no political or economic power from the services he renders to the community. Although an *i'yan* can offer protection from metaphysical attack, this does not appear to influence the residential strategies of individual hearth groups. That is, unlike the Piaroa, the Panare do not tend to group themselves around recognized shamans in order to take advantage of their supernatural protection (Kaplan 1975 : 53 *et seq.*). Nor did I come across or hear of any case of a Panare *i'yan* exercising some sort of legal or political power by means of making sorcery accusations against other members of his settlement group (see for examples, Butt 1965/6; Dole 1973). Although *i'yan* sometimes charge for their services, the payments involved are usually very small and are not sufficient for *i'yan* to become significantly more wealthy than their fellow Panare (Harner 1968). A Panare *i'yan* is a servant rather than a leader of his settlement group. His authority is confined to the spheres of the supernatural, ceremonial and music, and does not reach over into other domains of social life.[7]

The Panare's fear of the supernatural threat posed by the *i'yan* of distant settlement groups is merely the most extreme expression of a set of social attitudes that both reflect and serve to reinforce the independence of Panare settlements one from another. In Panare society there are no descent groups to foster a sense of social identity between members of independent settlement groups who have little or no social contact with one another. Due to the preference for local endogamy, the conjugal families that engage in marital exchange

6. In this connection, it is interesting to cite the remarks of a relatively acculturated Panare adolescent from the community of Caño Amarillo. This boy was taken to the town of Mérida in the Venezuelan Andes by my colleague Dra M -C. Müller to work with her on linguistic data. Coming across a stand of plants in the vicinity of Mérida that, in external appearance, bore a great resemblance to the Ischnosiphon from which the Panare prepare the elements used in the manufacture of baskets, Dra Müller suggested to her informant that he might like to experiment to see if the Andean plants could be used for this purpose also. But the boy replied that he could not possibly do this until he had consulted with his father, an *i'yan,* in order to find out whether or not this stand of plants 'belonged' to *amana*.

usually live either within the same settlement or in settlements that are geographically close to one another. Even those settlements whose members are closely related genealogically to one another are completely independent of one another in the course of day-to-day life.

As I noted in the preceding chapter, the independence of settlement groups is expressed in the generally negative opinions that the members of any given settlement group have for the members of any and all others. The members of other settlement groups are said to be unable to speak properly, unable to construct decent houses or weave good baskets, to be generally stupid—in short, to be *tincakeihkye,* a term used to describe ignorance both of basic technical skills and of correct social behaviour. Any form of violent behaviour is regarded as the most extreme manifestation of being *tincakeihkye.* The more distant a settlement, the more the Panare suspect its members of being *tincakeihkye* in this extreme sense and the more their chauvinistic attitude to outsiders shades into fear. For example, the members of the settlement group in which I was living in Colorado regarded the members of the other settlements in the valley, to whom they were closely related genealogically, as being decidedly less skilled than themselves in technical activities but in no sense as dangerous. The people from settlements such as Trapichote to the south-west and Manare to the north-east, about a day's walk away but with whom the people of Colorado had a number of kinship ties, were regarded as no more than potentially dangerous. On the other hand, the people of El Pajal, slightly further afield still, were not merely suspected of being dangerous, they were known to be so. It was said that they had the anti-social habit of tipping a substance resembling crushed glass into the beer canoe during dances, which could be fatal if one drank enough of it. But the Panare of Colorado did nevertheless recognize a very small number of kinship ties with the people of El Pajal, and the fact that they visited one another for dances demonstrated that some social contact between the two communities was maintained.

7. It would appear from the intriguing account in Dumont's second book (1978) that political machinations were far more prevalent in Túriba Viejo, the settlement group in which he was living, that they were in the Colorado group in which I was based. I believe that this difference can be put down largely to differences in the characters of the leading men in the respective groups. Furthermore, although the men of Túriba Viejo may have been busily engaged in domestic politicking, this does not alter the fact that, in Panare society generally, formal political institutions are virtually non-existent, nor that those who occupy the ill-defined role of headman lack any coercive power over the other members of their settlement groups. Under these circumstances, one would expect the personal qualities and particular interests of the individuals to play a large part in determining the degree and kind of political activity that takes place within the settlement group.

Moreover, although one had to keep an eye on the Pajal people during dances, they were not suspected of harbouring *i'yan* who might make nocturnal supernatural attacks. Not so with the people of the Eastern and Southern regional populations. There was no doubt in the minds of the Colorado Panare that the *i'yan* of these communities were quite ready to assume the form of *mahtikëdi*. The worst of them all for the Colorado people were the Panare from the most distant corner of Panare territory, those of the upper Cuchivero. Very few people in Colorado had ever visited this part of Panare territory and they recognized no kinship ties with the people living there. They were believed to be extremely dangerous and were reputed to have visited the Colorado valley, one night long ago, and to have plunged invisible lances into the chests of unsuspecting victims asleep in their hammocks.

But there is a contradiction underlying this antipathy to outsiders, for the autonomy of the settlement group is not absolute. Although the settlement group may be both economiclly and politically independent of others, it is rarely self-sufficient in the sense that it can supply all its junior members with spouses. If a man cannot find a wife for his son in his own settlement, he will look to neighbouring settlements. If he is unsuccessful there as well, he will be obliged to remember that he has a distant classificatory sister, living in a settlement with which his own settlement maintains very few social contacts, but who might have a nubile daughter. Although the Panare prefer to marry locally, marriage with women from distant settlements is not formally prohibited. Moreover, even the people living in settlements with whom there are no known kinship ties are still regarded as falling within the pale of Panare society. Even though they may be suspected of supernatural treachery, they are neverthless *e'nyëpa*, Panare, sharing similar institutions and cultural traits and speaking a recognizable language. They are quite clearly different from the criollos and the members of other indigenous groups. Although the Panare have no interest in descent nor any mythological tradition, they are still prepared to recognize that all Panare, however distant, are descended from the first people who burst out of the mountain at the headwaters of the Cuchivero at the beginning of time.


In summary, then, the position of the settlement group in relation to Panare society as a whole is much the same as the position of the conjugal family in relation to the individual settlement group. As I suggested earlier, the settlement group can be conceived of as an unstable compromise between the autonomy of the conjugal family units of which it is composed and the ties that cross conjugal family boundaries, binding them one to another. Panare society as a whole can be viewed in a similar sort of way: in this case, as a compromise between the autonomy of individual settlement groups and the common social and cultural attributes shared by all Panare. I now want to conclude this chapter (and hence also the part of the book that deals with the Panare's internal social system) by putting this analysis of Panare social organization to the test by showing how it can illuminate certain aspects of their male initiation ceremonies.

As I described in Chapter 3, when I discussed their economic aspects, these ceremonies involve three major dances (the *murankinto,* the *kaimoyonkonto* and the *katayinto*) spread out over a dry season, each lasting approximately twenty-four hours, from nightfall to nightfall. Prior to the last of these dances, there are a number of minor dances lasting not more than five or six hours, usually from midnight to daybreak. Throughout this series of ceremonies, the process of male initiation is linked with the celebration of subsistence activities.[8] This series of ceremonies represents the most elaborate form of ritual activity in which the Panare engage, and, as such, are worthy of a far more detailed treatment that I shall give them here. However my present purpose is merely to isolate the features of these ceremonies that are directly related to the theme that has formed the central thread of my analysis of Panare social organization: namely, the autonomy of the conjugal family within the organization of the settlement group and the autonomy of the settlement group within the context of Panare society as a whole.

As I observed in Chapter 3, the production of the material for a dance involves a degree of collective effort that is unknown in everyday subsistence production. Although the bulk of the sugar cane used to manufacture the beer is provided by the *tihcen,* who, in the case of the initiation dances, are the fathers of the boys to be initiated, this supply will be supplemented by the other members of the settlement who have some sugar cane to spare. All the men of the settlement help in the production of material means for the dances by contributing meat to the *kaimo'* and their labour in the preparation and installation of the beer canoe. All the women of the settlement generally help the *tihcen's* wives to prepare the sugar-cane beer.

8. The description I give here is of the male initiation ceremonies in the Western Panare region. Male initiation ceremonies are less frequent in Southern Panare territory and, moreover, may even be integrated into the ceremonies connected with death which appear to be more elaborate than the death ceremonies in Western Panare communities. I have no information whatsoever about initiation ceremonies in Eastern Panare territory.

Plate 12. Men and boys arrive at the beginning of a *kaimoyonkonto* held in the Colorado valley. They carry specially woven baskets packed with smoked meat and around their shoulders cloaks of green and yellow palm leaves. The people in the background play panpipes whilst the two men nearest the camera play *aramëtaime,* a pair of matched instruments (one being slightly more bass than the other) which produce a deep resonant note similar to that of a tuba (photograph by Jean-Paul Simonin).

The men of the settlement also prepare for the initiation dances by manufacturing the ritual paraphernalia that the initiands will put on during the course of the ceremonies. Although the *tihcen* and their conjugal families are allowed to provide the materials that will be used, they are expressly forbidden from participating in the actual manufacture of this paraphernalia. Thus, for example, although the *tihcen* may provide the toucan pelts and the monkey teeth necessary to manufacture the *amsïrïyën,* the special mantle that initiands will don during the *katayinto,* they are not allowed to make it themselves. Similarly, although it is usually the initiands' mother and/or sisters who weave the loincloth that the initiands will put on, they have to be painted with special designs that identify them as *katayinto* loincloths by men who are *not* members of the initiands' various conjugal families.

This exclusion of the initiands' conjugal families from the preparation of the ritual paraphernalia is merely one moment of the process that continues throughout the series of ceremonies. Although the initiands' conjugal families are permitted to play an active role in the general singing and dancing, at no point do they take part in the ritual events that directly affect the initiands. Throughout the series of ceremonies each initiand is guided by a young man. The man who adopts this role has no specific title but one might call him the initiand's 'second'. On no account should the second be a member of the initiand's conjugal family. Ideally, he should not even be a close *piyaka,* and for this reason, an initiand's second usually comes from a neighbouring settlement group rather than from the initiand's own. A second is responsible for telling an initiand where to stand during the ceremonies, when to dance, when to retire and so forth. The second is also charged with taking the initiand out to a special spot in the forest to take a series of emetics and other medicines. It is also the second who organizes the various preparatory mortification rites through which the initiands have to pass. These include nose-piercing and ritual whipping on the back of the legs. These rites are actually carried out, however, by anyone who feels like doing so—provided of course that they are not members of the initiand's conjugal family.

But if the initiands' immediate relatives are excluded from the preparatory stages in their initiation, in the culminating event of the whole series of ceremonies, the dressing of the initiands with their loincloths and other ceremonial paraphernalia during the *katayinto,* all the members of the initiands' settlement are excluded, not merely those most closely related to them. The *katayinto* differs from the other two major dances in the initiation series in two important respects. Firstly, the songs sung during the *katayinto* are not dedicated to the *kaimo'* as are the songs sung in the first two dances. Instead they are dedicated to the items of ritual gear that the initiands will put on. This difference indicates a shift of emphasis from the celebration of subsistence activities to a celebration of the act of initiation itself. The second major difference lies in the role of the so-called *panakon,* that is, the visitors from other settlements. Ideally, the *panakon* play a part in every Panare dance regardless of the motive for it. If no real outsiders are present, several men of the host settlement will act out the role of *panakon.* In a death dance and *tëwënmën,* that is, 'for nothing' dance, the *panakon* are supposed to approach the settlement in which the dance is taking place, armed to the teeth, and to stand in a challenging posture at the edge of the dancing arena. After ostentatiously ignoring the *panakon* for a while, the *tihcen* and other members of the host settlement group approach the *panakon* and engage them in a conventionally hostile dialogue. The *panakon* are told, against all the evidence of their senses, that there is no beer in the settlement and that for this reason they might as well go home. The *panakon* then accuse the hosts of being stingy: the hosts retort by accusing the *panakon* of being *tincakeihkye*. The dialogue continues in this recriminatory fashion for a while until, gradually, it becomes more amicable, finally reaching a point where the hosts and *panakon* begin to fondle one another's testicles. At this point, the *panakon* are given calabashes of sugar-cane beer and are invited to participate in the dance.

In the first two dances of the initiation series, the *panakon* arrive on the scene shortly after the dance has begun, and start to participate in the festivities straight away without any preliminary dialogue with the hosts. But in the *katayinto,* the arrival of the *panakon* is far more dramatic, more dramatic even than their arrival at the death dance or a *tëwěnmën*. In a *katayinto,* the entrance of the *panakon* is delayed until midday, after the hosts have spent the whole night dancing away by themselves. At this point, the *panakon,* who are usually camped at a short distance, are advised by a blast on a cow horn that the moment for them to enter the proceedings is at hand. The hosts then retire into the communal house and the entrances are firmly blocked up with palm leaves and matting. The hosts then begin to dance inside in the customary Panare fashion: the men dancing in a circle moving in one direction around the perimeter of the house and the women dancing in the opposite direction in a circle within that of the men, around the central house post. As the hosts wheel about the house, singing the song known as *panakon can,* the '*panakon* are coming', excitement begins to mount. Suddenly the palm leaves blocking the entrance to the house are smashed down, the women dancing in the centre of the house scatter to the perimeter and the *panakon* enter, screaming, yelling and brandishing branches. They stamp about furiously in the centre of the house, thrashing the house posts and the beer canoe with their branches, as if they wanted to bring the house down. Meanwhile the circle of male dancers has come to a standstill but they continue to sing as if nothing is happening, doing so even when the *panakon* approach them and, with their faces no more than six inches away, scream at them at a high and resounding pitch. After a few minutes of these antics, the *panakon,* having failed to produce any reaction from the dancers, run out of the house, still screaming and yelling and brandishing their branches. The hosts begin to dance again but having completed a few revolutions of the house, they stop singing and file out of the house to meet the *panakon* who are now stationed at the edge of the settlement.

Here the usual dialogue with the *panakon* ensues to give way eventually to mutual fondling of genitalia. The hosts then try to persuade the *panakon* to dress the initiands with their loincloths. At first the *panakon* put up a show of being reluctant to do so, but finally a

Plate 13. Women **dancing** in the open during a 'for nothing' dance, moving backwards in a circular fashion.

Plate 14. Initiands leaning on their sticks at the edge of the dancing arena during a *katayinto* ceremony. Their belts are made of tree bark and their headdresses of macaw feathers set in plaited palm crowns. Behind them stand their 'seconds', armed with the paraphernalia that the initiands will put on later in the ceremony.

number of them agree and they are led over to the initiands who by this time have adopted the posture in which they have spent a large part of the initiation ceremonies—leaning with their foreheads on poles at the edge of the dancing arena.

For the next hour or so, the *panakon* dress the initiands with all their paraphernalia, berating them verbally as they do so. Meanwhile the hosts hover in the background. Throughout the dressing period, the initiands must keep their eyes closed because it is said that if they look upon a woman whilst they are being dressed they might die. When the dressing has been completed however, the women of the settlement approach the *panakon,* leading young children or bearing infants. The *panakon* then turn their attention to piercing the ears of these children with blowgun darts. Once the ear-piercing is completed, the dancing begins again, hosts and *panakon* dancing together. The initiation process is still not quite complete, so the initiands return to leaning on the sticks at the edge of the dancing arena, now dressed in all the symbols of adulthood. As night approaches, both the dancers and the initiands move inside the house. As in all Panare dances, the longer the dancing continues, the more ragged it becomes and mixed-sex couple dancing begins. The dance ends when no-one is capable of dancing any more.

In the morning of the following day, the initiands are taken off to the forest once again by their seconds to take yet another dose of medicines. Meanwhile, back in the settlement, one of the *panakon* shares out the *kaimo'* amongst all the people present and a large meal is prepared. The rest of the day is dedicated to lounging in hammocks. At nightfall, after the initiands have returned, there is a short bout of dancing, following which the bark belts which the men have been wearing throughout the *katayinto,* and the palm leaf wrappings in which the *kaimo'* has been kept since the *kaimoyonkonto,* are hung up on a nearby tree in the forest. Even now, the *katayinto* is not quite finished. The next morning, the initiands will leave the settlement once again and go into the forest by themselves. Only when they return at midday will the whole series of ceremonies that have stretched over several months be finally completed.

The exclusion of the initiand's immediate family from the most important *rite de passage* of his life is rather curious at first sight and invites some sort of explanation. The Panare say that the boy's immediate family do not like to participate in the rituals that directly affect him for they do not like to make him suffer. Yet whilst one might accept this as a perfectly reasonable explanation for their non-participation in the mortification of the initiand, it does not really explain why they do not participate in the aspects of the ritual that do

Plate 15. A loincloth is decorated for one of the initiands by a young man from a nearby settlement group.

not involve suffering, such as the preparation of the initiand's gear for example. Moreover, although one might accept the Panare's explanation at face value, I think it is quite compatible with an explanation of a more sociological character.

From a sociological point of view, the exclusion of the initiands' conjugal families from the most important events of the initiation ceremony can be seen as a symbolic denial of the independence of the conjugal family. Although the conjugal family may enjoy a high degree of autonomy as the basic social unit both of production and reproduction, it cannot bring its offspring to social adulthood without the intervention of others. In the early stages of the initiation process, these others are the other members of the initiands' settlement group and the seconds who, if they are not members of the initiands' own settlement group, come from those situated close by. But neither these other members of the initiands' settlement group, nor the seconds, can bring the initiation process to completion. Ultimately, the initiands can only achieve social adulthood at the hands of the *panakon*. The role of the *panakon* in the *katayinto* symbolizes in the most dramatic fashion the ambiguity in the Panare's feelings towards outsiders. Their violent and aggressive behaviour when they first arrive testifies to the feeling that outsiders are *tincakeihkye* and therefore dangerous. In acting in this way, the men playing the role of *panakon* are acting as if they were outsiders from distant settlements whose *i'yan* are known to make supernatural attacks on other Panare. And yet despite their *tincakeihkye* behaviour, the *panakon* are invited to take charge of the culminating events of the *katayinto:* the dressing of the initiands and the sharing out of the *kaimo'*.

The handing over of these critical ritual duties to outsiders can be interpreted as a symbolic denial of the independence, not only of the conjugal family, but also of the settlement group. As such, the *katayinto* represents an expression of the solidarity of Panare society. It is a solidarity that has both a synchronic and a diachronic aspect. The Panare believe that ever since the first people broke out of the mountain at the headwaters of the Cuchivero, the Panare have brought their sons to social adulthood in the same way. During the *katayinto* I witnessed in Colorado, the hosts were most concerned to point this out to me. Gazing contentedly over the scene in front of the house where the *panakon* were dressing the initiands and piercing the ears of the infants, they commented, 'Look, Manyën, we are happy now because this is how the first people of long ago did things.' In effect, each series of initiation ceremonies is an affirmation of the continuity of the Panare tradition. Once the *panakon* have dressed the initiands, they turn to piercing the ears of the infants of the host settlement. As the members of one generation of Panare are ceremonially inducted into social adulthood, the next take their first step in the same direction by having their ears pierced. And it is fitting that the *panakon* should do this, for although they may be *tincakeihkye*, they too are descended from the first people. The initiation ceremonies therefore unite the Panare both with the past and present: by performing the initiation ceremonies in the traditional manner, the hosts are linked with the first people; by handing over responsibility for the culminating events of these ceremonies to the *panakon,* they are giving ceremonial recognition to the fact that their offspring belong not merely to their conjugal families, nor merely to the settlement group in which they are living, but to Panare society as a whole.

In the *katayinto*, then, the ambiguity of the Panare's feelings towards outsiders is finally resolved in favour of an expression of solidarity. Yet it is difficult to assess the practical social effect of these ceremonies; that is, it is difficult to say to what extent the ceremonial expression of solidarity that they involve actually promotes the social integration of the highly autonomous elements of Panare social organization. But it seems reasonable to suppose that in uniting all the members of the host settlement group in a common effort to produce the material means of the dances, and in bringing them into contact under convivial circumstances with members of other settlements with whom

Plate 16. (left). A *panakon* dresses an initiand in his loincloth, berating him verbally as he does so. The boy covers his eyes since it is believed that he may die if he sees a woman during this process.

Plate 17. (right). The *kaimo'* is shared out by one of the *panakon* at the conclusion of the *katayinto*.

they have little contact on a day-to-day basis, the initiation ceremonies serve to foster a sense of common social identity amongst the participants. To the degree that the initiation ceremonies do foster this sense of common identity, they also promote the possibility of marital exchanges between conjugal families from different settlements, and even co-residence, some time in the future. As such, the initiation ceremonies can be considered an effective ideological counterweight within the order of Panare social organization to the atomism of their economic system and kinship system, and a partial compensation for the absence of any form of socially integrative political organization.

The autonomy of the constituent elements of Panare social organization affords a considerable degree of personal freedom, particularly to men. Although there is no doubt that women are subject to the domination of men in Panare society, this is not an absolute domination, since each sex has its rights and its duties. Moreover, although men direct affairs in Panare society, women are usually consulted informally about any decisions to be taken. Taking each sex by itself, there is very little interpersonal domination: each woman has the same rights and duties as every other, just as each man has the same rights and duties as every other man. There is no active competition between generations since age brings responsibilities rather than privileges in Panare society. If a man attains a certain degree of authority through seniority, this authority is always vulnerable to the freedom that hearth groups have to secede from his settlement group. If a man achieves a certain measure of respect for attaining the condition of *i'yan*, this respect is always vulnerable to the scepticism of his fellow Panare. Nor are there any corporate groups that direct or constrain the activities of individuals. Each hearth group can choose between a number of different settlements in deciding where to live. If the members of a hearth group do not like any of the extant alternatives, they can set up a settlement of their own. They owe no political or economic allegiance, nor are they absolutely dependent on anyone. Far from producing a state of anarchy in which life is nasty, brutish and short, this atomistic social organization underlies a way of life in which there is very little interpersonal aggression and very few disputes, for the simple reason that the grounds for conflict are few. When conflicts do arise, they are resolved by the expedient of one of the parties going to live elsewhere, an action which in view of the social and economic autonomy of the conjugal family in Panare society involves no great hardship.

But whatever the advantages of such an atomistic social organization, it also has its weaknesses. Latent even in a traditional context, they are clearly exposed to view under present circumstances as the Panare begin to modify their settlement pattern in order to establish closer contact with the criollos. The socially integrative forces that hold Panare settlement groups together are comparatively weak. The ideology of food-sharing that holds the settlement together as a collective economic entity is vulnerable to the impoverishment of local natural resources that attends the changes going on in the Panare settlement pattern. The kinship system and the political system, such as it is, provide no strong barrier to the break-up of the settlement group into its constitutive conjugal families under conditions of scarcity. Nor do they provide the organizational basis for uniting the Panare to resist the incursions of criollo society, be these incursions physical, economic or cultural.

Even so, for the best part of a century, the Panare have maintained contact with the criollos without undergoing any radical change in their way of life. There is no doubt that part of the reason why the Panare have been able to do so, is the sense of independence and self-respect which the Panare possess as individuals and which derives from the personal freedom they enjoy within their own society. Thus the role which criollo society has to offer them, as members of the lowest social stratum of a hierarchical society, has no attractions whatsoever for the Panare. But this can only form part of the explanation for the Panare's cultural resilience, since the egalitarian constitution of their society is characteristic of most indigenous societies of lowland South America, many of which have broken up or undergone radical social change within a few years of making contact with modern industrial society. More important than the properties of the internal social system of the Panare in explaining their immunity to externally induced change are the properties of the system of relations they have maintained with the local criollos. It is with this system of external relations that the last three chapters of the book will be concerned.

# CHAPTER SIX

# The National Frontier

The way in which the Panare's relations with the local representatives of Venezuelan society are dealt with in the following three chapters owes a great deal to my reading of *Os índios e a civilização*, Darcy Ribeiro's work on the relations between indigenous groups and the national society of Brazil in the period 1900–60. The basic proposition put forward in this work I would summarize as follows: in situations where an indigenous society survives the 'bio-ecological' effects of the first years of contact (i.e. the effects of epidemic diseases and the destruction of the local natural environment), the social and economic relations of the contact situation itself are more important in determining the outcome than the predisposition of the members of that society to adopt, adapt or reject new ideas and forms of social behaviour in conformity with their own social and cultural traditions. Ribeiro recognizes that, in order to understand the way in which any particular indigenous society reacts to contact, one must refer to 'the specific circumstances that derive from the indigenous cultural context prior to contact'; but, he argues, the reaction of an indigenous group will always be constrained by the nature of the social and economic relations that the members of the national society seek to impose on them (Ribeiro 1970: 225–6).

Ribeiro distinguishes this approach to the study of contact from that of the classic 'acculturation' studies:

> The majority of acculturation studies are confined to the analysis of the diffusion and selective adoption by indigenous groups of alien cultural traits, the consequences of the integration of these traits into the traditional context being given special emphasis. Yet this is only one side of the problem . . . and certainly does not constitute the most fundamental aspect . . . In reality, these cultural traits pass from one context to another by means of the relations between people. And these relations operate between people situated within specific economic systems. It is the study of the relationship between the tribal and the national economic structures that is therefore the most important for the understanding of this process. More relevant than the analysis of the specific qualities of a cultural trait is the study of the economic mechanism whereby this trait is

introduced into tribal life and the effect of this mechanism on the social relations within the tribe and on relations between the tribe and the national society (Ribeiro 1970: 337–8).

I think that Ribeiro presents something of a caricature of the 'acculturation' approach in this passage, but in doing so, he gives a succinct account of the theoretical principles underlying his own.

Ribeiro points out that the effect of contact on Brazilian indigenous societies has not been uniform: whilst some groups have become extinct in a matter of years, others have survived literally centuries of contact, preserving a sense of their identity as Indians even though they may have undergone radical changes in their culture and internal social organization. In accordance with his general theoretical position, Ribeiro seeks to explain this variation in terms of the different types of social and economic relations that the various contingents of the national society have sought to establish with indigenous groups. These contingents of the national society, Ribeiro terms 'fronts of national expansion'. Ribeiro himself does not give a precise definition of this term but for present purposes, a 'front' can be defined as any group of members of the national society who share a common interest, economic or otherwise, in establishing themselves in a region inhabited by indigenous groups. Ribeiro applies the term 'front' to any contingent of the national society in contact with an indigenous group, irrespective of whether it is newly settled in a particular region, has been established there for centuries or has followed on historically from an antecedent front motivated by some other interest.

Despite his assertion that it is 'the study of the relationship between the tribal and the national economic structures' that is the most important for understanding the effects of contact, Ribeiro deals at length with fronts of national expansion that are not motivated exclusively by economic interests. Fronts of this latter kind he terms 'protectionist' and includes within this category fronts composed of government functionaries and missionary fronts. Economic fronts he subdivides into various types, according to the nature of the economic activity in which their members are engaged: extractive (that is, the collection of raw materials); pastoral (mainly cattle-raising) and agricultural (Ribeiro 1970: 15).

Ribeiro argues that the effect that a front has on the indigenous groups it comes into contact with is a function of the interests underlying the front, since it is these interests which determine the nature of the social and economic relations that the members of the front seek to establish with the Indians. In dealing with the economic fronts that have operated in twentieth-century Brazil, he attributes particular importance to the way in which the interest that the members of these fronts have in recruiting indigenous labour and/or appropriating indigenous lands determines the effect that they have on local indigenous groups. He also argues that the social composition and cultural attributes of an economic front are a function of the type of economic activity on which the front is based. He suggests that to the degree that these features of a front affect the nature of the social relations the members of a front seek to establish with the local indigenous population, they also play an important part in determining the effect of contact on the indigenous groups of the region in which the front operates (Ribeiro 1970: 435–7).

Elsewhere I have offered a number of criticisms of this typology of fronts, arguing that it is neither comprehensive nor sufficiently sensitive to differences between fronts based on the same general type of economy (Henley 1978). Nevertheless, I find the notion of a 'front' useful for describing the relations between national societies and indigenous groups. I also share Ribeiro's view that in the majority of cases ('bio-ecological' considerations permitting), it is the nature of the social and economic relations that the members of the national society seek to establish with the Indians, rather than the reaction of the Indians, that is the principal determinant of the outcome of any contact situation. Why this sould be so is no theoretical mystery: in almost all contemporary contact situations in lowland South America, the national society is far more powerful than the indigenous societies with which it comes into contact. Under these conditions, it is only too obvious that the reaction of an indigenous group to contact will be constrained by the sheer physical presence of the national society. On the other hand, it is equally clear that it is not always the case that the interests underlying a front of national expansion are so specific as to require its members to impose a very particular, well-defined set of social and economic relations on local indigenous groups. When they are not, the Indians have a much higher degree of freedom to decide the outcome of the contact situation. As we shall see, the Panare are in this fortunate position.

Throughout these final three chapters, I make use of the terms 'acculturation', 'assimilation', and 'integration', which it is convenient to define here. The term 'acculturation', I use in the most general sense to refer to the adoption of social and cultural features of the criollos' way of life by the Panare. The terms 'assimilation' and 'integration', as I use them, are an elaboration and modification of the terms used by Ribeiro (1970: 14–15). The term 'assimilation' I use to describe a situation in which the members of an indigenous group lose all sense of their common ethnic identity and become immersed in the national society as an indistinguishable part of it. The term 'integration', on the other hand, describes a situation in which the members of an indigenous group, whilst retaining some notion of a distinctive ethnic identity, become in some sense participant in the life of the national society. If the members of an indigenous group depend on the national society for certain goods and/or derive at least part of their livelihood from working for non-indigenous employers, but are not otherwise involved in the general social life of the national society, then they can be said to be integrated only in an economic sense. However, should their participation in the national society become more general (as measured by such indices as whether or not they send their children to national schools, register as voters, join political parties or unions, perform military service, intermarry with non-indigenous individuals, etc.), they can then be said to be socially integrated as well. Although the boundary between a condition of exclusively economic integration and a condition of more general social integration may often be difficult to draw in practice, it is nevertheless a distinction that is useful for describing the condition of many contemporary indigenous groups of lowland South America, including the Panare.

It is for the entirely pragmatic reason that the information available on earlier periods is extremely sparse that I deal only with Panare –criollo relations in the course of the present century in this book. If the historical reconstruction I made in Chapter 1 is correct, the Panare, as the Oye or one of the other groups identified on the middle Cuchivero by Gilij, were already in contact, albeit indirectly, with the colonial predecessor of modern Venezuelan society in the eighteenth century (see pp. 5 *et seq*.). One of the main reasons for their subsequent expansion out of the Cuchivero basin during the course of the nineteenth century seems to have been a concern to establish closer relations with the criollos. But the only documentary evidence available on Panare–criollo relations in this period is Chaffanjon's brief observation that at the time he was in the area, the mid-1880s, the Panare used to visit a criollo village on the lower Cuchivero in order to sell agricultural produce.[1]

No thorough study of the social and economic life of the criollos who inhabit the hinterland of Caicara has ever been carried out. Consequently, even my account of Panare–criollo relations in the course of

1. Chaffanjon 1889: 73. A few pages before, Chaffanjon relates that at the time he visited Caicara, Indians used to come into the village to sell sarrapia. However it is not clear whether or not he is referring to Panare in this passage.

this century has been cobbled together from a number of different sources. The information concerning the first three or four decades of this century derives mostly from interviews conducted with elderly inhabitants of the region, both Panare and criollo. Official statistics on the demography and certain criollo economic activities have been collected since the 1930s, but I have reservations about the reliability of these, even when they refer to the last two decades. I have also been able to make use of the reports of a number of anthropologists, sociologists and other visitors to the region since the 1940s. However all these sources tend to be rather superficial and some of them are not entirely reliable. Thus even my account of Panare–criollo relations in the last few years relies heavily on the interviews that I conducted myself.

Until the 1960s, the region in which the Panare live was something of a social and economic backwater as far as the rest of the national society was concerned. This was largely because access to the region was difficult. Although the Orinoco permitted access to Caicara and La Urbana, terrestrial communications between these towns and the rest of the country were very poor. Communications within the hinterland of Caicara were worse still: only the lower reaches of the Cuchivero and the Suapure are navigable, and prior to the 1960s the roads in this hinterland were little more than jeep tracks that became inundated and impassable in the rainy season. Thus although Panare territory is closer to the urban and industrial centres of Venezuela, until recently it remained just as isolated, if not more so, than the upper Orinoco region of the Territorio Federal de Amazonas where the presence of large and navigable rivers made penetration of the region comparatively easy during the rainy season.

In colonial times, La Urbana attained considerable local importance. It grew up on the site of a Jesuit mission founded in 1748 and housed a Spanish garrison which controlled river traffic on the Orinoco (Del Rey Fajardo 1971: 67). But over the years, the importance of La Urbana has diminished as its port has silted up. Today it is a town in the process of decline, its population dwindling steadily. In 1960, it had just under 450 inhabitants. Its position as the criollo town of greatest local importance has been taken over by Caicara, which was first founded in the 1770s (the exact date is a matter of dispute). By 1960, the population of Caicara was estimated at 3281 individuals.[2]

2. Del Carmen Perez *et al.*, 1973: 45. Unless otherwise stated all census data in this chapter come from this source, which provides tables compiled by the Ministry of Economic Growth (*Ministerio de Fomento*), the government body at that time responsible for censuses in Venezuela.

Less information is available on the colonization of the hinterland of Caicara. It appears that there was already a criollo community at El Tigre by 1815, because the contemporary historical accounts record that Cedeño, one of the heroes of the War of Independence, was billeted there very briefly (Yánes, 1943: 248). From Chaffanjon's account, it appears that the hinterland was lightly settled by criollos over the course of the nineteenth century. Around the turn of the present century, a criollo community became established in the vicinity of the present Hato San Pablo, and a few years later another was founded at Túriba by a group of settlers from Coro in Falcón State (see Maps 2 and 3). Since then, the rural population has gradually been on the increase. Coupled with the simultaneous tendency of the Panare to move towards the criollos, this has produced the present situation in which the great majority of Panare settlements are no more than half a day's walk from a criollo house.

Most of the area occupied by the Panare falls within the Municipality of Caicara which, together with three other Municipalities, makes up the Cedeño District of Bolívar State. Census information is available on a municipality basis at roughly ten-year intervals from 1950. When I refer to the demographic trends indicated by these census figures, I will be referring to the figures collected for the Municipality of Caicara only. These show that in the period 1950–60 the population increased by about a third, from 6387 to 8534, a result that can be attributed primarily to the natural increase of the local inhabitants, since immigration to this area from other parts of the country at that time was minimal. At the same time however, the proportion of the population living in the rural hinterland of Caicara declined from approximately 70 per cent to 60 per cent of the total population of the municipality.

Prior to the 1960s, the Panare very rarely visited Caicara, even though they were in regular contact with the rural criollo population. This rural population was engaged in one or both of two principal types of economic activity: cattle pastoralism and the collection of sarrapia (see p. 4 above). Although many of those engaged in these activities also practised slash and burn subsistence agriculture, the soils in the hinterland are generally poor and it is only in certain very restricted areas that, in the absence of considerable capital investment in machinery and fertilizers, they permit any form of commercial agriculture (CODESUR 1970: 22–8).

In the 1960s, the economic organization of the contingent of the national society in contact with the Panare began to change. There is no clear cut-off point between one stage and another, but one can identify 1964 as a turning point because it was in this year that the collection of sarrapia ceased. The history of sarrapia collection is less dramatic but essentially the same as the better-known history of rubber collection. From about 1885 until 1940, sarrapia had an important place in the list of Venezuelan exports. But after 1940, the market value, and hence the volume collected, began to fluctuate wildly from year to year (CODESUR 1970: 68–70). Finally, the market for the wild product disappeared entirely when a laboratory method was devised to synthesize the chemicals which had been extracted from sarrapia. The people who had worked in the collection of sarrapia, which included the Panare, were obliged to turn their hands to other things.

The 1960s also saw the beginning of a series of road-building programmes that would make terrestrial communication between Caicara and its hinterland and between Caicara and the remainder of the country much better. The road connecting the left bank of the Orinoco opposite Caicara to the industrial centres of Venezuela was greatly improved, as was the road connecting Caicara to Cuidad Bolívar and the other large urban and industrial centres at the mouth of the Orinoco. Shortly afterwards, the construction of roads through the hinterland of Caicara capable of withstanding rainy season flooding began. In 1969 the road that may eventually connect Caicara with San Juan de Manapiare in the Territorio Federal de Amazonas was started. Although the construction of this road has been sporadic over the last three or four years, it has already reached some 200 km south of Caicara and is used to supply the newly-established diamond mines in the middle reaches of the Guaniamo. Since the early 1970s, two other major roads running south from Caicara have been under construction: one of these will eventually reach La Horqueta at the junction of the Cuchivero and Guaniamo rivers, whilst the other will run to the south-west across the Suapure and on to Puerto Páez and Puerto Ayacucho. During the period when I was in the field, both these roads were still under construction, but I have subsequently heard that they have now been completed (see Map 4).

The most obvious effect of the new roads has been to encourage a rapid expansion in the size of Caicara. Between 1960 and 1971, the population doubled, reaching 6867. Between 1971 and 1976, the population more than doubled again, reaching approximately 15,000 individuals.[3] This rapid increase is largely due to the influx of individuals who come to work on the construction of the roads and other public amenities within the town. A large proportion of these immigrants are from the hinterland of Caicara itself. They have abandoned the countryside in favour of what they regard as the brighter social, economic and educational prospects of the town. Although the census figures indicate that the rural population of the Municipality of Caicara increased by 60 per cent, from 5253 to 8320 between 1961 and 1971, the proportion that the rural population formed of the total population of the Municipality fell from approximately 60 per cent to 48 per cent.

One should point out however that whereas at the time of the 1950 and 1961 censuses the only urban centre in the Municipality of Caicara was Caicara itself, by 1971 this was no longer the case. Shortly before the 1971 census was compiled, a rich field of diamonds was discovered on the middle Guaniamo. Despite the fact that the site was set in the middle of forest and was completely inaccessible by road, a mining community sprang up there immediately. By the time the data for the 1971 census were collected, the population was already estimated at approximately 2000. One source puts the population of the mines at 8750 by the end of the same year (Maziarek 1975: 58–9). Subsequently the population of the mines has fluctuated greatly, exceeding 10,000 at times but at other times falling as low as 4000. Although the inhabitants of Caicara complain that most of the wealth generated by the diamond mines flows out of the area, they have nevertheless contributed to the development of Caicara indirectly, in the sense that the miners are obliged to pay certain taxes to the Municipality and represent a market for the merchants and food producers of the town and its rural hinterland.

But more important than the presence of the mines in explaining the economic development of the region around Caicara is the fact that the new roads, by creating a better link between the food producers of the rural hinterland and the markets in the urban and industrial centres of Venezuela, have encouraged capital investment in the area. At the time that I was in the area, the first steps were being taken to modernize the local cattle industry and to introduce mechanized agriculture. This capital investment is already beginning to transform the economic organization and the social composition of the fronts of national expansion that are in contact with the Panare and hence to affect relations between the Panare and the national society.

3. The source of this last figure is the Caicara office of the Malaria Control Division of the Ministry of Health. The functionaries of this body make a record of all the people to whom they give anti-malaria pills and whose houses they spray with DDT. They attempt to visit every house and give pills to all the inhabitants. Another government source (CVG 1979: 124) puts the population of Caicara at 9564 in October 1977. However I would tend to rely more on the Malaria Control Division figures since they have more direct contact with the population. A local priest has recently estimated the population to be 'close to 20,000' (Arango Montoya 1979).

The Panare's relations with the national society are also being modified by the presence of several new 'protectionist' fronts, that is, fronts composed of missionaries or of government functionaries. It is difficult to explain why no attempt was made to evangelize the Panare in earlier periods, although the difficulties of communication within the area may have been a contributory factor. Whatever the reasons, by 1974 there were three mission stations in Panare communities whereas in 1968 there had been none. The first to be established was the Roman Catholic mission on the middle Cuchivero, which was founded in 1969. Three years later a New Tribes Mission station was established in the Colorado valley. In 1974, as reported in Chapter 1 (see p.24), a group of Panare moved down from the headwaters of the Cuchivero and took over the New Tribes Mission station on the Caño Iguana originally set up for the Hoti. As is the case in many parts of Venezuela, the missions have been far more effective at maintaining a corps of representatives in the field than the agencies of the government. It was only in 1974, that the government body at that time specifically in charge of the administration of indigenous affairs, the *Oficina Central de Asuntos Indígenas* (OCAI), made any direct attempt to intervene in the affairs of the Panare.[4]

Having identified the principal fronts of national expansion that operate or have operated in the course of the twentieth century in the region in which the Panare live, I will now turn to examine the way in which the interests of the members of these fronts have influenced the form of the social relations they have sought to maintain with the Panare. But before doing so, it is necessary to point out that the fronts that I have identified are not always mutually exclusive in terms of the personnel of which they are composed. For example, in the era of sarrapia collection, many of the individuals involved in this front were also cattle pastoralists. Nevertheless, it is useful to distinguish between these two fronts on the grounds that as pastoralists the interests of these individuals with regard to such matters as engaging Panare labour or appropriating their land were different from their interests as sarrapia collectors.

Of all the fronts that have operated in Panare territory in the course of this century, the cattle pastoralist front has been by far the most important. In the hinterland of Caicara, there are a few large ranches, but the great majority of pastoralists have small or medium-sized herds.[5] All pastoralists are required by law to register their brand marks and the number of cattle they possess in the Prefecture of the municipality in which they live. The relevant figures for the

4. A short history of Venezuelan indigenist legislation and the various government bodies that have been in control of indigenous affairs is to be found in Appendix 4.

Municipality of Caicara in 1974 indicate that of the 410 registered concerns owning ten or more head of cattle, approximately 65 per cent owned less than 100 head and a further 30 per cent less than 500 head. A fact of considerable local importance is that of the remaining 5 per cent of registered concerns, one is far greater than any of the others, possessing over 11,000 head (Ferrer Perez *et al.*, 1975: 17–18). This concern belongs to the Garridos, a wealthy family which exercises great political influence both at a local and at a state level. Similar information for earlier periods of time is not available, but according to local informants the pattern of cattle ownership described by the 1974 figures has 'always' been true of the region around Caicara.

The pattern of land ownership amongst the members of the front has also remained largely unchanged over the years of this century. About a million hectares of land are used for cattle pastoralism in the Municipality of Caicara. This area of land is more or less equally divided between three forms of tenancy: private property, common land *(tierras ejidales)* and land belonging to the nation *(tierras públicas)*. Since 1960, when the Agrarian Reform Law was passed, the legal machinery has existed for handing over title to the lands falling into the last category (and to private lands not used economically) to small or medium-sized pastoralist concerns. However, by 1971 the area of the Municipality of Caicara which had been handed over under the terms of the Agrarian Reform Law amounted to no more than 58 hectares! Although the public lands handed over to producers in the other municipalities of the Cedeño District is admittedly larger, it is still generally true to say that in the region in which the Panare live, the Agrarian Reform Law has not yet brought about the transformation of the social and economic organization of the agrarian sector it was designed to achieve (Ferrer Perez *et al.*, 1975: 122 *et seq.*)

The lands falling into the category of private property in the Municipality of Caicara belong to a few large landowners, almost half of them (160,000 hectares) belonging to the Garridos. These privately owned lands are not exploited intensively by their owners and parts of them are leased to smaller cattle pastoralists who pay rent, usually in the form of a certain proportion of the number of calves their herds produce each year. In some cases, private lands have simply been occupied by small pastoralists. Most of the lands belonging to the nation and the common lands, the latter mostly situated in the vicinity

---

5. In terms of socio-economic organization and culture, the pastoralists of Panare territory share much in common with the ranchers of northern Brazil described by Rivière. As Rivière points out, it is difficult to fit this type of pastoralist into the sociological categories that are conventionally used to classify the members of the rural communities of Latin America (see Rivière 1972: 2).

of Caicara itself, are used as pasturage by individuals who have no title to them.

This pattern of land ownership and use is consonant with the generally backward state of the cattle-raising activities in the area. The methods employed are the traditional methods of the Venezuelan Llanos: the cattle are left to roam the savanna at will, finding pasturage and water where they can. The only control exercised over the herds are periodic round-ups for the purposes of milking or de-lousing. Fences and corrals are few and little attempt is made to sow artificial pastures or control reproduction. Both the quality of the natural pasturage and of the cattle stock are poor in the region around Caicara, and the fertility of the herds is well below the national average. In the rainy season, a large number of animals are lost through parasitic infection, whilst in the dry season many die for lack of water. The animals that survive the annual hazards of disease and drought rarely attain a good weight on account of their poor diet and the walking they have to do to find it.

The majority of the pastoralists in the region either lack the technical knowledge or the capital to make the investment in fencing, artificial pasturage, irrigation systems, medicines and dietary supplements that would be necessary for them to bring about a significant improvement in their stock. Many of them find it difficult to make ends meet and become heavily indebted. They breed their herds primarily for sale as meat, but in order to supplement their income many of them make cheese, an activity which merely exacerbates the poor quality of their animals since it deprives the new-born calves of their mothers' milk and thereby inhibits their physiological development (Ferrer Perez et al., 1975: 142–56).

Most of the labour needs of the pastoralists with small or medium-sized herds are met by themselves and their families. There are also a number of traditional arrangements whereby one man will work for another at some task requiring a large labour force (such as a round-up or the construction of a fence) on the understanding that the beneficiary will either reciprocate in the same way at a later date or lay on a large amount of food and drink. The larger concerns tend to be staffed by a nucleus of permanent employees which is supplemented when necessary by casual labourers. But even the labour needs of the large ranches are not great and can easily be met by the local criollo population. The casual labour force is in fact often made up of smaller producers who wish to supplement their incomes or who are prepared to work for private landowners in exchange for being allowed to use their lands as pasturage for their own animals (Ferrer Perez et al., 1975: 206–8).

Being self-sufficient in meeting their labour requirements, the members of the pastoralist front have not been concerned to contract the Panare as labourers. Nor, until recently, have the members of the pastoralist front come into competition with the Panare over the use of natural resources. Until the mid 1960s, most Panare lived in the mountains, which are totally unsuited to cattle-raising, and came down to the plains only on a temporary basis. When they come down to the plains, it is the rivers and the clumps of forest that the Panare utilize rather than the savanna itself. Since it is primarily the savanna which the pastoralists are interested in, the two groups have had no reason to dispute the use of the available natural resources.

The Panare have long visited the homesteads of the pastoralists with small herds for the purposes of trade. Since the time about ten years ago when it became more frequent for the Panare to establish their permanent settlements on the plains, these contacts have become more frequent. Most of the small producers, and many of the middle-sized producers with whom the Panare maintain this contact are themselves natives of the region, and as a result are accustomed to the idea of the presence of Indians in the vicinity. They know that they have no reason to consider the Panare as a threat either to their lives or to their livelihood. Over the years, certain individual criollos and Panare have become very familiar with one another and intimately acquainted with one another's biographies, even though the Panare speak only a very limited amount of Spanish and the criollos even less Panare. This familiarity can be institutionalized in the form of a *compadrazgo* relationship. This relationship is sanctified by a simple ceremony in which the criollo baptizes his Panare *compadre* with his own name (that is the criollo's Spanish name) and gives him a few simple gifts. The basis of this relationship is supposedly the preferential exchange of goods between the parties involved. But as far as I could see, the Panare generally get the better of these arrangements since, whilst the criollo believes that it behoves him as an agent of civilization to be generous with the Panare, the Panare rarely if ever give their *compadres* anything free of charge. It is even rare for the Panare to sell their *compadres* something at a price lower than they would charge anyone else. Although the basis of the *compadrazgo* relationship is essentially economic, it is often something more than that as well. The Panare like to visit their criollo *compadres'* houses just to see how they are getting on, to hear their gossip, perhaps to drink a little aguardiente if there is any. For their part, the criollos sometimes visit the Panare's settlement on the occasion of a dance. Although they do not join in the dancing, they are not averse to sampling the sugar-cane beer and any food that might be served.

Plate 18.   Pedro Cabeza, a criollo who lives at the entrance to the Colorado valley, making cheese with the aid of a basketry mould woven by one of the local Panare.

Generally speaking, the attitude of the small pastoralist producers towards the Panare is one of patronizing benevolence. Although the criollo will admit that the Panare are very knowledgeable about the local flora and fauna, he regards the Panare as essentially inferior because they lack what the criollo considers to be the benefits of civilization: clothes and the ability to speak Spanish. This sense of superiority is enshrined in the criollos' use of the traditional Hispanic distinction between *indios*, in this case the Panare, and *racionales* (literally, 'rational beings') which is the term they apply to themselves. But apart from baptizing the Panare with their names when initiating a *compadrazgo* relationship, the local criollo cattle pastoralists make no attempt to convert the Panare to their way of life.

The Panare for their part have shown no interest in becoming cattle pastoralists. There have been a number of reports of cases of the

6. The reports of Panare keeping herds of cattle usually refer to the Panare of the region around the criollo village of El Tigre (see for example, Lopez Ramirez 1944: 254–5; Antolinez 1952: 258; Layrisse and Wilbert 1966: 57). Krisólogo (1965) reports that the Panare of this region used to be given a calf in exchange for every jaguar paw they brought in. In this way, the criollos hoped to keep down the jaguar population that was preying on their herds. But since a moratorium on the hunting of wild animals was put into force by the government in 1974 the criollos have discontinued this practice. It is conceivable that the herds that these earlier anthropologists came across did not represent any serious intention on the part of the Panare to become cattle pastoralists but were merely the animals which they had been given by the criollos. If this were indeed the case, the fact that the source of these animals has dried up would explain why these Panare no longer have any cattle. Presumably the animals they once had have either been eaten or sold.

Panare keeping cattle, but all these attempts have been short-lived.[6] The reason for this lack of interest in cattle is straightforward: the Panare think that cows are dirty, smelly, ugly animals, whilst bulls they consider positively frightening. They have no great admiration for beef as a food, and cheese they find disgusting. Nor is there anything intrinsically attractive for the Panare about the cattle pastoralists' way of life. Both the pattern of their working life and their diet are far more monotonous than those of the Panare. Although the cattle pastoralists may have certain material articles that the Panare want, most of these they can acquire through trade with the criollos.

Compared to the relations between pastoralist fronts and indigenous groups in other parts of lowland South America, the relations between the Panare and the local criollo cattle front have been relatively peaceful. In Brazil, for example, the relations between cattle pastoralists and Indians have generally been extremely violent. Where Indians have not been murdered, they have been dislodged and harassed. In some cases, cattle ranchers have been attempted to eliminate entire communities in order to 'clear' them from the region and take their lands.[7] The main reason for the extremely aggressive character of the cattle pastoralist fronts in Brazil has been the desire of the cattle ranchers to gain control of the land and other natural resources which they want for their animals but on which the local indigenous groups depend for their livelihood. But in Panare territory, the cattle pastoralists had no motive for such agggressive behaviour since they were not in direct competition with the Indians for natural resources.

However, there is often more to the clashes between cattle fronts and indigenous groups than straightforward competition for natural resources. This was amply demonstrated by the case of the Cuiva of the northern Colombian Llanos, whose case attracted worldwide publicity following the massacre of eighteen of them by a group of local criollos in December 1967 (Arcand 1972). Competition between the Cuiva and local criollos over natural resources was not acute since the Cuiva met most of their subsistence needs from riverine or forest sources whilst the criollos relied principally on the savanna as pasturage for their animals. Indeed, in this sense, the situation of the Cuiva appears to have been very similar to the present situation of the Panare. The difference between the two cases appears to lie in the social composition of the criollo fronts. Although relations between the Cuiva and the local criollos had never been easy, they deteriorated

7. See Ribeiro 1970: 437. For a specific example, see Melatti 1967: 48–50. Several such cases came to light during the investigations following the disbandment of the Indian Protection Service in Brazil in 1967.

significantly after 1960 when, in the aftermath of the *Violencia* (the civil war between the followers of the two dominant political parties), a large number of immigrants from other parts of Colombia settled in the region. It seems that these immigrants came armed not only with guns but also with the most derogatory view of the Indians. In this social climate, no great stigma was attached to the murder of Indians since they were regarded as less than human beings. Even so, in this particular case, the murderers were eventually brought to trial. In their defence, they ingenuously explained that they had carried out the massacre because the Indians had been making a nuisance of themselves stealing pigs and industrial goods from their homesteads. In contrast to the Cuiva situation, most of the criollo cattle pastoralists in the Panare area are local people, many of whom have had *compadrazgo* ties with individual Panare most of their adult lives. Although these men will complain that some Panare are not above stealing pigs or industrial goods, they would never attempt to justify the murder of a Panare on the grounds that they were less than human. Unfortunately for the state of interethnic relations in Panare territory, this state of peaceful co-existence is being upset by changes going on in the economic organization and social composition of the cattle pastoralist front. I will return to look at the significance of these changes in the following chapter.

In contrast to cattle raising, in which no more than a handful of Panare have ever been directly involved, most Panare communities have taken part at some time or other in the collection of sarrapia. The local government authorities attempted to control the collection of sarrapia by means of licences that entitled the holder to exploit a given area. These licences were often bought up by entrepreneurs who contracted other men to do the actual collecting. The collectors brought the sarrapia to depots belonging to the entrepreneurs who took charge of marketing the product. Old-timers claim that in the early years of the sarrapia business, certain individuals were able to amass large fortunes acting as entrepreneurs. In later years, however, the government attempted to undermine the entrepreneurs by setting up its own collecting depots (see Hurtado Izquierdo 1961).

Apart from the cost of the licences, the collection of sarrapia required no great capital investment. In fact, all one needed to become a collector (as opposed to an entrepreneur) was a knife, an axe and something to carry the sarrapia in. So it was not long before the Panare became involved. Sarrapia grew in the forest of the mountains which they inhabited, so they did not have to go far to gather it. Furthermore, the collecting depots in which they sold or exchanged the fruit were often also located close to where they lived. The criollo informants to whom I talked about the matter disagreed as to what extent the Panare respected the licences held by criollos. Certainly the Panare never held licences of their own. But if there were disputes between the two groups, these never erupted into violence.

In the early years of their involvement in the sarrapia-collecting business, the criollo entrepreneurs appear to have been able to make large profits on their exchanges with the Panare. The following passage is an extract from the transcript of an interview I conducted with Pedro Castro of Caicara who was a sarrapia entrepreneur in the 1930s. The extract is interesting, not only because it shows how the Panare were exploited at that time, but also in that it reveals how the Panare went about trading before they had the skill they have today at handling criollo money:

> Those Indians only collected sarrapia. They didn't know how to extract the oil of the coroba palm and they weren't interested in *balatá*. . . . They used to live in the mountains, they were the masters of it. *'Patriota no come araguato'*, (literally, 'criollos don't eat howler monkey'), they used to say. They didn't come to Caicara like they do now. Oh no, if you wanted to trade with them you had to go to where they lived—in the bush out there, up in those mountains . . . But you had to know how to trade with them. For an envelope of four aspirin you got a small basket of sarrapia; for a machete you got a basket of sarrapia; for a shirt— one basket and so on. You had to be prepared to lose out sometimes. Say they wanted a shirt worth Bs.20, well, you had to hand it over for a basket of sarrapia that wasn't worth more than Bs.4. But then another time they'd give you a basket for an envelope of aspirins worth Bs.0.25. . . . When the government sent its functionaries down here they didn't understand this and that's why they were a failure. But in the old days, if you knew what you were doing, you could load up an *arreo* of eight donkeys for a box of aspirins. Ah, but you couldn't do that now. Those Indians are nobody's fool nowadays.

Other criollos who were involved in the sarrapia business deny that the Panare were ever as gullible as Pedro Castro's account suggests. Certainly by the 1950s they had become very adept at handling these commercial exchanges. The following account was given to me by José Perdomo who established a sarrapia depot in the Colorado valley in 1953:

> Yes, you had to know how to deal with those Indians. They were all right as long as you kept a tight rein on them. Otherwise they'd cheat you. I've never known an Indian who wouldn't try to cheat you if he could. It's not as if they know they're doing wrong: it's

their way . . . They had a good idea of what sarrapia was worth. They used to judge it by the size of their baskets. What they used to do, would be bring you a basket weighing 2 kg and then ask for goods worth, say, $2\frac{1}{2}$ kg. Then they'd claim not to have any more, hoping to get you to say, 'Oh, all right, here you are.' But I'd give it all back to them and say, 'Come back when you've got enough.' And then generally it would turn out that they did have a bit more tucked away somewhere, behind a tree, and back they'd come immediately with it. Just like that . . . Also, I always traded each object individually. If a man had enough for a bowl and a bit left over that he wanted to go towards a knife, well, I'd give him back the sarrapia that corresponded to the bowl and tell him to come back for the knife when he had a bit more . . . Otherwise they'd get confused and say you were cheating them . . . Another thing I did to stay on good terms with them, was charge them a little more for the goods they wanted. Because, you see, after the business had been done and the sarrapia was all weighed, they'd want something given free. Well, by charging them extra I could give them all sorts of little gifts without losing on it and they'd still go away thinking that I was a good man and good to trade with.

In summary, although the Panare were more directly involved in the collection of sarrapia, this involvement had no more impact on their society than their contact with the cattle pastoralist front. The criollos never attempted to make the Panare work for them by ensnaring them in cycles of debt-peonage, nor did they ever come into conflict with the Panare over access to the sarrapia trees. The Panare worked at the collection of sarrapia when it suited them, which was when they wanted to acquire some industrial goods; they were 'target workers' in the classic sense. Nevertheless, their involvement in sarrapia collection did serve to increase their dependence on the local criollo economy, because they became used to having the relatively wide range of industrially manufactured goods which they acquired through the sale of sarrapia. When the market for sarrapia collapsed in 1964, the Panare were therefore obliged to look for some other means of exchange for these industrial goods.

It is interesting to compare the impact of the sarrapia collection on the Panare with the effect of the extractive fronts on the indigenous groups of Brazilian Amazonas. According to Ribeiro, the commercial extraction of forest products in this area has had an extremely destructive effect on the local indigenous popualtion, the worst period being around the turn of the century when the most commercially important forest product was rubber. The particularly destructive effect of the extractive front at this time can largely be attributed to the fact that the front was operating in an area that had never been systematically colonized by the national society before. The members of these fronts brought diseases against which the indigenous population had no biological defence whatsoever and who therefore succumbed in large numbers to epidemics. The forces of law and order in these frontier regions were extremely weak, if present at all, and violence, murder and gross economic exploitation of both the indigenous and non-indigenous population were common. Under these circumstances, if members of an extractive front wanted to use the Indians as labourers, they had no qualms about enslaving them by means of debt-peonage. The extremely harsh working conditions to which the Indians were obliged to submit further contributed to the high mortality rate amongst the indigenous population. Another feature of these fronts to which Ribeiro draws attention was that they were primarily composed of single males who turned to the indigenous women to meet their sexual needs, sometimes resorting to raiding Indian villages in order to steal them (Ribeiro 1970: 21–9, 437).

In contrast to these Brazilian extractive fronts, the sarrapia collecting front of Panare territory was not operating on an entirely new frontier of colonization. By the time that sarrapia collecting became an important part of the local criollo economy, in the last two decades of the nineteenth century, the rural hinterland of Caicara had long been settled by criollos. As I suggested in Chapter 1, by this time the Panare appear to have built up a certain degree of immunity to the diseases introduced by the criollos (see p.22). Although there was indeed a certain amount of immigration into the area at the turn of the century, these immigrants moved into an essentially stable social situation. Many of them brought their families with them and therefore did not have to look to the Panare to provide them with sexual partners. Although there were very few agencies of government authority in the area, all accounts indicate that life in the hinterland of Caicara never had the violent and 'Wild West' character that it had on the rubber-collecting front of early twentieth-century Brazil.

A second factor that distinguishes the sarrapia-collecting front from the fronts described by Ribeiro was that the local criollo economy was not based entirely on the collection of sarrapia. The collection of sarrapia only took place in the dry season, and for the remainder of the year the people involved in it dedicated themselves to other activities—mostly cattle raising and, to a lesser extent, agriculture. They were people settled permanently in the region who were well acquainted with the Panare as trading partners and *compadres*. Even though the Panare were not integrated socially, in the sense defined above, the local criollos were entirely familiar with them. In contrast, a large part of the labour force involved in the rubber front of the Brazilian Amazonas was made up of individuals from outside the region who were completely dependent on the collection of forest products as a source of livelihood. This labour force moved about the area as the market value of the various products collected rose and fell (see Ribeiro 1970: 248). As Da Matta's account of the extractive front in Gaviões territory suggests, under these circumstances, the members of an extractive front tend to view the local indigenous population as animals, lying outside the pale of human society and therefore not deserving of the treatment normally accorded to human beings (Da Matta 1976: 39).

A third distinguishing feature concerns the use of indigenous labour. In Brazil, the *patrões,* the men who recruited labourers for extractive enterprises, were keen to supplement their labour force with Indians, since their knowledge of the natural environment gave them certain advantages over labourers from other parts of the country. The *patrões* often managed to persuade Indians to leave their communities and go to work in other parts of the region where they soon became embroiled in debt-slavery. The *patrões* would charge the Indians exorbitant sums for the fare to the site of collection, for the alcohol provided *en route* and for the equipment needed to tap rubber. Prices were fixed so that Indian labourers were never able to free themselves of their debts. In contrast, although the Panare sold their sarrapia to the entrepreneurs in their depots, they came and went as they pleased: they were never formally recruited. Instead the entrepreneurs relied mainly on the local criollo population to provide the necessary labour power. Since the criollos were native to the region, just as the Panare were, they had sufficient knowledge of the local topography to find their way around the forested mountain slopes whilst on collecting expeditions. For all these reasons, the entrepreneurs in the Panare area did not rely on indigenous labour to nearly the same degree as did the *patrões* of early twentieth-century Brazil.

It is these differences that explain why the sarrapia-collection front did not have the destructive effect on the Panare that rubber collection had on the indigenous populations on the Brazilian Amazon. If anything, sarrapia collection had a beneficial effect for the Panare since it enabled them to acquire steel tools and other goods that allowed them to reduce the time and effort spent on mundane subsistence activities.[8]

Compared to the pastoralist and extractive fronts, the agricultural front with which the Panare were in contact prior to 1960 was

relatively unimportant in the local criollo economy. Although most of
the small producers of the pastoralist front also practised a subsistence agriculture, it was only in one or two restricted areas that the
criollos' main source of livelihood was derived from the sale of
agricultural produce. Until very recently, almost all the individuals
involved in commercial agriculture practised a simple form of swidden
agriculture, on land to which they had no legal title. Each man
worked for himself and, together with his family, provided his own
labour force. These peasant agriculturalists had no capital to invest in
improving the efficiency and productivity of their operations.

Prior to the mid 1960s, one of the few places where the criollo population's principal means of livelihood was derived for agriculture
(and still is to this day) was in the vicinity of the village of Túriba. The
social and economic relations that the Panare maintained with the
criollos of this village were much the same as the relations they maintained with the small cattle pastoralists; they traded with them, made
social visits to their homesteads and often were *compadres* to them. But
the Panare never attempted to integrate themselves any further into
the social life of the village, nor did the criollos attempt to force them
to do so. Since the Panare lived for the most part in the mountains at
that time, there was never any competition over land suitable for
agricultural purposes. Although the Panare would work for the
criollos occasionally, they would only do so when they wanted particular goods which they had no other means of acquiring. The way of
life of the argiculturalists held no more attractions for the Panare than
the way of life of the small cattle pastoralists. From the Panare point
of view, the agriculturalists had to work far too hard to make a living
and the daily round of unremitting toil in the gardens was totally alien
to the Panare's own varied work pattern. As a result, the agricultural
front had no more impact on the Panare than any of the other fronts of
expansion operating in Panare territory in the period prior to the
collapse of the sarrapia trade.

From the foregoing account, it is easy enough to see why the Panare
should have been able to sustain regular contact with the criollo fronts
of expansion during the course of the first six decades of this century
without this having any significant impact on their culture or on the
social organization of their traditional way of life. On the one hand,

8. Ribeiro's ideal-typical model of the effects of an extractive front on local indigenous
populations is very much based upon the example of the rubber collecting front of
Amazonas in the early twentieth century. But as the case of the Panare shows clearly,
this model is too simplistic, as it stands, to be applicable to contact situations in
lowland South America generally. Even within Brazil, its general applicability is
questionable (see Da Matta 1976: 38 *et seq.*).

the Panare were under no pressure from the criollos to change their ways. The criollos did not seek to appropriate their lands, nor their labour, nor their women and they had no strong ideological motive for 'civilizing' the Panare and assimilating them into their own society. Nor did the Panare have any motive for assimilating themselves with the criollos. In material terms, they could get what they wanted from the criollos by means of trade whilst from a social point of view, criollo society had no advantages to offer over the way of life they already had. And, in the absence of any dispute over natural resources, the two populations were able to live in comparatively close geographical proximity without this producing any serious confrontation between them.

Thus in the mid 1960s the Panare remained readily distinguishable from the criollo population. This was true even of the communities of the most northerly segment of Panare territory that had the greatest degree of contact with the criollos. Today, the Panare still preserve a large measure of their social and economic autonomy. They continue to live outside the bounds of local criollo society. Cases of individuals who have left their communities to go and live more or less permanently with the criollos are extremely rare. The number of Panare who speak Spanish has probably increased in the last fifteen years, but those who speak it really fluently still number less than ten. Cases of sexual unions, stable or otherwise, have if anything become more rare rather than more frequent in the course of the last decade. The Panare are still very reluctant to work for the criollos and all communities continue to meet most of their food needs from their own subsistence activities.

And yet, over the course of the last few years, a number of subtle changes have been taking place both within Panare society and in their relations with the criollos. In the following chapter, I will describe these changes and examine to what extent they can be attributed to changes that have been going on more or less simultaneously in the criollo fronts of expansion operating in Panare territory.

# CHAPTER SEVEN

# Recent Developments

The most evident change that has taken place in Panare society over the last ten years is the general tendency of communities to move down from the mountains and establish their principal settlements closer to those of the criollos on the plains. In Chapter 1, I suggested that the gradual migration of the Panare to the north and north-west, which has been going on for probably as long as a century, if not more, can be attributed, at least partly, to their concern to establish better access to the criollo settlements. But in the last ten years this process has intensified. For example, fifteen years ago in Western Panare territory, very few communities were established on the plains, but by 1976 almost all were. Those Panare who had not moved down to the plains said that they intended to do so in the next two or three years, when the gardens they had in the mountains had passed their peak. This tendency to move progressively closer to the criollos is found all over Panare territory with the exception of the communities still located on the upper reaches of the Cuchivero.

In many of the communities that have established themselves on the plains, there is no longer a large communal house; instead, the members of these communities prefer to live in a series of small dwellings, housing no more than one or two conjugal families. In the communities closest to Caicara, these houses are often built in the criollo style with mud walls rather than with palm thatch. Most of the members of these communities have also abandoned traditional dress; in the communities situated on either side of theVía del Guaniamo, a loincloth has become a rare sight.

The reasons that the Panare give for these changes are usually pragmatic. They no longer want to live in the mountains because there are too many snakes there and the paths are bad; they no longer build communal houses because it requires a great deal of work to gather together the necessary palm, especially down on the plains; they no longer wear loincloths because these require a great deal of effort to weave. But although it is true that living in the mountains involves certain physical hardships, and that traditional forms of housing and clothing require a certain amount of physical effort to manufacture, the fact that the Panare are no longer prepared to accept these hardships is symptomatic of a changing attitude towards traditional forms of social behaviour. Many Panare now appear to accept with fatalistic resignation that their customs will sooner or later give way to those of the criollos and, although they show no eagerness to embrace criollo customs, they do not make any vigorous effort to reject them either.

The closer they are to Caicara, the more Panare communities have adopted criollo cultural patterns. Thus, when I was in the field, it was the communities that were located around the Hato San Pablo, along the Vía del Guaniamo and around the criollo village of El Tigre that had undergone the greatest degree of acculturation. In these communities, there are also signs of incipient changes that, in the long run, will probably have far more significant repercussions on Panare social organization than mere changes of dress and housing arrangements. For example, I found that the young male informants in these communities were remarkably inept at handling the categories of the kinship system, and some even claimed that they no longer considered it important to marry women of the approved category.[1] Nevertheless, even the most acculturated communities preserve a high degree of economic autonomy, continuing to meet almost all their food needs through their own subsistence activities. Furthermore, although the Panare, as a whole, have been moving closer to the criollos in simple spatial terms over the last decade and some have begun to adopt a number of criollo cultural traits, there is no indication that they are about to become integrated in a general *social* sense into local criollo society. If anything, the social boundary between Panare and criollos has hardened over the last few years rather than diminished. Both Panare and criollo informants were agreed that there had been a deterioration in the quality of their relations with one another over this period, for reasons that are essentially economic.

The cumulative experience of years of trading with the criollos has made the Panare comparatively skilled at the basic arithmetic involved in commercial transactions. Although the attitudes of the criollos who trade with the Panare vary considerably, from the patronizing but basically honest to the frankly exploitative, it appears that the Panare have learnt from past experience that it is best to work on the assumption that all criollos are out to cheat them. The criollos for their part do the same with regard to the Panare, as the statement of José Perdomo that I quoted in the last chapter clearly shows. Now

1. David Thomas (personal communication, 1975) reports that although young Pemon informants told him that they no longer regarded it as important to marry women of the correct category, in practice the great majority of them continued to do so. Unfortunately, my genealogical material from the most acculturated communities is not comprehensive enough to say to what extent this is true of the Panare also.

that the Panare have mastered the basic techniques of trading, they are determined not to allow themselves to be cheated by the criollos and invariably drive a very hard bargain.

A good example of this determination is the reaction of the Colorado Panare to the increase that has been taking place over the last few years in the prices that criollo traders charge for industrial goods. These price increases are a consequence of national and even international economic factors, just as far beyond the control of the local criollos as they are beyond the control of the Panare. The traders are merely passing on to their customers, Panare and criollo alike, the increase in the market price of the goods they sell. But the Panare tend to hold the local criollos as a whole responsible for this price increase. Even if the Panare are aware that the criollos themselves are paying more for the merchandise as well, they have only the local criollos on whom to take out their discontent.

Since the collapse of the sarrapia market, the Panare of Colorado have raised the cash they need to buy trade goods through the sale of decorative basketry. In response to the increase in the price of trade goods, they have increased the price they charge for these baskets. Indeed, the Panare have become quite familiar with the idea of progressive inflation. On one occasion when I purchased a basket in the dry season 1975–6, the man who had made it pointed out that at Bs.20, which was the sum he was asking, the basket was cheap because by the time the rainy season came round it would cost Bs.25, by the following dry season Bs.30, Bs.35 the rainy season after that and so on. A comparison of the prices charged by the Colorado Panare in 1975–6 with those paid for a museum collection made in 1969 shows that the price of baskets increased between three and five times between 1969 and 1976.[2] But over the same period, very few of the items that the Panare buy from the criollos more than doubled in price. When one asks the Panare why they charge so much for their baskets, they reply in a truculent manner that the baskets they make now are better than they were in the past and therefore they should be paid more for them. Whilst this is certainly true, there is no doubt that the real increase in the prices the Panare now charge for their baskets also represents a way of getting their own back on the criollos for the high prices they now charge for trade goods. The element of retribution involved was clearly apparent in a case involving not merely an increase in the price charged for basketwork, but a total embargo. In the rainy season of 1975, a number of men in Colorado agreed not to

2. This collection was made by R. Lizarralde and is presently held by the Ethnography section of the Research Institute of the Faculty of Economics and Politics in the Universidad Central de Venezuela.

sell any more basketry cheese moulds to the local criollos. The local criollos who produce cheese are absolutely dependent on the Panare for these moulds since they have no idea how to make them themselves. The Panare explained that they had started this embargo because the criollos were charging high prices for their cheese. The fact that they, the Panare, do not eat cheese and the majority of them consider it absolutely disgusting, did not matter. It was the principle they objected to. They were aware that the high price of the cheese was related to the high price of trade goods—perhaps their only mistake was to get the causal relationship between the two the wrong way round. Whilst the embargo lasted, the Panare laughed amongst themselves at the thought of the criollos using old sacking for moulds. But the agreement did not last very long, and by the dry season of 1976, everybody in the valley was selling cheese moulds to the criollos once again.

The criollos describe the Panare's current hard bargaining approach to trade relations by referring back to the old distinction between *indios* and *racionales*. 'What has happened,' they say, 'is that the *indios* have become more *racional* than the *racionales*.' The Panare's attitude to economic relations with the criollos disrupts the customary relationship between the two groups, which is something that the criollos find annoying. They say that the Panare have become impossible to deal with because they have become too demanding. Since the principal basis of Panare–criollo relations is, and always has been, economic, the tensions that arise in the assessment of the material value of goods tend to overflow into the social domain of relations between the two groups. Symptomatic of the incipient discord between the two groups is the gradual erosion of the *compadrazgo* system. The criollos are no longer willing to enter into these relationships because, they claim, once they do so they find themselves continually pestered by the Panare for gifts, whilst they themselves never manage to get the Panare to do or give anything free of charge. The Panare for their part complain that the criollos have become stingy All senior Panare men in Colorado have Spanish names which they acquired through a *compadre*, but many young men do not. This is either because they have been unable to find a criollo who is prepared to become a *compadre* or because they have found their *compadre* to be so stingy that they do not want to use his name any more. Other Panare in Colorado have several Spanish names because they have changed their *compadres* several times over the last few years as, displeased by the stinginess of one *compadre*, they have initiated a new *compadrazgo* relationship with someone else instead.

But a far more dramatic testimony to the deterioration of Panare

–criollo relations than the decay of the *compadrazgo* system is the number of cases of open confrontation between the two ethnic groups that have occurred in the last few years. During the period that I was in the field, I collected information about four of these, which I describe below. I did not witness any of these incidents and the accounts I was given of them varied greatly. These however appear to be the essential details:

*Case 1.* The community of Macanilla (see Map 4) is located on private property belonging to a prominent criollo family. For some time, the landowners have been keen to get the Panare to move off their land and have been badgering them to do so: the Panare claim that they have gone so far as to order their men to uproot manioc in their gardens. Events came to a head in early 1975, when one of the landowners' men castrated a donkey belonging to a Panare, after the donkey had eaten some of the criollo's clothes as they hung on a fence to dry. The Panare responded by throwing boiling water over a donkey belonging to the criollos (in the more lurid accounts they are supposed to have tied the donkey up and lit a fire underneath it!). Shortly afterwards, the landowners' men and the Panare came face to face, the latter supposedly armed with poles. Blows were exchanged but no-one was seriously hurt. When I left the field in June 1976, the incident had apparently passed over with the Panare still living where they were.

*Case 2.* In July 1975, a group of young Panare from the community of El Pajal killed a cow belonging to a local criollo. They were caught red-handed on their way to Caicara to sell the meat. It then turned out that the cow belonged to a criollo whose family had lived in the region for a long time and with whom the Panare of El Pajal were on generally friendly terms. When they discovered this, the culprits said in their defence that they would not have killed the animal if they had known it had belonged to this man. But, they claimed, the brand mark on the animal had not been very clear and they had thought it belonged to another local pastoralist whom they disliked. This man had moved to the area only recently and he did not have the rapport with the Panare that the owner of the animal did. When the latter heard about the incident, he was initially very annoyed since the animal in question was of a good quality breed and was worth several hundred *bolívares*. But apart from reporting the matter to the local representatives of OCAI, he took no further action on the matter.

*Case 3.* In September 1975, another criollo cattle-owner came across a group of Panare from the community of El Valle cutting up a dead cow. The Panare claimed that the cow was dead when they found it and pointed to the maggots in it as evidence of this fact. But the criollo would not believe their story (cattle can be infested with maggots whilst still alive) and went to fetch the local National Guard. When the National Guard arrived, with their guns at the ready, the Panare fired on them as they approached. One of the Guardsmen was hit in the arm and the Guard withdrew. On the way back to Caicara, they took out their anger on an innocent Panare standing by the side of the road, roughing him up and confiscating his shotgun. The matter was then referred to the military authorities based in Caicara who got in contact with the OCAI personnel. Together they investigated the incident and came to the conclusion that it was a case of much ado about nothing. It seemed unlikely that the Panare had in fact killed the cow and the owner had clearly over-reacted in calling in the National Guard. The National Guard had been at fault in entering the Panare settlement with guns in hand because this had frightened the Panare, leading them to fire on the Guardsmen in what they thought was self-defence. The incident was reported on the national radio network, but after a few weeks tempers cooled and it became no more than an item of local gossip. But even though some local criollos had sympathized with the Panare in this dispute, the incident served to increase the general feelings of mutual suspicion and hostility between the two ethnic groups.

*Case 4* took place in early 1976 when a Colorado Panare came across a cow eating the crops in his garden. Infuriated at the prospect of losing his food, he shot the cow dead on the spot. But when he returned to the settlement and reported the matter, everyone became worried about what the local criollos' reaction would be. The man's father-in-law who was friendly (though not actually a *compadre*) with the criollo whose cow had been killed, took it upon himself to act the role of mediator and went to report the matter to the owner. The owner's reaction was to persuade the Panare to accept a fence halfway down the valley which would have the effect of keeping the cattle out of the Panare's gardens in the future. The criollos provided the materials and the Panare helped to cut the poles. Although the Panare accepted this arrangement, they only did so with the greatest reluctance because they suspected that the criollo would then regard the half of the valley in which his cattle were allowed to roam as his. I subsequently discovered that the Panare had been perfectly justified in their suspicions since the criollo in question had made an application to the *Instituto Agrónomo Nacional* (IAN), the body responsible for making grants of land under the terms of the Agrarian Reform Law, for title to this part of the valley. This application had been refused on the grounds that there were indigenous inhabitants. In constructing the fence where he did, the criollo was attempting to lay a *de facto* claim to the same section of the valley that he had been refused *de jure*. Some months after the construction of the fence, IAN intervened more directly in the affairs of the valley when they gave the Panare title to the whole of the valley; it also undertook to construct a fence at the mouth of the valley to keep out the criollos' cows. This fence would have made the other fence obsolete. But the money for the new fence never materialized, and the old fence collapsed, so that within a few years the cattle were once again invading the Panare houses and gardens.

In summary then, in the last ten years there have been changes both within Panare society and in their relations with the criollos. Contemporaneous with a tendency to adopt certain criollo cultural patterns of dress and housing arrangements, there has been a marked deterioration in the relations between Panare and criollos. I now propose to consider in what ways these changes can be attributed to changes that have also been taking place in the economic organization and social composition of the local fronts of national expansion.

The most dramatic change that has taken place in the configuration of fronts of national expansion in Panare territory is the sudden emergence of the Guaniamo diamond mines. It is convenient to describe the social and economic features of these mines independently before passing on to consider their effect on the Panare. These mines began in 1970 when a group of prospectors discovered a field of diamonds on a minor branch of the middle reaches of the Guaniamo. Although the quality of these diamonds was very much lower than that of those found in other parts of Venezuela, they were present in great quantities and as news of the discovery spread, there was a rush to the site. (Such rushes are known in Venezuelan miner's argot as *bullas*.) Most of the in-coming population were professional miners who, up until that point, had been working in the diamond mines in the Gran Sabana, further to the east in Bolivar State (see Map 2). They were readily attracted to Guaniamo because the mines in the Gran Sabana were apparently nearing the end of their lives. The diamonds were located at a spot that was completely inaccessible by river or road, and the first wave of miners came in by foot from the Raudal Alto on the Upper Cuchivero (see Map 4). Shortly afterwards, airstrips and helicopter pads were cut near the mine and most supplies were then brought in by air. By the end of 1971, there were supposedly 8500 people living in the shanty towns that had sprung up at the site (Maziarek 1975: 58–9).

Plate 19.   The collective house at Tiro Loco in September 1975. Even though it was one of the finest current examples of Panare architecture, it lay no more than a kilometre away from one of the Guaniamo diamond miners' shanty towns.

Plate 20.   The diamond miners' shanty town at El Milagro, Guaniamo, in September 1975. Whenever a new strike is made, another section of the forest is cut down and the corrugated iron huts are dismantled and moved to the new site.

Since then, it is clear that the population of the mines has fluctuated greatly, although it has never been possible to compile an accurate census. As in the case of Caicara itself, the functionaries of the Malaria Control Division have the most accurate idea of the size of the population. Probably more than half of the miners are foreigners, mostly Colombians. Many of these foreign miners are *indocumentados*, that is, they have no official permits to be in the country. (This is one of the reasons why it has been difficult to compile an accurate census: the last thing that the *indocumentados* want is for someone to record that they are there.) Another striking feature of the population is that a high proportion, often said to be more than half, are women (Villasmil Febres 1976: 23). A handful of these women work as miners, others work as cooks and waitresses, whilst some simply live there with their husbands. But the majority of these women make a living as prostitutes. Like the miners themselves, many of these women have followed the mining camps around all their lives, moving from one site to another as the *bullas* come and go.

Since 1974, the government has attempted to impose some sort of control on the activities in the mines through the *Comisión Presidencial del Guaniamo*. This body is composed of representatives of all the government agencies that have some brief to intervene in the affairs of the mines: the Ministry of Mines, the Ministry of Health, the Ministry of Public Works, etc. This body was made responsible for maintaining law and order in the mines and to this end, the *Cazadores,* a battalion of soldiers trained in anti-guerilla techniques, was also sent to the mines. Up until the arrival of the *Cazadores*, according to the government, the mines were frequently the scene of murder, robbery and other violence. The *Cazadores* disarmed everybody, imposed a curfew and a ban on all forms of alcohol except beer. Since then, life in the mines has been a great deal quieter.

From a legal point of view, mining in Guaniamo is regulated by the system known as *libre aprovechamiento* (literally, 'free exploitation') dating from the 1940s. According to this system each individual miner can apply for a licence from an office of the Ministry of Mines set up in the immediate vicinity of the diamond zone. This licence entitles him to exploit an area of no more than ten square metres. In actual practice however, it is very common for a number of miners to take out licences to adjoining areas and work them together, dividing up the spoils between them. Although the laws regulating diamond-mining in Venezuela contemplate the possibility of much larger concessions, in Guaniamo no one has taken advantage of this for a number of pragmatic reasons: concessions take up to two years and Bs.20,000 to negotiate, whilst past experience has shown that when a rich deposit

Plate 21. A group of miners using a pump and high pressure hoses on the pit which they work together. Once the earth has been softened up by the jets of water, everyone gets in and starts to dig out the material that will then be sifted for diamonds. In the picture, the hoses, having fulfilled their function, are about to be turned off.

of diamonds is discovered the floating population of miners will converge on the region in question and begin digging with scant regard for the rights of the concession holders (Maziarek 1975: 73–4).

The *libre aprovechamiento* regulation has the effect of discouraging large capital investment, and as a result the mining methods used in Guaniamo are very primitive. All miners work in open-cast pits. Some pits are simply excavated with pick and shovel and the resultant material washed through a sieve manually in a nearby source of water. It is becoming increasingly common however for the miners to use certain items of plant such as high-pressure hoses, pumps, diesel engines and crude mechanical sorters to separate the diamond-bearing material from the remainder of the contents of a pit. Strictly speaking, these items of plant are not permitted under the terms of the *litbre aprovechamiento* regulation which was designed to meet the requirements of a labour force of itinerant miners with few capital resources. Miners of this kind still make up the majority of the mining population, but there is no doubt that these items of plant make excavation far more efficient, and for this reason the authorities take what they call a 'flexible' attitude to them. At the time that I was in the mines, their policy was to allow machinery already in the mines to be replaced but not to allow any more in.

The presence of these items of plant affects the relations of production between the miners who take out licences to adjoining plots. If one of the licence holders owns a pump or a hose, he will get a larger proportion of the spoils from the joint enterprise than one who does not. The conventional arrangement is for a man to get one and a half shares, or *plazas* as they are known, for every pump he contributes. A man who contributes a high-pressure hose or a sorter or some other item of machinery will also get more than a man who has only his labour and his right to exploit ten square meters to offer to the enterprise. Such a man only gets half a share. An individual who owns several items of machinery often does not work in the pit at all himself; instead he may well spend most of his time running a store in one of the shanty towns that have sprung up at the mines or buying diamonds off other miners for re-sale in Cuidad Bolivar. In fact, these individuals often spend a great deal of time outside the mines, restricting themselves to periodic visits just to keep an eye on things. In addition, they will often appoint a foreman to act on their behalf, directing operations, maintaining the machinery and making sure that they are not swindled. Such foremen usually get a whole share of the profits. Each joint enterprise also normally has its own cook who gets a half-share. At the end of the life of the pit, all the money received from the sale of the diamonds that the pit has produced is divided up amongst the shareholders according to the number of shares they have.

In effect then, although nobody works for a wage in the mines, this system of dividing up the spoils serves to create two categories of miners: those who own the machinery, who often do not work in the pits themselves and get the lion's share of the profits, and those who do all the manual work and get a much smaller share. However, by discouraging large capital investment the ambiguous *libre aprovechamiento* regulation has the effect of inhibiting the development of a system of production in which owners of the means of production and wage-earners are clearly distinguished.

Even when these items of machinery are used, the methods used to mine diamonds in Guaniamo are highly inefficient. It has been estimated that they involve a wastage rate of 40 per cent of the diamonds a pit contains (Maziarek 1975: 93). In 1976, the Ministry of Mines reckoned that given this system of production and their estimate as to the extent of the diamond reserves, the mines would not last much beyond the end of 1980. Already there were signs in 1976 that the large quantities of diamonds that had been found in the early stages were a thing of the past. However, despite the short projected life of the mines at Guaniamo, the government has invested a large amount of money in public works in and around the mines. The rationale underlying this investment is the government's general policy for the economic development of the region. By mere coincidence, the mines lie close to the road being built from Caicara to San Juan de Manapiare, originally intended to encourage the colonization of the interior of the Distrito Cedeño and the Territorio Federal de Amazonas. According to government functionaries working in the mines, the government hoped to take advantage of the human and material resources already in place there, by creating a small town of approximately 2000 inhabitants and encouraging at least some of the miners to stay on and become agriculturalists once the diamonds ran out. However, to the best of my knowledge, no studies have been made either of the agricultural potential of the soils in the immediate vicinity of the mines or of the attitude of the miners to the idea of remaining at Guaniamo. Judging by other parts of Panare territory, it seems unlikely that the soils around the mines will be fertile enough to sustain commercial agriculture without a large capital investment, whilst my impression from conversations with individual miners was that most of them would be prepared to stay in Guaniamo only so long as there was no prospect of a *bulla* breaking out elsewhere.

Although there are now about 150 Panare living within half a day's walk of the mines, there were none there when the mines first started. A few years previously there had been a Panare settlement at the site within the mining area presently known as La Salvación but this was abandoned before the first miners arrived in 1970. At that time, most of the Panare now living in the vicinity of the mines were settled around the junction of the Cuchivero and the Zariapo rivers, close to the Raudal Alto. It was from there that the first miners entered the diamond area on foot in 1970. The Panare were therefore aware of the existence of the mines right from the start, and it was not long before they also made the three-day walk south and built themselves houses close to the shanty town of the miners.

This segment of the Panare population had been involved, in earlier periods, in the collection of sarrapia, and for a long time had been in regular contact with the criollo settler population around the junction of the Cuchivero and the Zariapo. But since the collapse of the sarrapia market, they had found it hard to acquire the steel tools and other industrial goods on which they had come to depend. They therefore saw in the mines a chance to return to their former position of relative affluence in these items. However, with two exceptions none of these Panare has ever worked as miners. These two exceptional individuals, both of them adolescents, spoke some Spanish because they had been boarders at the Roman Catholic mission school at Laguna Sucia on the middle reaches of the Cuchivero. There were also four other Panare working in the mines, also all adolescents, but these boys came not from the Raudal Alto area but from the more acculturated communities presently situated along the Vía del Guaniamo.

Instead of working in the mines, the Panare have been content to acquire trade goods by selling agricultural produce and game to the miners. Since the miners grow very little food of their own, large quantities have to be brought in from Caicara and Cuidad Bolivar. In the dry season, these supplies can be brought in by road, but at the height of the rainy season they have to be brought in by air. It has been estimated that in 1975 the miners consumed thirty-five tons of food and drink a day (Villasmil Febres 1976: 84). By the time these supplies reach the miners, they are far more expensive than they are in the towns they come from. The prices of most items of food and drink in 1975–6 in the mines were between three and five times the prices of similar items in Caicara and Cuidad Bolívar. Consequently the Panare never find it difficult to find a customer for any food they have to sell.

Although they generally get paid less by the miners than the prices charged by the shopkeepers in the mines, the Panare get paid more than they would anywhere else in Panare territory. Even though the trade goods are also more expensive than anywhere else, the Panare reckon they are better off than they were when they lived at the mouth of the Zariapo.

The mines, despite their rapid growth and large population, have so far had very little impact on the Panare communities that live in the vicinity. The Panare can get what they want from the mines with relative ease by selling food, whilst the miners, as an economic front, need neither the Panare's land nor their labour. Under the system of *libre aprovechamiento*, the area of land exploited by the miners is relatively restricted; in the absence of concessions, nobody can lay claim to the land on which the Panare live. In theory this land belongs to the Venezuelan nation. Similarly, given the method of organizing labour in the mines by the share or *plaza* system, nobody is in a position to recruit the Panare as casual labourers to an enterprise. Even if the Panare wanted to become involved in mining, which most do not, they would have to undergo a considerable degree of acculturation before they would accept the conditions of work and the system of sharing out the profits from a pit. It is not surprising therefore that all the adolescents who have become involved in the mines have either come from relatively acculturated communities or have attended the Roman Catholic mission school.

Nor did I hear of any case of miners seriously abusing the Panare. The miners have brought their own camp-followers with them, so they feel no need to resort to the Panare to meet their sexual needs; nor do they consider the Panare to be any sort of threat that it might be necessary to eliminate. Although many of the miners are new to Panare territory, most of them have previously worked in areas occupied by indigenous groups. In fact, some of the miners in Guaniamo are Indians themselves, being Pemon from the Gran Sabana who joined the rush to Guaniamo when the diamonds ran out in their own area. The miners constitute a most heterogeneous population from a social and cultural point of view, and this seems to encourage a certain tolerance amongst them for all kinds of unconventional behaviour. The Panare therefore fit quite readily into the world-view of the average professional miner. They might regard the Panare as inferior to themselves but many would nevertheless recognize that they behave in the way they do because they have a distinctive way of life with its own social codes and not simply because they are incapable of copying the criollo way. Playing on the popular association between the term 'indio' and stupidity or primitiveness, one expressed this point of view to me in the following way: 'What do I think of those Indians? They're all right. They've got their thing, their laws, their customs and all that shit. I tell you that there are a lot of "mothers" in these mines who are more indio than those Indians out there in that forest.' In short, the miners have no motive for disturbing the Panare, and since the Cazadores established law and order in the mines the miners have had good reason to believe that any major abuse of the Panare will, at the very least, get them expelled from the mines. Yet the Panare freely recognize that even before the Cazadores arrived, they had never had any open confrontation with the miners.

Perhaps the most significant effect of the mines on the Panare has been biological. At the time that I visited the mines in September 1975, six Panare had died in the previous three months of 'gripe', that is of colds that the Panare believed they had contracted from the criollo population. Most of the remaining members of the communities around the mines had heavy colds and coughs. The individuals who had died of 'gripe' had been of all age cohorts, from infants to people over sixty. It is impossible to know to what extent these deaths can be attributed to infection with diseases that the miners had brought with them. However given the diverse origins of the mining population, it seems likely that new viruses have been introduced into the area against which the Panare have very little natural defence. Nevertheless, despite the risk of infection, the Panare say that they intend to stay in the mines as long as they remain open.

The impact of the mines on the Panare in the future is difficult to predict. If the government's plans to build an agricultural township come to fruition, this will no doubt significantly modify Panare–criollo relations. But at the present time, this scheme appears to be in doubt; apart from the practical difficulties that would have to be overcome if the township were to be viable, the fact that it is the road to Puerto Ayacucho running parallel to the Orinoco rather than the road to San Juan de Manapiare that is being built at the moment (see above, p.2), suggests that the government may have decided to encourage the development of the Territorio Federal de Amazonas by means of this route instead.

The other major change in the local criollo economy that has been taking place over the course of the last decade is the modernization of the cattle pastoralist front. This modernization process has only just begun in the hinterland of Caicara but future trends can already be identified. New and better breeds of cattle are being introduced, artificial pastures are being sown, reproduction is being more closely controlled. Partly as a result of these and other technical improvements, and partly as a result of the natural increase of the herds, the number of head on the plains in the hinterland of Caicara is growing steadily. At the same time, the number of Panare who have their principal settlement and gardens in the forest at the edge of the plains is also growing. As the number of cattle increases, the more they tend to penetrate the clumps of forest where the Panare now live, damaging their houses, defecating all over their settlements and eating their crops. As in Case 4, reported above, the Panare have occasionally responded to those intrusions by shooting the offending animals. The Panare say that since the cattle belong to the criollos, it is they who should put up fences to stop them intruding; the criollos for their part appeal to the traditional *llanero* convention that it is the responsibility of the agriculturalist to protect his gardens, not the cattle owner.[3] Some pastoralists have acceded to the Panare's point of view just to avoid any future trouble. Others have threatened the Panare with burning down their houses in order to frighten them into leaving.

3. This traditional law of the Llanos is however directly contradicted by one of the provisions of the Laws of the Indies of 1532. This provision is quoted with approval by the editor of the ninth edition of the Agrarian Reform Law and reads as follows: 'Our justices should not allow cattle to enter the land worked by Indians and should arrange for any as there might be there to be expelled, imposing and carrying out severe penalties against any persons who should act to the contrary.' (Hernandez-Bretón, 1969: 6).

Thus, to the degree that the modernization of the local cattle industry
has led to an increase in the number of head on the plains, it has also
contributed to the general deterioration of relations between the
Panare and the criollos, since it brings them into direct competition
for natural resources in a way that did not happen before.

Another change going on in the cattle pastoralist front which is
likely to affect relations between the two ethnic groups in the future is
the change that appears to be taking place in the social composition of
the front. Many of the small producers who were born and grew up in
the hinterland of Caicara are leaving the countryside. Their place is
being taken by more entrepreneurial pastoralists, some of whom
dispose of a certain amount of capital. These newcomers have been
attracted to the area by the new roads, the low density of settlement
and by the fact that much of the land in the hinterland of Caicara
belongs to the nation. The immigrants hope to be able to acquire title
to a tract of land under the terms of the Agrarian Reform Law and
apply for government credits to develop it. In the absence of any
statistical data, it is impossible to say how far this process of replacement of one type of criollo cattle pastoralist by another has gone.
However the local representative of IAN in Caicara receives between
twenty and thirty visits a month from people outside the area seeking
titles to local tracts of land. These new settlers do not have the rapport
with the Panare that the native criollo pastoralists have from a
lifetime's experience dealing with them. The potential consequences
are exemplified by the second case of dispute reported above in which
a group of Panare from El Pajal ingenuously sought to justify the
slaughter of a cow on the grounds that it belonged to a man whom
they considered stingy. Unlike the man who was in fact the owner of
the cow, this man had only recently moved to the area and was not on
good terms with the Panare. Although nothing came of this particular
incident, it constitutes a most ominous precedent for the future of
Panare–criollo relations.

At the present time, however, most of the cattle pastoralists in the
region around Caicara still have no title to the lands they occupy and
use for pasturage. But as the competition for land intensifies, it is to be
anticipated that the small and medium-sized producers will become
increasingly concerned to establish their control over a certain area of
land by means of a legal title. Although it is well known that the
official policy of IAN is not to give title to lands that are occupied by
indigenous groups, this has not stopped cattle pastoralists from
applying for title to lands occupied by the Panare. As we have seen,
this is what the criollo involved in the fourth case described above did.
Fortunately, the local IAN officials were well acquainted with the

facts of this case and the criollo's application for title to half the valley of Colorado was refused. But in other parts of Panare territory, where the Panare have only recently established themselves on the plains, it may be more difficult to identify the Panare's rights. And even if IAN does continue to support the Panare's interests against those of the cattle front, this will have the effect of increasing the competition between the two groups for access and control over natural resources. Judging by the reaction of the criollo involved in the Colorado case, the granting of land titles to Panare communities will be greatly resented by many criollos who argue that the Panare should not be allowed to stand in the way of their own economic ambitions, on the grounds that they do not work hard enough and do not have the ability to exploit local natural resources 'properly'. Clearly, this is also ominous for the future of Panare–criollo relations.

Like the cattle-pastoralist front, the agricultural front is also in the process of being modernized. Small groups of entrepreneurs have begun to set up mechanized agricultural enterprises in various parts of Panare territory. The area of land which these enterprises will bring under cultivation is much more extensive than the area cultivated by the peasant agriculturalists who used to make up the agricultural front in Panare territory. Many of this latter type of agriculturalist, like their counterparts in the pastoralist front, are leaving the countryside and settling in Caicara. If the mechanization of local agriculture results in the deforestation of large sections of Panare territory, this may well have the most serious repercussions for the Panare, for not only will it reduce the area available for their own agricultural activities, but it will also deplete the silvine game population on which they presently depend for protein. However, so far the new mechanized operations have not come into direct competition with the Panare.

It is not only changes in the economic fronts of the national society that have been taking place in the last decade in Panare territory. Their relations with the national society have also been modified by the establishment of a number of 'protectionist' fronts in the area, i.e. those composed of missionaries or of government employees. I have already alluded in passing to the activities of OCAI and IAN but I will begin by describing the missionary fronts.[4]

In 1975–6, there were two basic types of missionary front in Panare territory, one Roman Catholic, the other Evangelical Protestant. The Roman Catholic front consisted of the mission station on the middle

4. The activities of both these types of 'protectionist' front are supposedly regulated by a large but confused body of laws and government decrees. A brief summary of these is given in Appendix 4.

reaches of the Cuchivero and an independent missionary working in the Panare communities around the criollo village of Túriba. In addition, the mission also intervened in the affairs of other Panare communities on occasion, most notably the communities situated in the vicinity of the Hato San Pablo. The Evangelical front consisted of two mission stations: one in Colorado and the other at Caño Iguana, both of which belong to the New Tribes Mission. In addition, another Evangelical mission, the Orinoco River Mission, which works primarily on the criollo population, has a house in Caicara where the Panare often go during visits to the town.

The Roman Catholic mission station was founded in 1969 under the direction of the Archbishop of Cuidad Bolívar, Monseñor Mata Cova. The name of the mission is *Corazón de Jesús* but is situated at a spot known locally as Laguna Sucia. Nearby there is a small criollo hamlet called La Candelaria, most of whose inhabitants are involved in cattle-raising and related activities. The mission station is staffed by half-a-dozen nuns of the Madre Laura order, assisted by lay personnel. The day-to-day activities of the mission are primarily educational, and to a lesser extent medical. The nuns run a school which gives instruction up to the sixth grade of the standard Venezuelan school curriculum. In 1976, about seventy children attended the school, of whom approximately fifteen were Panare. These Panare children spent most of their time living in the mission station along with about a dozen criollo children.

As far as I could tell, neither the living conditions within the school nor the instruction given in class were in any way adapted to take into account the Panare's distinctive social and cultural traditions. None of the nuns has ever succeeded in learning Panare and all instruction is therefore given in Spanish. The Panare children who attend the school are obliged to dress in criollo clothes and sleep in dormitories separated by sex. They are expected to attend prayers and to say Grace before meals which are eaten in criollo fashion, at a table with knives and forks. The nuns' ambition is to bring one of their Panare pupils up to the sixth grade standard, whereupon he or she will be sent off to Cuidad Bolívar to continue his or her education there. By 1976, however, no Panare child had got beyond third grade.

The mission was originally built close to the present site of the Panare community of Manteco, which is situated on the level of the plains at the foot of the range of mountains that separate the Cuchivero and the Caura river basins. Most of the Panare children who attend the mission school come from this community. The mission was subsequently moved to a point about 10 km away on the banks of the Cuchivero, in order to improve its communications with

Caicara. (In the rainy season, Manteco becomes inaccessible to wheeled vehicles.) The parents of the children who live as boarders in the school are able to visit their children whenever they want, and they have built themselves a traditional collective house right in front of the mission station on the banks of the river. They stay in this house when visiting their children or when taking advantage of the simple medical service that the nuns provide. During school holidays, the children return to their communities.

The general attitude of the Panare of Manteco towards the mission is one neither of enthusiasm nor of antipathy. They talk about the mission with an air of apparent indifference. They do not like to be separated from their children but accept the nuns' judgement that it is important for their children to be educated in the criollo fashion. Even though their parents continue to wear loincloths, the children attending the school no longer do so. Nor have they been given Panare names; and there are no plans to initiate them ceremonially into adulthood some time in the future. When one asks their parents why they are no longer concerned to initiate their sons, their answers are characteristically pragmatic, being some variation on the theme that it takes a great deal of effort to collect together all the materials necessary for an initiation ceremony.

And yet, although the Panare of Manteco appear to be resigned to the fact that their offspring, if not themselves, will become acculturated to the criollo way of life, so far the presence of the mission and contact with the criollos of La Candelaria has produced few changes in the social life of the adults of the community. Few speak more than a trade Spanish and most continue to wear loincloths, at least within their own settlement. When they visit the criollos or the mission station, they tend to put on criollo-style clothes. But none of the adult Panare has been converted to Christianity in anything more than the most nominal way. Given that the nuns of the mission speak no Panare and the Panare very little Spanish, the linguistic barriers to proselytization are considerable. But to the best of my knowledge, no systematic attempt to convert the adults has been made.

Indeed it seems that the mission's operations have been directed more towards changing the material conditions of life in the Manteco community than they have been directed towards changing the community's belief system. All the mission schemes designed to change the material bases of the community appear to have the same end: to turn the Panare into peasants on the criollo model. Another thing that these schemes have in common is that all of them have been failures. When the mission was first set up at Manteco, the Archbishop arranged for all the criollos living in the immediate vicinity to be bought out. The Panare were then encouraged to come down from the mountains and build their houses there. I do not know whether it was the Panare's own idea or the Archbishop's, but the houses they built at Manteco were for one or two conjugal families only and were in the criollo architectural fashion, with mud walls. Several of them were built with zinc roofs, the material for which was donated by the Archbishop. But although some members of the community now spend a large part of the year living at Manteco, they continue to maintain their traditional collective houses up in the mountains, at a spot known as La California. They go off there regularly to hunt and hold dances. Some members of the community even have gardens up there and live up there more or less permanently. This is no more than one variant of the traditional settlement pattern described in Chapter 2. When I asked the Panare why they did not build a collective house on the plains, their replies were as pragmatic as ever: 'Too much wind down here for large collective houses', or alternatively 'We already have houses.'

The mission has made two attempts to encourage the Panare to keep herds of domesticated animals. Shortly after the establishment of the mission, the Panare were given a herd of fifty goats. According to the Panare, this experiment was a failure because the goats were very weak and quickly died of the cold! I never heard the nuns' explanation for the failure of this experiment, but my own observations of the attempt to encourage the Panare to herd cattle suggest that the death of the goats had nothing to do with their condition on arrival. The latter experiment began in February 1975 when the Panare were given a herd of thirty cattle. In addition, four criollo stockmen were sent to show the Panare how to look after them. In June 1976, I visited Manteco and was curious to find out how the Panare had got on with the herd of cattle. On my way to the village, I passed a dead cow riddled with parasites. The village itself was a sorry sight with cow droppings all over it. Most of the members of the community were away in the mountains at the time and the cattle had broken into their houses and defecated inside. I asked the headman's son what had happened to the herd. 'They're out there somewhere,' he said. Naïvely wondering whether the Panare milked the cows or simply intended to breed them for their meat, I asked what the purpose of the herd was. 'To get themselves lost,' was the reply. Since many of the local criollos who have been involved in cattle-raising all their lives find it difficult to overcome the problems of managing cattle in the sort of natural environment that Panare territory affords, it is little wonder that this experiment to make pastoralists of the Panare, who have no interest in cattle and very little knowledge about them, should have been such a failure.

It is not only the Panare of Manteco who have been affected by the policies of the Archbishop of Cuidad Bolívar. He has visited most parts of Panare territory and has persuaded a number of Panare parents to allow him to take their children off to school in Cuidad Bolívar. The number who have acceded to this request has not been large. I do not know the exact number of children who have gone to Cuidad Bolívar but I estimate that it cannot be more than ten. This group includes both boys and girls. During my period in the field, I talked to three Panare who had spent some time at school in Cuidad Bolívar. All of them said that they did not like being there, mainly because they missed their families, but also because, in addition to attending classes, they were made to work very hard at domestic chores around the school. For these reasons, all three of them had returned to their communities.

The Archbishop was also responsible for persuading the Panare of the communities in the vicinity of the Hato San Pablo to leave that area and re-settle on a site to the south of the Guaniamito river known as Perro de Agua (see Map 4). The Panare of these communities had been living very close to the local criollo population and on land that was privately owned by a number of powerful criollo families. In the years leading up to 1976, relations between the two groups had been deteriorating rapidly. The criollos accused the Panare of stealing pigs and killing cattle and were keen to get the Panare to move. In fact, three of the four cases of dispute described above took place in this area. In contrast, at that time, there were very few criollos living in the vicinity of Perro de Agua.

It would appear therefore that the Archbishop's motive for persuading the Panare to move, was to remove them from an area where they were beginning to come into conflict with the criollos, to one where the likelihood of such conflicts would be much reduced. Most, though not all, of the Panare living in the vicinity of the Hato San Pablo complied with the Archbishop's plan. They and their belongings were taken to Perro de Agua in a truck in May 1976. The Archbishop gave them a few sacks of rice to tide them over until such time as their new gardens came into production. The land on which these Panare now live belongs to the nation and they could therefore be given title to it under the terms of the Agrarian Reform Law. Without such a title, the Panare at Perro de Agua will find themselves in the same situation as they were in the vicinity of the Hato San Pablo, given that once the new road to San Juan de Manapiare is opened, criollos will soon begin to settle in this area also.

The Archbishop also pays the salary and expenses of Padre Gonzalo Tosantos, who at the time that I was in the field was living more or less permanently in the community of Portachuelo, close to the criollo village of Túriba. Padre Gonzalo is a Spaniard who lived and worked in Caicara for many years before setting himself up in Portachuelo in 1974. He lives in a small house similar to those of the Panare, eats with them and joins in their daily subsistance activities. With their help, he has cut himself a garden. Otherwise his activities in the community are confined to providing very simple medical aid and trade goods which he brings from Caicara and sells at wholesale prices. He has also been active in lobbying the head office of IAN in Caracas in order to get them to make grants of land to the Panare. As we shall see, the grant made to the community of Colorado in July 1976 was a result partly of his efforts. His principal ambition at the time I was in the field was to learn to speak Panare. Although not a linguist, he wanted to work out a system for writing Panare using, as far as is possible, the letters of the Spanish alphabet. When this has been achieved, he hopes to be able to teach the Panare to read and write, not only in their own language, but in Spanish as well.[5] Padre Gonzalo claims that at this stage of his work amongst the Panare, he is not interested in converting the Panare to Christianity. Rather his present concern is to help the Panare confront the problems that further integration into the national society will bring. Only once the material bases of their society have been secured—their land and their health—and they have the knowledge of Spanish that will allow them to look after their own interests within the national society, will it be appropriate, to Padre Gonzalo's mind, for one to think in terms of proselytization.

The attitudes of the nuns of the Corazón de Jesus, the Archbishop and Padre Gonzalo vary considerably in the degree of respect they accord Panare social and cultural traditions. But all these representatives of the Roman Catholic front are alike in that they are all working in some sense towards the further integration of the Panare into the national society. They all believe that what they are giving or teaching the Panare will improve their condition *within* the national society. A concern to turn the Panare into Christians forms no more than one aspect, and indeed, a relatively minor aspect of this general policy. The attitude of the members of the Evangelical Protestant front towards proselytization is in sharp contrast to that of the Roman Catholics. As far as the New Tribes Mission is concerned, conversion

5. The results of his first two years of learning Panare have been published in the form of a small handbook (Tosantos 1977). This book indicates that he still has a long way to go before mastering the language.

is the objective of overriding importance. Although they also get involved in medical, economic and educational activities, these they regard as merely a means to the end of spreading the word of God.

The headquarters of the New Tribes Mission (NTM) are in Sanford, Florida in the southern United States. It is a world-wide organization, with over 1500 missionary members at work in 16 countries amongst more than 100 different tribal groups. In Latin America, in addition to Venezuela, the NTM has missionaries at work in Peru, Colombia, Brazil, Bolivia and Paraguay (Holland 1980: 36). The activities of the mission are reported in its journal, *Brown Gold*, where 'gold' refers to the souls of the tribal peoples they hope to save, and 'brown' to the colour of the bodies where these souls are temporarily housed. Although the mission has an office in Caracas, its main base of operations in Venezuela is at Tamatama on the upper Orinoco (see Map 2). From there, radio contact is maintained with the mission stations dotted all over the Venezuelan Amazonas, parts of Bolivar State and the State of Apure. Recently, the activities of the mission have been the subject of investigation by various government commissions, following allegations that the missionaries' religious activities were merely a front for espionage and paramilitary activities (see Appendix 4). In the field they are assisted by a sister organization, the so-called *Alas de Socorro* (literally, the 'Wings of Succour') which is composed of North American Evangelical Protestant pilots. This organization flies people and supplies in and out of the mission stations. Although the New Tribes Mission has two mission stations in Panare territory, it was only the station at Colorado that I was able to visit personally. But since there was frequent exchange of personnel between the two stations, it is safe to assume that the attitudes and policies of the two stations are much the same.

The New Tribes Mission station in Colorado was set up in 1972. It is staffed by two North American families. Although they buy some food from the Panare, most of the station's supplies are brought in from the outside. Like all New Tribes missionaries, the work of these two families is paid for by the congregations of their local churches back home in the States. Their religious beliefs are radically fundamentalist and they believe the Bible to be a literal account of historical fact. The Panare they consider to be host to the Devil and therefore condemned to burn in everlasting Hell—unless they can be saved by being introduced to the word of God as it is enshrined in the Bible. The principal practical objectives that the missionaries have pursued in their first few years in Colorado are to learn the language, work out a method of transcribing it and then teach the Panare to read it.

These objectives are identical to those of Padre Gonzalo but the motives the Evangelicals have for pursuing them are significantly different. Whereas Padre Gonzalo's concern to teach the Panare to read is primarily motivated by a desire to make the Panare better equipped to handle the problems that further integration into the national society will bring for them, the Evangelicals' principal objective is to save the Panare's souls. This they hope to do by translating the Bible or parts of it into the Panare language, thereby making the way of salvation open to them.

All four of the missionaries in Colorado received some training in descriptive linguistics before they left the States, although one of the women reached a more advanced level than the others. By 1975 when I arrived in the valley, it was only she, Jana Price, who had achieved any real fluency in the language. With the aid of half a dozen young adult male informants, she had managed to work out a means of transcribing the language on the basis of syllables and had prepared a series of 'primers', with which to teach the Panare to read. The missionaries began their literacy classes in late 1975. These classes were open only to the male members of the community, although at a later stage the missionaries said they intended to teach the women as well. In addition to the primers, Jana Price has also prepared a booklet giving simple accounts of the best-known stories of Genesis: the Creation, Adam and Eve, Noah's Ark. But by the time I left the field it was only one or two of the informants who had helped Mrs Price work out the system of transcription who were able to read this document.

Only when most Panare are capable of reading the Bible stories for themselves do the New Tribes missionaries intend to attempt to convert the Panare systematically. In the interim, they are content merely to explain what their beliefs are in the daily conversations they have with the Panare who visit the mission station to buy trade goods, to receive medicine or simply on a social call. There are a number of central features of Panare society that the missionaries believe will have to change if the Panare are to achieve salvation. Firstly, they will have to accept Jesus as their Saviour and reject the Devil. For the missionaries, the Panare's belief in *mahtikëdi, wori,* etc., are not illusions: these evil spirits are manifestations of the Devil who is a very real person. One of the missionaries explained that, for her, it was no coincidence that *amana* manifests itself in the form of a boa constrictor since, after all, it was also in the form of a snake that the Devil seduced Eve. Secondly, the Panare will have to give up all fermented drinks since these give rise, inevitably, to drunkenness and 'immorality'. If sugar-cane beer is no longer brewed, this will mean an end to the Panare's dances in their present form. As the Panare very much enjoy their dances and are prepared to dedicate a large amount of economic

Plate 22.  Two young men at work early one morning learning to read the syllables of their own language with 'primers' prepared by the New Tribes missionaries in the Colorado valley. The boy on the left is learning to read them upside down.

effort towards producing the means for them, the missionaries realize that it may well be very difficult to get the Panare to abandon them, unless they can replace them with something else. This replacement is likely to be Evangelical hymn-singing. Thirdly, the Panare will have to abandon the practice of polygyny which the missionaries consider to be sinful in the eyes of the Lord and degrading to women. On the question of dress, the missionaries' views are more ambiguous. They say that they are happy that the Panare should go on dressing in the traditional way, 'even the women'. On the other hand, the women who work as servants in the missionaries' homes are encouraged to wear dresses.

There is no doubt that the Panare welcome the presence of the Evangelical missionaries in the valley. To a certain extent, this approval is due to the material benefits that the missionaries' presence implies. The missionaries sell all sorts of minor trade goods or exchange them for food. The prices that the missionaries charge are generally lower than those charged by the local criollo population. The missionaries also give medical attention every morning and evening. They can arrange for serious cases to be flown out to the hospital in Puerto Ayacucho. The missionaries sell goods to any Panare who can afford them and give medicines to any Panare who needs them: they do not require the Panare to show any sign of conformity with their religious beliefs before giving or selling them what they want. The only time that they do withhold medicines is when the Panare come to the dispensary complaining of a headache the morning after a dance or a heavy drinking session.

So far the most visible effect of the mission in Colorado has been on the Panare's settlement pattern. Although there have been Panare settlements on the valley floor for many years, in 1972, when the missionaries first arrived, a large proportion of the present population of the valley had their principal houses and gardens in the forested mountains that encircle the valley. The missionaries built themselves a house at the heart of the valley, close to one of the settlements on the valley floor. But no sooner had they done so, than the members of this settlement group abandoned the site and built themselves a new house further away. But since then this trend has been completely reversed. Over the last few years, as the Panare have become accustomed to the presence of the mission and aware of its potential benefits, they have been moving their houses progressively closer to the mission station. By 1975, all the collective houses in the mountains had been abandoned and no one intended to cut new gardens up there ever again. Many of the Panare now live no more than two or three hundred yards from the mission station. In 1974, there was only one Panare house next to the mission and it belonged to the man mentioned in Chapter 4, who was somewhat ostracized socially because he had married a classificatory sister. He lived there alone with his wife, his children and his 'real' sister, who was also something of a social outcast because she was unmarried, even though she was in her thirties. In 1975, the population living within a stone's throw of the mission increased to about forty, and the following year it increased by a further twenty-five. In other words, by 1976, almost a third of the population of the valley was living no more than two minutes' walk from the missionaries' houses. The remainder of the community had their settlement within a radius of no more than three-quarters of an hour's walk. The reason these settlement groups had not also built houses next door to the mission had more to do with their antipathy to the other Panare living there than it had to do with their reservations about the missionaries.

This change in settlement pattern has been associated with a tendency to build smaller dwellings, housing one or two conjugal families only, instead of the traditional collective house. This is particularly noticeable in the group that has established itself right next door to the mission station, all of whom live in small conjugal family houses. The Panare say that they now live in small houses because 'the *musiú* (i.e. the missionaries) don't like big houses.'[6] The missionaries for their part deny that this is true and claim to encourage the Panare to go on building collective houses. But whatever they might actually say to the Panare, it is clear that in some sense they do prefer conjugal family dwellings, because each of the two missionary couples lives in its own house. So it may well be that, in the case of the Colorado Panare at least, the present tendency to build smaller houses could in part be an expression of their respect for the missionaries and their consequent desire to imitate them. On the other hand, one should bear in mind that the tendency for Panare settlement groups to break up into conjugal family dwellings is found amongst all those who have moved down to the plains in recent years, regardless of the presence or absence of missions. The reasons for this general tendency are complex and somewhat difficult to identify and I will leave further consideration of them until the final chapter.

Although the most obvious of the effects of the mission may be that on the settlement pattern in Colorado, perhaps the most significant effect that the mission has had on the Colorado Panare is on their belief system. The missionaries have not yet started systematic proselytization but they have already begun to sow the seeds of conversion in their private conversations with the Panare. When I first arrived in Colorado, I was bombarded with questions that were clearly the result of these conversations: 'Do you know God?' 'Have you spoken with Jesus?' 'Have you seen him?' 'How tall is he?' 'Where is he now?' Most of all, they were concerned to know about what they called *yuwĕhtamin* (or sometimes *anakïmĕkĕn*), that is, the end of the world. During my time in the field, I was given several versions of how this would occur, horror rather than internal consistency being their common characteristic: the earth would crack, huge fires would rage, waters would come from under the earth and cover everything, jaguars and snakes would roam the world attacking men and eating children.

This belief in *yuwĕhtamin* has widespread currency amongst the Panare and is held even by those who have no direct contact with missions, either Roman Catholic or Evangelical. In fact, it seems that the Panare had a belief in some sort of apocalypse even before the recent welter of missionary activity in their territory. Since the idea of a future apocalypse is rather unusual in indigenous Guianese belief systems, it seems likely that it was introduced to the Panare at some prior stage in their long history of contact with the criollos. But whatever the origin of this idea, it is now being strongly reinforced by the Evangelicals in Colorado who do not merely believe that the world in its present form will end, but that it will end soon. Many Panare are

6. The term *'musiú'* which the Panare use to refer to the missionaries has been adopted from the Spanish. This term is said to be a corruption of the French title 'messieur' and is the popular Venezuelan term for all foreigners.

very worried by this prospect and they often asked me about it. I once encountered a Panare from the community of Macanilla in the Caicara bus station on his way to Cuidad Bolívar in order to ask the Archbishop whether all this talk of an imminent *yuwëhtamin* was true or not. In fact, it seems to be this fear of collective extinction rather than their individual mortality that motivates the Panare of Colorado to contemplate seriously the message of hope and salvation that the Evangelical missionaries have to offer. To the Panare, confronted as they are on a daily basis by the preponderant power of criollo society, the threat of collective extinction must seem just as real a prospect as their own individual deaths.

It is clear that the New Tribes missionaries have won the respect and confidence of the Panare of Colorado, even if they have not yet entirely won their souls. The Panare have responded with great enthusiasm to the missionaries' literacy programme, attending classes diligently and even building thesemves a school house in front of the mission station. This enthusiasm is partly an expression of their desire to master a skill which they know, from their dealings with the criollos, to be very useful in a number of straightforward practical senses, not least in an economic sense. But it is also, and perhaps even primarily, motivated by an interest in finding out about this God of whom the missionaries so frequently speak. Some Panare are more sceptical than others about what the missionaries have to say but I never heard any Panare denounce their message as false. But so far, the Panare have not been called upon to give up anything. For the time being, they have no qualms about saying that they will one day give up the things the missionaries disapprove of, without this serving in any way to dampen their enthusiasm for drinking and dancing now. Whether or not they will be quite so ready to embrace the missionaries' ideas once they are under pressure to abandon what the missionaries consider to be sinful ways of behaving, remains to be seen.

The enthusiasm the Panare of Colorado show the the Evangelical missionaries is in marked contrast to the apparent indifference shown to the Roman Catholics. This difference in attitude cannot be explained by the greater material generosity of the Evangelicals: if anything, it is the Roman Catholics who are more generous in this sense, because whilst they will sometimes give away goods to the Panare, the Evangelicals always insist that the Panare pay for the goods that they receive. Nor can this difference in attitude be explained in terms of the Panare's reaction to the doctrinal differences between the two fronts, since in neither case have the Panare been subject as yet to any thorough indoctrination. Rather the difference in the attitude the Panare display towards the two types of missionary front appears to be best explained in terms of the way in which the two missionary orders fit into the general context of the Panare's relations with local criollo society.

The goal of the Roman Catholic front, in all its various forms, is to make available to the Panare the economic and educational means to handle the problems that further integration with the criollos will inevitably bring. But however well-intentioned this policy may be, it is not one that the Panare themselves find inherently attractive, since they have no desire to become part of the national society. It is not that they have any doctrinaire belief in the importance of maintaining their own customs; indeed, as we have seen, many Panare communities have begun to adopt certain superficial criollo cultural traits. What the Panare do reject, however, is the subordinate role that criollos always seek to impose on them. In the context of economic exchanges, the Panare feel that the criollos are always trying to make dupes of them; in all social exchanges, the criollos are invariably supercilious. The Panare, who recognize virtually no hierarchy in their own society, resent being treated in this way. So whilst there are no material pressures on them to do so, they have no motive to seek to become any more integrated with the criollos than they are already.

From the Panare's perspective, the Roman Catholic missionaries are easily identified with the local criollo population: they attend the local criollos as much as they attend the Panare, speak the same language as the criollos, look much the same, eat the same food, wear the same clothes and, worst of all, tend to be patronizing just as the criollos are. The Panare's attitude to the Roman Catholics is therefore much the same as it is towards the criollo population in general; they are interested enough in enjoying the material benefits that the Roman Catholic missionaries have to offer but they show no enthusiasm for changing their patterns of social behaviour in the ways that the missionaries want. Thus the Panare of Manteco were happy enough to accept the herd of cattle that the Archbishop gave them, but they made very little effort to ensure that the venture was an economic success.

In contrast to the Roman Catholics, the Evangelical missionaries can in no way be identified with the local criollo population. Like the Panare themselves, they are outsiders to criollo society. They look different, speak differently and eat different foods. They also treat the Panare in a different way. They attempt to communicate with the Panare in their own language and as equals. They sell trade goods at prices that undercut those of the criollos. Although their ability to do this is due to the fact that, unlike the local criollos, they do not attempt to make a living out of the sale of trade goods, the Panare take the lower prices of the Evangelicals as confirmatory evidence for their suspicion that the criollos are intent on swindling them. The Panare appreciate the Evangelicals because in all these ways their behaviour contrasts favourably in Panare eyes with that of the criollos. But what the Panare appreciate most of all is the fact that the Evangelicals are quite clearly there to serve the Panare and the Panare alone. Their trade goods and medicines, the literacy classes, the message of salvation—all these bounties are exclusively for the Panare. This special attention confirms the Panare in their belief that they are different from the criollos and worthy of respect. It is as if the Panare were looking to the Evangelicals as allies in their struggle to retain their self-confidence in the face of the all-too-evident and overwhelming power of the criollos. Thus the effect of the Evangelical missionaries' presence has been to reinforce the social boundary between the Panare and the local criollo population.

It should be emphasized however that this is in no way the explicit intention of the missionaries. In order to win favour with those who are responsible for authorizing their visas, they have shown themselves to be very willing to co-operate with any and all government agencies. For example, they recently produced a number of simple Spanish-Panare language primers in order to counter the frequently-voiced public criticism of the New Tribes Mission that it does not attempt to prepare indigenous groups to become part of the national society. But ultimately, the principal aim of the New Tribes missionaries is to save the Panare from Hell-fire, not to ease their integration into the national society. And it is precisely for this reason that the Evangelical missionaries have been welcomed in a way that the Roman Catholic missionaries have not.

The intervention of the other type of 'protectionist' front, government agencies in the affairs of the Panare has been far less intensive than the intervention of the missions. The Panare's welfare is affected indirectly by the activities of innumerable government agencies, but at the time that I was in the field there were only three government bodies that intervened directly in their lives. Of these, the body that has been involved the longest with the Panare is the Malaria Control Division of the Ministry of Health. This body maintains posts throughout the country, even in the most isolated areas. Each post has a small team of functionaries who travel the surrounding countryside dispensing anti-malaria pills and spraying houses with DDT. In isolated areas, they penetrate as far as a mule or an outboard motor canoe will go. Most Panare communities are visited by one of these functionaries every two or three months. The Panare are sceptical about the value of DDT but usually allow the functionary to spray their houses. They dislike taking the pills but most adults will do so when they are given them. One of the problems with giving the Panare malaria pills is that they have to be taken once a week to be effective. Since the Panare have no way of computing a week, and the functionary only comes once every two months at the most, this means they do not take the pills at the correct intervals, if, that is, they take them at all. It would appear therefore that the pills actually do very little to protect the Panare against malaria. Whether the DDT is any more effective, I am not qualified to say.

In addition to the Malaria Control teams, the Ministry of Health also has small units touring the countryside dealing with yellow fever and dermatological problems. These units make occasional visits to the Panare communities that are accessible by road. But apart from these services and those provided by the missionaries, the Panare receive no medical attention. If they are seriously ill, they are obliged to travel to Caicara, just as the rural criollo population is, and wait their turn at the public hospital there. Since the Panare are afraid to allow themselves to be taken into the hospital, they in fact rarely go to it, preferring instead to suffer at home, hoping to be cured by an *i'yan* or by the patent medicines of the local criollos.

The national body responsible for the administration of indigenous affairs, the *Oficina Central de Asuntos Indígenas* (OCAI), only established itself in the Panare area in 1974. In that year, as part of a general expansion of OCAI's activities on a national level, it set up a small office in a private house with two paid employees. When the new office was set up, it was given a brief to realize a number of ambitious projects, including the following: a survey of land titles in the area with a view to identifying lands that were not yet privately owned and which could therefore be granted to the Panare under the terms of the Agrarian Reform Law; the construction of a school near the Hato San Pablo; a small pilot project of economic development in the community of El Pajal designed to encourage the Panare to become cash-croppers; the selection and training of a number of Panare *promotores indígenas*, i.e. individuals who would act as intermediaties between government agencies and their own communities; the construction of a Reception Centre in Caicara where the Panare could stay during visits to the town and where they could be given medical attention.

By the end of my time in the field, by which time the OCAI office in Caicara had been in operation for approximately two years, it had had very little success in achieving any of its objectives. The efforts of the two employees in Caicara were hampered by a number of factors that have dogged the operations of OCAI throughout Venezuela. In this sense, the office in Caicara was no more than a microcosm of OCAI at a national level (see Appendix 4). Firstly, the office in Caicara was chronically short of resources. The two employees simply did not have either the capital or the human resources to put their projects into operation. Salaries and budgets were always late in arriving in Caicara, if they arrived at all. As a result, both the employees of OCAI, as well as the *promotores indígenas* they had contracted, became disillusioned with their jobs. The second major obstacle to OCAI's operations in Panare territory was its lack of coordination with other public and private bodies. The most dramatic example of this lack of coordination was the removal of the communities in the vicinity of the Hato San Pablo to Perro de Agua by the Archbishop of Cuidad Bolívar in May 1976, described above. This intervention was carried out entirely at the Archbishop's own initiative and he neither informed nor consulted the OCAI representatives in Caicara. By the time the latter heard of it, it was already a *fait accompli*. They were annoyed to discover this because the move clearly made their plans for a school and the pilot economic development project, both of which were to be situated in one of the communities close to the Hato San Pablo, entirely obsolete. In the long run, the move to Perro de Agua may well turn out to be beneficial to the Panare but the case nevertheless shows how in Panare territory, as in Venezuelan indigenism generally, the left hand often does not know what the right is doing.

The third and perhaps the most fundamental obstacle that prevented OCAI from having a powerful impact on the problems it confronted was the fact that there is no clear government line on what the ultimate objectives of indigenist policy in Venezuela should be. In the absence of clear directives from above, it is understandable that the local OCAI functionaries should often have had no comprehensive idea of what they were trying to achieve. In the case of the OCAI representatives in Caicara, their ability to have a significant impact on the problems they confronted was further limited by the fact that they had only an outsider's knowledge of the needs and aspirations of the Panare. Although one of them was an anthropologist and the other a native of Caicara, neither had spent more than a few days actually resident in a Panare community. They lived in Caicara and made brief visits to those communities accessible by road or by air from there. Since they spoke no Panare and most Panare speak only the most rudimentary Spanish, they found it very difficult to communicate with them and overcome their suspicions.

It is little wonder that the new OCAI office, confronted with all these obstacles, despite the good intentions of the employees, managed to achieve very little in its first two years of operation. However as my account of the cases of dispute that have occurred over the last few years indicates, the OCAI representatives did play a very important role as mediators between the criollos and the Panare. Indeed, it was indubitably partly due to their intervention that none of these disputes became more serious than they did. But whether OMAFI, the government agency set up to replace OCAI, shortly after I left the field in 1976, will be able to play a more active role than this in the future, will very much depend on whether the problems of Venezuelan indigenism are solved at a national level.

The other government body that directly intervened in the affairs of the Panare when I was in the field was the *Instituto Agrónomo Nacional* (IAN). This body is empowered, under the terms of the Agrarian Reform Law, to give legal titles to settlers on lands that belong to the nation or which have been confiscated from private landowners because they are not used economically. Although the Agrarian Reform Law also recognizes the rights of Indians to the land and other natural resources on which they depend, it provides no machinery for implementing those rights in a way that takes into account the special needs of indigenous populations. Nevertheless, from about 1972 onwards, certain individuals within IAN began to use the machinery of the law as it was devised to meet the needs of criollo peasant communities to endow indigenous communities with land titles.

This group within IAN became involved in the situation of the Panare as a result of representations made to the head office by P. Gonzalo Tosantos, Dra. M.-C. Müller and myself. It was decided to make a start by granting a title to the community of Colorado. At the time, this community was the largest extant Panare community and was a fairly straightforward case because there were no criollos living in the valley at the time. Accordingly, two employees of IAN and myself compiled a census in the valley in June 1976, a necessary preliminary to putting an application before the Directory of IAN, the body that approves the granting of titles. In making the application, the problem arose of how much land to ask for. As I described above, the general tendency over the last few years has been for the Panare to move down from the mountains and establish themselves on the plains. At the time that the census was compiled, all the Panare of Colorado had their principal houses and gardens on the plains. But the community still derived a significant part of its subsistence resources from hunting and collecting in the mountains. Moreover, since there appears to be some danger that the Panare may exhaust the forest resources on the valley floor, they may at some future date be obliged to derive a larger part of their subsistence resources from the mountains than they do now. Under these circumstances, they might return to living in the mountains. Alternatively, rather than return to the mountains, they may decide to take up cattle raising. In this way, they would be able to use the savanna area of the valley floor, which at the present time is little more than useless to them, whilst remaining in close contact with the sources of industrial goods, medicines, etc., that have become so important to them. For all these reasons, it is difficult to predict how much land the Panare of Colorado will need in order to sustain themselves indefinitely, especially since it is impossible with the data presently available to make any accurate prediction of future demographic trends in the valley. Although the population of the valley presently appears to be on the increase, this increase may well be compensated for in the future through emigration from the valley, as the Panare become generally more acculturated (see Chapter 2, p.53).

The reaction of the group within IAN to this problem was entirely pragmatic. It was noted that the valley of Colorado falls within four squares formed by the coordinates on the 1 : 100,000 map of the area. Rather than allow the application to get bogged down by arguments about the future land needs of the Panare, it was decided to make an application on the Panare's behalf for the area enclosed by the four squares, which in point of fact amounted to 14,400 hectares. This application was ratified by the Directory of IAN in July 1976. IAN also agreed to pay for the erection of a fence at the entrance to the valley in order to keep the local criollos' cattle out of the valley.

At the time that I was in the field, there were hopes that it would be possible to extend this policy of granting land titles to other Panare communities. Unfortunately the group within IAN that had been responsible for this policy was subsequently disbanded. Their activities had never had the full approval of the higher echelons of IAN and when the individuals involved found that all their schemes were being blocked higher up in the organization, they resigned.

The general overall effect of the changes that have taken place in the local criollo economy over the last decade has been to increase competition for natural resources in the hinterland of Caicara, particularly for land. So far, it is only in the parts of Panare territory where the cattle pastoralist front operates that the competition between the criollos and the Panare has broken out into open confrontation. But, although these confrontations have been relatively few and very localized, accounts of them circulate as rumour, both amongst the Panare and the criollo population, and in the process become grossly exaggerated. In this form, they serve to encourage an attitude of mutual resentment and hostility, not only between the individuals directly involved in the dispute but between the criollo and Panare populations generally. It is by encouraging this hostility that competition over natural resources has played an important part in maintaining the social boundaries between criollos and Panare, even at a time when they are in more frequent contact than ever before. Under these circumstances of mutual suspicion, the attitude of the criollos toward the Panare begins to turn from paternalism to authoritarianism. Consequently, the Panare, even whilst becoming progressively more integrated economically with the criollos, are discouraged from seeking to integrate themselves socially. And yet, if the social boundaries between the two ethnic groups are hardening, why is it that some Panare communities have begun to adopt criollo customs? One would have thought, perhaps, that the current drift in the attitudes of the criollos would have encouraged the Panare to reject criollo customs rather than to adopt them. This question I shall try to answer in the following and final chapter of the book.

# CHAPTER EIGHT

# Present and Future

Amongst themselves, the Panare will often denounce the criollos as stupid, mean, violent, in short, as generally *tincakeihkye,* but they are only too painfully aware that in addition to being far less numerous, they are much weaker than the criollos in technological and economic resources. There is no doubt that this is one of the reasons why they find it so galling to be treated as inferiors. The tendency of some Panare to adopt criollo styles of dress and housing might be interpreted as an attempt to avoid such treatment by showing that they are capable of behaving in the ways that the criollos themselves do. On a day-to-day basis, the disparity between the power of criollo society and that of their own is brought home most forcibly to the Panare living closest to Caicara. It is not surprising therefore that it is these communities that have undergone the greatest degree of acculturation.

As a result of the development of the hinterland of Caicara, the technological and economic disparity between the two ethnic groups has become much greater in absolute terms over the last decade than it ever was previously. The disparity between them has also increased in a social sense. In the mid-sixties, the criollos with whom the Panare were mostly in contact were pastoralists with small herds, and peasant agriculturalists who were little better off materially than they themselves. Now many of these traditional rural inhabitants have left the countryside and have gone to Caicara, their place being taken by men who live in more substantial houses, equipped with all sorts of technological artefacts that the traditional inhabitants never possessed, who drive lorries and jeeps, and in some cases fly light aircraft. By means of the new roads, these men are in constant contact not only with Caicara, but with Caracas, and the other large urban centres of Venezuela. In contrast, the criollo population who inhabited the hinterland of Caicara prior to 1960 were almost as isolated from the urban centres of the country as the Panare themselves. To the traditional criollo inhabitant, the Panare was a *compadre,* but to the new settler the Panare is, at best, a poor creature who needs to be helped and at worst, a squatter who ought to be moved.

Plate 23.    Some of the earth moving vehicles used by the army engineers to build the new road between Caicara and Puerto Páez.

It is only to be expected that under these circumstances the Panare should become awed by the presence of the criollos and lose confidence in their own traditions. And yet, whilst not discounting the demoralizing effect of the changes that have recently taken place on the criollo fronts of expansion, I now want to propose another explanation for the acculturative trend evident in certain communities. It is an explanation that complements rather than contradicts an explanation of the kind just discussed. However I put it forward as no more than a working hypothesis, since the time that I spent in the most acculturated communities was comparatively brief and I do not therefore have all the data necessary to substantiate it fully.

Briefly stated, the hypothesis I propose is that the acculturation that has taken place in the communities closest to Caicara is the result of changes over the course of the last decade or so, in the form of the trade relations that these communities maintain with the local criollos. There are several steps to the argument underlying this hypothesis: the present system of trade with the criollos undermines the internal economy of the Panare to a degree that trade in earlier periods of contact did not; as I sought to show in Chapter 3, the internal system of economic relations plays a central part in promoting and maintaining the internal solidarity of Panare communities; thus by disrupting the internal  economic system, trade relations can serve to weaken the solidarity of a community; as a result the members of the community lose confidence in their own cultural traditions and become more susceptible to acculturation. In offering this hypothesis, I am in effect putting into practice Ribeiro's theoretical dictum, quoted above at the beginning of Chapter 6, to the effect that in order to understand why an indigenous group adopts an alien cultural trait it is necessary to study 'the economic mechanism whereby this trait is introduced into tribal life and the effect of this mechanism on the social relations within the tribe and on relations between the tribe and the national society'.

Although the Panare have long been dependent on industrially manufactured goods which they can acquire only from the criollos, they have always been reluctant to acquire these goods by means of selling their labour. It is only when the wages offered are particularly good, or when they have no goods to exchange but need some items urgently, that the Panare will work as casual labourers. But cases such as these are exceptions to the general rule. Moreover, even when they do work for the criollos, the Panare will not normally work for more that two or three days in succession. Many local criollos regard the reluctance of the Panare to work for them as an indication of their savagery and congenital laziness. Even those criollos who are favourably disposed towards the Panare are inclined to emphasize the need to 'civilize' them by 'teaching them how to work'. The Panare for their part see it differently. They dislike working for the criollos because they make them work too hard and pay them too little. Criollos of Western Panare territory know better than to try to get the Panare to work for them when they need cheap labour for harvesting. Instead they import Piaroa and Guahibo from settlements to the south-west of Panare territory.

Most of the industrially manufactured goods that the Panare acquire from the criollos they acquire through the sale or exchange of goods of their own manufacture or production. One can identify three material consequences that these trade relations have had for the Panare: it has permitted them to acquire a large number of goods they cannot manufacture themselves; it has encouraged them to change their settlement pattern so as to be closer to the criollo settlements; it has obliged them to dedicate labour to producing a means of exchange for these goods. I shall now consider the social repercussions of each of these consequences separately.

It is not of course material goods themselves that have social repercussions but the way in which they are used that does, and the way in which the Panare of the traditional communities such as Colorado have used these goods is, for the most part, entirely compatible with their traditional system of social relations. In Table 2 I gave a list of the most important of the goods the Panare obtain from the criollos. In Chapter 2, I examined the way in which the goods I classed as 'means of production' have affected Panare subsistence activities. I concluded that although the use of industrially manufactured tools and weapons may have made these activities more efficient from a technical point of view, as far as it is possible to tell, these items have not brought about any major changes in the social relations of production. Much the same can be said for all the other goods in Table 2: in the traditional communities they have simply been accommodated to the traditional system of social relations. No social prestige is attached to ownership of trade goods and they do not therefore serve as a basis for any form of social differentiation. Amongst men, the number and type of trade goods that an individual has varies with age. Adolescent and young men tend to be well supplied with goods for self-adornment as well as with radios, record players, bicycles. They like to pay visits to the criollo settlements to buy soft drinks and bread. Mature adult Panare men in the twenty-five to forty-five age range tend to be those best-equipped with the goods that serve as means of production. Men over the age of forty-five tend to be the poorest of all in trade goods. They are unlikely to have shotguns or new machetes; they never wear beads. But these inequalities in the distribution of trade goods tell one nothing about social status, since if anyone exercises any sort of social or political authority in Panare society it is the men of the most senior age group. The trade goods owned by women are generally fewer than those owned by men and the number and type of women's goods do not vary with age so much. Most women wear large bunches of beads until they are very old, all will have at least two or three aluminium pots or bowls, a knife, possibly a machete, a mosquito net and a piece of cloth to wrap around themselves. But as amongst men, ownership of these goods does not serve as the basis for any form of social differentiation. [1]

Many of the goods that the Panare acquire through trade are indicative of an active interest in criollo customs. But in the traditional communities, an interest in these customs does not entail the abandonment of their own indigenous customs. Many Panare like to listen to the criollo radio stations and to records of *llanero* music but this does not mean that they are no longer interested in making their own music. Many Panare, especially young men, will walk (or ride, if they

1. Although the Panare are by no means unique in not using the trade goods as a basis for social differentiation within their society, this is not always the case amongst tribal groups in contact with industrial societies (see Harner 1968).

have bicycles) a long way to purchase sugar, soft drinks, biscuits and so forth but these items are eaten as 'treats' and do not form an important part of their diet. Indeed the Panare of the traditional communities are reluctant to spend their money on staple foodstuffs. In Colorado, for example, in the rainy season of 1975, when there was a shortage of food, the members of the settlement in which I was living were extremely unwilling to spend any of their cash on food, preferring to go hungry instead. The same is true of their attitude towards criollo alcohol. Although many Panare men like to cadge nips of *aguardiente* when they go on visits to their criollo *compadres*, it is not often that they are prepared to spend money on it themselves.

In a traditional community like Colorado, the value of the trade goods owned by any individual hearth group is often over Bs.500. Some hearth groups in Colorado owned goods worth about Bs.1500. In the more acculturated communities closer to Caicara, although the value of the trade goods that individual hearth groups possess is not necessarily higher, the degree to which they have replaced items of indigenous manufacture is greater: criollo clothes are replacing the loincloth; in some communities the indigenous diet is occasionally supplemented with food that has been bought; *aguardiente* sometimes replaces sugar-cane beer at dances; industrially produced hammocks are used instead of hammocks of domestic manufacture. But the fact that goods bought from the criollos are beginning to replace articles of indigenous manufacture in the communities closest to Caicara is obviously an effect rather than a cause of acculturation. Thus, in order to explain the acculturation taking place in these communities, one must look to the two other consequences of trade relations identified above, namely the tendency to move settlement sites closer to the criollos and the need to dedicate labour to the production of a means of exchange.

In the long term, both consequences can undermine the economic organization of Panare settlement groups by producing conditions of food scarcity. When a community moves down to the plains, it is moving to a locality where natural resources of the type the Panare exploit are less abundant than they are in the mountains. Furthermore, the plains communities are generally larger than those of the mountains, since several independent groups tend to gravitate towards a single criollo settlement or mission station. In effect then, a move down to the plains in order to gain readier access to criollo settlements produces a situation in which there are a larger number of Panare competing for fewer resources.

The need to produce a means of exchange can also produce conditions of scarcity by diverting labour from the production of food for domestic consumption. As I showed in Chapter 3, under the conditions of scarcity produced by seasonal fluctuations in the availability of food, the system of collective consumption within Panare settlements tends to break down, as the members of each hearth group, being barely able to feed themselves, become reluctant to surrender their product to the collective pool. Under these circumstances, hearth groups revert to a number of conventional procedures in order to remove from public view the fact that they are eating. Alternatively, they may leave the settlement site entirely, on a temporary basis, and retire to a small house in the gardens or up in the mountains.

From this decription of the effects of seasonal scarcity one can extrapolate to the effects of scarcity induced by the maintenance of trade relations with the criollos. But first, one must note the essential differences between the two forms of scarcity; whereas seasonal scarcity is by definition transistory, there is no reason why the scarcity induced by trade relations should not be permanent. It is reasonable to suppose that under permanent conditions of scarcity the effects observed during periods of seasonal scarcity would tend to become permanent also. That is, one would expect individual hearth groups to remove themselves entirely from the system of collective consumption. The most obvious way to do this would be for each hearth group to live in its own dwelling where it could consume the food that it had produced without feeling any obligation to share it with other members of the settlement. In this way the social solidarity of Panare communities would be entirely undermined. Their mutual economic interdependence ruptured, their social intimacy reduced, the relationship of the hearth groups within a settlement would become the same as the relationship between the families of a local criollo hamlet: they would become no more than a series of more or less independent economic entities, consuming and producing in isolation, living in spatial proximity to one another for social rather than economic reasons. Under these conditions, one would anticipate that the members of such a group would become less concerned to maintain indigenous cultural traditions and correspondingly more disposed to adopt criollo patterns of dress, housing and economic behaviour.

I now propose to examine the value of this hypothesis by applying it to the data that I have on the history of the Panare's commercial exchanges with the criollos. The goods that have been most important to the Panare as a means of exchange have varied over time and from place to place within Panare territory. Until the mid-sixties, what most Panare communities produced for exchange was sarrapia. Although some communities had already moved down to the plains by this time and produced a small agricultural surplus, this means of exchange was not nearly as important to the Panare as a whole as sarrapia. After the collapse of the sarrapia market in the mid-sixties, the Panare began to produce one or other or both of two types of goods: agricultural produce and decorative basketry. Some of the Panare who produce an agricultural surplus also raise pigs, whilst those who produce decorative baskets also produce a few items of functional basketry such as manioc sieves, presses and cheese moulds for sale to the local pastoralists. The degree to which trade with the criollos has encouraged the Panare to change their settlement pattern or divert their labour from subsistence activities into the production of goods for exchange has varied with the type of exchange goods produced. Thus, if the hypothesis I am putting forward is correct, one would expect the degree of acculturation that has taken place in a community to be dependent on the type of goods that it has produced for exchange.

Since the trade in sarrapia finished long before I reached the field, my information about it is derived exclusively from informants' accounts. From these, it appears that the collection of sarrapia neither provided the Panare with any strong impetus to move their settlements closer to those of the criollos, nor interfered in any significant way with their own subsistence activities. The sarrapia fruit grew in the mountains close to where the Panare had their principal houses at that time, and they never had to go very far to sell the sarrapia they had collected since there were depots set up all over Panare territory, often at the foot of the mountains where they lived. Furthermore, the collection of sarrapia used to take place only during the dry season. As we saw in Chapter 3, it is at this time of year that Panare men have the least amount of work to do on subsistence duties. It is also at this time of the year that the Panare living in the mountains go down to the plains to fish. Thus the sale of sarrapia in the depots on the plains was easily integrated into this traditional subsistence strategy.

After the collapse of the sarrapia trade, the Panare were obliged to look around for some other means of exchange for the industrial goods on which they had become dependent. Even before the sarrapia trade collapsed, many Panare communities had produced functional items of basketry for the local criollos. But from the mid-1960s onwards, encouraged by the missionaries of the Orinoco River Mission in Caicara, a number of Panare communities became far more actively involved in the production of decorative basketry. Although the Panare continue to this day to produce functional basketry, decorative basketry is now far more important to them as a means of exchange. The principal customers for these baskets are no longer the local peasants but people from the urban centres of Venezuela. If these potential customers visit the Panare region during the dry season as tourists, the Panare are able to sell to them directly. But for the most part, Panare baskets only reach their customers *via* criollo inter-mediaries based in Caicara. These intermediaries take the Panare's baskets to Caracas and other cities where they re-sell them to gift-shop owners and the like. Each time the baskets change hands, they increase in price, so that by the time the ultimate customer buys a basket from the gift shop, it costs between two and three times the sum paid by the criollo intermediary from Caicara to the artisan who made it.[2]

The communities most actively involved in the production of com-mercial basketwork are those lying to the south and west of the Chaviripa river. In these communities, it is the principal activity by which a means of exchange is produced. The communities lying to the east of the Chaviripa as far as Caño Amarillo, close to the junction of the Cuchivero and Guaniamo rivers, also produce commercial basketry, but in these communities agricultural produce is at least as important as basketry as a means of exchange. The communities lying to the south of the Guaniamo are not engaged at all in the production of commercial basketry (apart from occasional pieces of functional basketry), the main reason being the isolation of these Panare from their potential customers. In contrast to the parts of Panare territory where the basket trade is important, access to this area by road is difficult, even in the dry season. For this reason, the Panare very rarely go to Caicara where the criollo intermediaries who buy decora-tive baskets are based.

Judging by the situation in Colorado, one of the communities most actively involved in the basket trade, the production of commercial basketry does not seriously interfere with food-producing activities. Although the collection of the raw materials requires a strenuous expedition to the mountains, the preparations of the materials and the actual process of weaving are comparatively leisurely activities, which the Panare perform at times otherwise used only for relaxation. As I showed in Chapter 3, Panare men take one out of every three or four days off from subsistence activities outside the settlement. They do this regardless of whether or not they are actually engaged in produc-ing a batch of commercial baskets. But if they are, a few hours of these rest days are often dedicated to weaving or preparing materials. In Colorado, the production of commercial basketry often seems to be nothing more serious than a pastime. Frequently, a man will return in

2. See Henley and Müller (1978) and Müller and Henley (1978), the latter being a slightly modified and better illustrated Spanish version of the former.

Plate 24. (left). Panare on a visit to a criollo store in the village of Turiba.

Plate 25. (right). A young Panare man negotiates a price for his decorative basketwork with a storekeeper in Caicara.

mid-afternoon from hunting or gardening, and, after bathing and changing into his best loincloth, he will set about casually weaving baskets whilst chatting to the other men in the settlement about the events of the day.

On the other hand, if the members of a community rely on basketry as a means of exchange, they have a clear motive for moving down to the plains. Here they are far more accessible to the criollo traders who deal in baskets or, if they have to go to Caicara themselves to sell their wares, they are much closer to the road. It might be argued, though, that the communities which now make baskets have no more reason to settle on the plains than they did when they were engaged in sarrapia collection. But there is one significant difference between the two forms of producing an exchange article that is relevant here: whereas sarrapia collection was a seasonal activity and the sale of the fruit could be integrated into the dry season pattern of going down to the plains to fish, the manufacture and sale of baskets takes place all year round. Thus the communities that now make baskets have more reason to settle permanently on the plains than they did when they collected sarrapia. Yet against the advantage of settling on the plains close to the road to Caicara, the Panare have to weigh up the disadvantages of separating themselves from the source of raw materials. A community in the *serranía* has the raw material close to hand, whilst the members of plains community have to go on a strenuous day's expedition to get it. In Western Panare territory, where the basket trade is most active, it would be possible for a community to live in the mountains and still be within a day's walk of the roads. Nevertheless, the general tendency amongst these communities, as all over Panare territory, is to leave the mountains and settle on the plains.

The communities most involved in the production of an agricultural surplus for exchange are those located closest to Caicara between the Chaviripa and Cuchivero rivers. The principal crops produced for sale are rice, maize and manioc which is sold in the form of cassava bread. A number of individuals in these communities also keep a few pigs for commercial purposes. The volume of the agricultural surplus produced by these communities is not large: I heard of the case of one man of the community of Santa Fé who had an annual contract with a shopkeeper in Caicara for fifty sacks of maize a year (about 2500 kg). I also came across a number of men who claimed to produce between twenty and thirty sacks of rice or maize a year for sale to the criollos. But generally speaking, the average size of the surplus produced by individual hearth groups is much smaller. Outside the area enclosed by the Cuchivero and the Chaviripa, the volume of the agricultural surplus produced is smaller still. The Panare from the communities to the west of the Chaviripa will occasionally sell a basketful of agricultural produce, but they rely principally on basketry as a means of exchange. The volume produced by the communities to the south of Guaniamo, even though they have very little else to exchange with the criollos, is also small.

A community that relies primarily on agricultural produce as a means of exchange has an even stronger motive for settling on the plains than one that relies on basketry. This is for the simple reason that the ratio of the exchange value to the volume and weight of the product is much lower in the case of agricultural produce than it is in the case of either basketry or sarrapia. All three products have to be taken to the local criollo settlements on the plains to be sold immediately or taken off to Caicara by road. In the last years of the sarrapia trade, a Panare could sell a 25 kg basketful for approximately Bs.100. A bundle of decorative baskets with a similar exchange value would weigh less than a couple of kgs and would be an insignificant load. But at 1976 prices, to earn Bs.100, a Panare would have had to deliver slightly more than 150 kg of rice. A man living in the mountains who wished to sell a sack of rice would have to carry it down to the plains on his back, or, if the slopes were not too steep, on the back of a donkey. Even a Panare would find it difficult to take much more than 50 kg at a time. On the other hand, a man living on the plains can sell his produce to a criollo trader who, in the dry season, will often be able to drive right up to the Panare settlement and load up as many sacks as the Panare has to sell. If the members of a community also raise pigs, as a number of Panare in the communities most involved in cash-cropping do, they have yet another reason for settling on the plains. Pigs cannot be raised in the mountains because they do not find the foods they like up there and they tend to get lost. Thus any man who wants to raise pigs is more or less obliged to live on the plains.

The production of an agricultural surplus also interferes more with traditional subsistence activities than does the collection of sarrapia or the production of commercial basketry. Unlike basketry, cash crops cannot be produced at moments that would be otherwise used simply for relaxation. Unlike sarrapia, which was collected at the time of year when Panare men do not have much work to do, the work required to produce cash crops has to take place precisely at the time when the Panare are very busy preparing the gardens from which they will meet their own food needs.

In short, the production of an agricultural surplus is more likely than the other forms of producing a means of exchange to result in a scarcity of food in the communities engaged in it and hence to provoke a breakdown in the system of collective consumption. This is because, firstly, it puts greater pressure on a community to move to an environment which is less rich in natural resources than the one in which the Panare traditionally lived, and secondly it interferes more directly in the production of food for domestic consumption.

There is yet another way in which cash-cropping is more likely to lead to the breakdown of the system of collective consumption than sarrapia collection or basket weaving. Neither of these latter two activities involves the commercialization of an article that is valuable to the Panare themselves. Although the sarrapia fruit is edible, it plays no part in the Panare diet, whilst baskets of the type that the Panare weave for sale they never use themselves. In contrast, cash-cropping, by giving a commercial value to food, also gives a commercial value to the principal material means of exchange *within* Panare society. Under these circumstances, any hearth group that produces a surplus of food over and above its own immediate needs will be confronted with the possibility of selling it rather than contributing it to the daily food pool of the settlement group. Since the system of collection consumption depends on individual hearth groups pooling the greater part of their daily food product, the system will soon break down if the constituent hearth groups of the settlement start to sell anything they have over and above their own immediate food requirements to the criollos.

If these arguments as to the social repercussions of the various forms of trade relations that the Panare have maintained with criollos are correct, then one would expect to find firstly, that it has only been in the years following the collapse of the sarrapia trade that the Panare have begun to move down to the plains and secondly, that of those that have moved down to the plains, it is the communities most involved in cash-cropping that have undergone the greatest degree of acculturation.

These expectations are only partially fulfilled by the data available. With regard to the first expectation: although the tendency to move down to the plains has become widespread only since the collapse of the sarrapia trade, there were some communities that moved down to the plains even before the collapse of the trade, whilst others continue to live in relative isolation in the mountains even today. With regard to the second expectation: it is indeed the case that the communities *most* involved in cash-cropping are also the most acculturated, but one has still to account for the fact that the groups south of the Guaniamo, who also rely on agricultural produce as an exchange article, have undergone very little acculturation. However since these communities south of the Guaniamo actually produce very little agricultural produce for sale to the criollos, one can save the general hypothesis by modifying it to the effect that it is only when involvement in cash-cropping reaches a certain point that it begins to have a disruptive effect on the internal economy and hence on the social solidarity of a community.

In sum, although the effect of changes in the system of trade relations with the criollos may be part of the answer to the question of why certain communities have begun to adopt criollo customs, this effect does not by itself appear to be sufficient explanation for the phenomenon. Moreover, it is obvious that further empirical evidence is necessary before the general hypothesis can be accepted. Amongst other things, it would be necessary to show empirically, firstly, that the pattern of consumption within the communities involved in cash-cropping is significantly less collective than it is in other Panare communities; and secondly, that this lack of collectivity is due either to the impoverishment of local natural resources on the plains and/or the diversion of labour from domestic subsistence activities into cash-cropping. I believe that it would be a relatively straightforward matter to collect data of this sort, but my own visits to the communities most involved in cash-cropping were never long enough to do so. Although the impression that I gained from these visits and from informants' accounts was indeed that the pattern of consumption in these communities is less collective than in a traditional community such as

Colorado, whether this was due to the conditions of food scarcity induced by cash-cropping I am unable to say.

Nevertheless, although further empirical evidence is needed before this hypothesis can be properly tested, I believe that it fits sufficiently well with the available data to be provisionally accepted as valid. Even so, as it stands, the hypothesis suffers from one notable defect: it does not explain why the various Panare communities differ in the type of goods they produce for exchange. In other words, it does not explain why the communities most involved in cash-cropping do not produce basketry and *vice versa*. If one asks the Panare of the cash-cropping communities why they do not produce baskets they say that it is because basketwork is very hard work. And, as if to emphasize how laborious it is, they enumerate in minute detail all the separate processes involved. But although it is true that the production of these baskets is hard work and requires considerable skill, I am not convinced, having mastered the skill myself, that it is any more hard work than producing cash crops. The exchange value of the labour invested in producing decorative basketwork is about Bs.15 a day. Thus, in two days a basket weaver can earn the same as a Panare producing cash crops earns from selling 50 kg of rice. From my personal experience of harvesting rice in Panare gardens, I consider it very unlikely that it would require *less* than two days' work to produce 50 kg of rice, given the primitive agricultural methods of the Panare. But statistics of this kind are of very limited value in explaining why some communities produce cash crops whilst others produce baskets, because it is quite clear that the Panare themselves do not think in these terms. They have neither the means nor the interest to calculate the exchange value of their labour. The immediate reason for the variation in the type of exchange article produced by the communities lying north of the Guaniamo is not so much economic as attitudinal: in the communities closest to Caicara, basketry is regarded as pure drudgery, whilst in the more isolated communities, although considered to be hard work deserving an adequate reward, basketry is something which people take pride and even pleasure in. And this attitudinal difference appears, in turn, to be a function of the different historical appearances of the various communities concerned.

Although all the communities north of the Guaniamo have been in regular contact with the criollos since at least the beginning of this century, it is those closest to Caicara which have had the social, economic, demographic and technological disparity between themselves and the criollos most forcibly impressed upon them. As I have argued above, these conditions favour the abandonment of traditional customs. I would suggest, then, that the preference that some communities show for cash-cropping can be seen as part of a general acculturative trend: in adopting criollo customs, the members of these communities have adopted not only criollo styles of dress and housing but also criollo patterns of economic behaviour. In the local context of Caicara and its hinterland, the production of basketry is an exclusively Panare activity whilst the production of cash crops is not. Although very few local criollos actually find their main source of livelihood in producing cash crops, it is nevertheless a form of economic activity that is respected by the local criollos. For the criollos, the production of cash crops is 'proper' work and if a Panare is engaged in it, they take it as a sign of how advanced and 'civilized' he is. In contrast, the production of decorative basketry is regarded as a rather quaint activity, ingenious perhaps, but not really 'serious'. It is consistent with the different cultural associations of these two means of producing exchange articles that it should be the Panare of the relatively traditional communities to the south and west of the Chaviripa who continue to practice commercial basketwork, whilst those living closer to Caicara, who have adopted criollo styles of dress and housing, should produce cash crops as a means of exchange.

Another way of putting this argument is to say that cash-cropping is both the cause and effect of acculturation. If the reasoning underlying this argument appears circular, this is because the process of acculturation is itself circular: as the maintenance of trade relations with the criollos gradually erodes the economic bases of a community, its members become more disposed to adopt criollo customs; the more the process of acculturation proceeds, the more the members of the community become disposed to adopt forms of economic behaviour that erode the internal economic order. This path of acculturation is one along which all Panare communities appear to be travelling: the communities closest to Caicara have merely proceeded furthest along it. With time, as the Panare become progressively acculturated, it is to be anticipated that they will eventually become not only more involved in cash-cropping but also in the dominant criollo economic activity in the area, cattle-raising.

There were already signs when I was in the field that the communities that now rely on decorative basketry as a means of exchange will also take up cash-cropping in the not-too-distant future. In 1976, a number of men from the valley of Colorado began selling agricultural produce in Caicara, either directly, or indirectly through a criollo intermediary. Strictly speaking, perhaps, this could not be considered cash-cropping since they were merely selling off what they felt they could spare and had not cut extra-large gardens the previous year with the specific intention of selling a surplus to the criollos.

Nevertheless, the experience opened the eyes of the Colorado Panare to the economic potential of selling agricultural produce. Whether this experience will turn out to be the beginning of a trend towards the partial or total replacement of basketry as a means of exchange will depend on a number of related factors: if the preference for cash-crops over basketry is a function of the degree of acculturation through which a community has passed, then the future importance of cash-cropping in the communities that presently produce commercial basketry will depend on how ready the Panare of these communities will be to adopt criollo customs in the forthcoming years. This in turn will depend on the economic effects of their present tendency to settle on the plains and the social and cultural effects of their relations with local criollos and missionaries.

Judging by the experience of the Panare's neighbours to the east, the Ye'kuana, the production of decorative basketry and other indigenous artefacts corresponds only to a certain stage in the acculturation and economic intregration of an indigenous group. Many Ye'kuana communities which once produced large numbers of such artefacts have now turned to cash-cropping and cattle-raising instead.[3] It is to be anticipated that the same will occur with the Panare communities that are still now actively engaged in the production of decorative baskets. This process is only likely to be interrupted if the production of commercial basketry becomes manifestly more profitable and reliable than other forms of producing a cash income with which to buy industrial goods. This is clearly not the case at the moment, and many of the artisans who produce baskets are beginning to become disillusioned with basketwork as a means of exchange. This trend is likely to be arrested only if one of the government agencies responsible for the administration of indigenous affairs intervenes in the basketry trade so as to cut out the criollo intermediaries and thereby ensure that the artisans receive a greater proportion of the sum paid for their work by the urban customers than they do under present circumstances.

The history of the Panare's relations with the criollos contradicts a number of commonly held assumptions about the effect of contact on indigenous groups. Contrary to the assumption that indigenous groups are doomed to disappear at the first brush with a national society, the Panare as a whole have retained a way of life that is socially and culturally quite distinct and independent from that of the

3. W. Coppens, personal communication. See also Arvelo-Jiménez 1971 : 39, and Hames and Hames 1976 : 32ff.

local criollos, despite regular contact with the latter since at least the beginning of the present century. This they have been able to do by virtue of a certain concatenation of historical circumstances: the members of the local fronts of national expansion have not sought to deprive the Panare of the material bases of their social existence, nor have they offered the Panare a way of life that would appear any more attractive to them than the one they have already.

In the Introduction, I suggested that the cultural resilience of the Panare in the face of contact marks them out as an exception to the general rule in lowland South America. Whilst this is undoubtedly true, they are by no means unique in having survived as a distinguishable ethnic group despite a long period of contact. This point is very forcibly argued by Ribeiro in the Introduction to *Os índios . . .* Here, he claims that the results of his study of relations between the indigenous groups of Brazil and the national society defy all conventional views:

> According to the almost unanimous view of the Brazilian historians and even of the anthropologists who have studied the problem, the confrontation [between the national society and tribal groups] leads to the disappearance of the tribal groups through absorption into the national society . . . Our study turned out to show exactly the opposite with regard to the period under consideration, the twentieth century. In fact none of the indigenous groups about whom we obtained reliable information were assimilated into the national society as indistinguishable parts of it. Contrary to this expectation, the majority of the indigenous tribes were exterminated and those that survived, remained Indian: no longer in their habits and customs, but in their self-identification as peoples different from the Brazilians and as victims of their domination (Ribeiro 1970 : 8)

In my view, Ribeiro overstates his case in this passage, since I believe that close examination of the period of Brazilian history that he is dealing with would reveal many examples of indigenous groups that, once deprived of the material infrastructure of their social life, broke up and were assimilated into the national society.[4] On the other hand, his study does show very convincingly that if an indigenous group does manage to retain its material bases, it can continue to survive as a group whose members preserve some sense of an independent ethnic identity, despite literally centuries of regular contact with the national society and the loss of most of its distinctively indigenous cultural traits. In *Os índios . . .* he reports a number of case histories

4. See Henley 1978 : 101 – 5, for a more detailed criticism of Ribeiro's contention that assimilation has never occurred in twentieth-century Brazil.

that give the lie, not merely to the assumption that indigenous groups are destined to disintegrate at the first touch of modern industrial society, but also to the assumption that acculturation and assimilation are concurrent and identical processes.[5]

The present situation of the Panare contradicts this latter assumption also. Even though some Panare communities are now beginning to adopt criollo customs, there is no evidence to suggest that they are on the point of being assimilated as an indistinguishable part of the national society. Even though the last decade has seen an increase in the degree to which they are economically integrated with the criollos, this process has not been accompanied by a similar increase in the degree to which they are socially integrated.

There is no doubt that criollo society has many immediate attractions for the Panare, particularly for young adult men, who like to sample the criollo way of life in Caicara: to eat criollo food, to drink criollo alcohol, to visit the cinema or simply sit in the main street watching the criollo world go by. Many cherish the ambition to visit Caracas and the other large cities of Venezuela they have heard of. But as a long-term prospect, living amongst the criollos offers the individual Panare little or no advantage over living in his own community. The economic role that criollo society has to offer the Panare is that of the lowliest casual labourer, a role that few are prepared to accept. If a Panare accepts this economic role on a temporary basis, he is obliged to confront the barrier of criollo ethnocentrism. Even today, there are very few Panare who speak Spanish. Consequently, when a Panare interacts with the criollos, even though he may be dressed in smart criollo clothes, he is immediately marked out by his speech, not to mention his physical type. As a result, wherever he goes in local criollo society, a Panare has to suffer the indignity of being treated as an inferior.

From a sociological point of view, perhaps the most telling consequence of the ethnocentrism of the criollos is the barrier it sets up to marriage between members of the two ethnic groups. Criollo women find the idea of marrying a Panare little more than incredible, whilst

5. Of course, Ribeiro is not the only author to make this point. Much of the work carried out in recent years on ethnic groups and their boundary-maintaining mechanisms points to the same conclusion. As Fredrik Barth, who, arguably, might be considered the *maître d'école* of this type of study has observed, 'Culture contact and change . . . is a very widespread process under present conditions as dependence on the products and institutions of industrial societies spreads in all parts of the world. The important thing to recognize is that a drastic reduction of cultural differences between ethnic groups does not correlate in any simple way with a reduction in the organizational relevance of ethnic identities, or a breakdown in boundary-maintaining processes.' (Barth 1969 : 32 – 3).

criollo men, although always ready to boast of their 'conquests' amongst the Panare women, generally claim that they would never marry a Panare woman because they are 'dirty' and 'do not know how to cook properly'. The Panare, for their part, show very little interest in seeking a criollo spouse. As I demonstrated in Chapter 4, the Panare are highly endogamous, both genealogically and geographically. Given that even within Panare society marriages between distantly related individuals are extremely rare, for an individual to marry a criollo would represent a most radical departure from Panare custom.[6] Instead of becoming more common, as one might expect in view of the incipient acculturation of the Panare, mixed marriages between members of the two ethnic groups actually appear to have become less frequent in recent years. Although there is no doubt that there were a number of cases in earlier periods of contact, I came across no evidence of any extant marriage or even of a recent temporary sexual union between Panare and criollo.

By discouraging individual Panare from seeking to assimilate themselves, the prejudices of the criollos play an important part in maintaining the social boundary between the two groups. But it is a boundary that few Panare seek to cross anyway. Accustomed to the highly egalitarian organization of their own society, the Panare reject the subordinate social role that the criollos seek to impose on them. Accustomed to the varied and intermittent work pattern of their own subsistence activities, they reject the economic role offered to them as unskilled casual labourers working at the most monotonous tasks. Brought up to believe that any form of violence is the height of immoral behaviour, the Panare find local criollo society, in which interpersonal violence is common and gun-toting soldiers, National Guardsmen and policemen are to be seen everywhere, truly disturbing. In effect then, the boundary between the Panare and the criollo population is maintained both from within and from without: from within by the Panare, who disdain the criollos because their social behaviour runs counter to the values they cherish; from without by the domineering attitude of the criollos who, used to living in a

6. Stephen Hugh-Jones (personal communication, 1979) reports that miscegenation between criollo and indigenous people in the Vaupés region of the north-west Amazon is comparatively common. One of the reasons why the Vaupés is different from the Panare area in this regard may be that the marriage rules of the indigenous population require an individual to marry someone from a different language group. Thus marriage with a criollo does not represent such a radical departure from their own traditions as it would for the Panare. It could perhaps be an interesting comparative project to investigate whether the degree of endogamy that is typical of an indigenous marriage system can in any way be correlated with the incidence of miscegenation between the members of that group and the local non-Indian population.

hierarchical society, cannot understand why the Panare will not accept the subordinate role that criollo society seeks to thrust upon them. The boundary-maintaining effect of these attitudes is now being reinforced by the sentiments of mutual hostility and resentment that have sprung up due to increasing competition for natural resources.

Yet even though there may be no evidence to suggest that the Panare are about to become assimilated as an indistinguishable part of the national society, they will only survive as a group capable of providing its members with the essential social and economic requisites of life if the material bases of their society are secured. In simple physical terms, the capacity of the Panare to resist the criollo frontier is minimal. The 1971 census showed that at that time there were already more than five times the number of the criollos living in the rural hinterland of Caicara than there were Panare. Since that census was compiled the demographic disparity between the two groups has become even greater. The disparity in technological and economic resources also increases with each passing year.

In terms of social organization also, the Panare are ill-equipped to resist the expansion of criollo society. Their economic organization is vulnerable to disruption by the trade relations they maintain with the criollos and to the impoverishment of local natural resources, not only by the criollos, but also by themselves, as, largely of their own volition, they become more sedentary. At the same time, the autonomy that Panare society affords the elements of which it is composed is antithetical to any form of politically organized resistance. Even within the domain of internal social relations, the solidarity of the Panare over and above the level of the settlement group is at best tenuous. Although they have shown themselves disposed to unite in opposition to the criollos when confronted by the threat of invasion, they lack the political traditions of chiefship and men's councils which have played such an important role in the resistance that their neigh-bours, the Ye'kuana, and further afield, the Shavánte of Central Brazil, have offered to the incursions of their respective national societies. In short, if the Panare's control over the natural resources on which their social life depends is to be secured, it will be primarily by virtue of the protection they are afforded by agencies of the govern-ment (or possibly by missionary organizations), rather than by virtue of the political or physical resistance that they themselves are capable of offering to the criollo fronts of expansion.

In this regard, the Panare are fortunate to have reached their present stage of integration with the national society at a time when, in principle at least, the rights of indigenous groups over the lands and other natural resources on which they depend are recognized by

Venezuelan law. At earlier periods of Venezuelan history, they would simply have been dispossessed. Yet the gap between the principles of Venezuelan indigenist legislation and their practical implementation remains wide, and it is difficult to predict the future effect of government intervention on indigenous affairs in general or on the affairs of the Panare in particular.

In the near future, however, the Panare are likely to be involved in what may become a test case of the government's policy towards indigenous groups. An estimated 500 million tons of high grade bauxite has been discovered in the *serranía* overlooking the criollo hamlet of Los Pijiguaos, in the southwestern corner of Panare territory (see Map 4). The *Corporación Venezolana de Guayana* (CVG), the government agency now responsible for the economic development of the whole of the country lying to the south of the Orinoco, has begun to put into effect plans to exploit these reserves commercially. According to the report of the feasibility study carried out by Swiss Aluminium Ltd, the mining area will be located roughly midway between the points where, in 1976, the Panare settlements of Rincón and Mata Brava stood. A processing plant, warehouses and residential buildings for the mineworkers will be built almost exactly on the spot where the Rincón group lived. The report makes no mention of the Panare, confining itself to the observation that 'in the vicinity of the bauxite plant there are only two little "pueblos" with less than 500 inhabitants, Los Pijiguaos and Turiba' (CVG 1978 : 36). This could mean that the Panare had already moved away by the time the feasibility study was carried out, or, alternatively, that their presence was simply overlooked. From Rincón, the ore will be transported by road to one of three possible port sites on the banks of the Orinoco, loaded on to barges and sent off downstream to Cuidad Guayana, where it will be further processed in a new aluminium plant presently under construction. The commercial value of the Los Pijiguaos reserves, even in their unelaborated form, is estimated at Bs.45,000 million (roughly £4,500 million at 1980 exchange rates) and CVG hopes that they will become the cornerstone of a totally self-sufficient Venezuelan aluminium industry, producing a million tons a year by the end of the century. Some of the mining infrastructure is already in place and it is anticipated that the mines will eventually come 'on-stream' in 1982. (CVG n.d. : 5 – 6, 104 – 7; CVG 1978).

This project is bound to have the most serious repercussions for the Panare, both directly, as it displaces those living in the immediate vicinity of the mine, and indirectly, as it gives rise to further colonization of the region by criollos. Clearly, the great economic importance that the Los Pijiguaos mines could have for the Venezuelan nation as

Plate 26. The settlement at Rincón in April 1976. According to the feasibility plans, the processing plant for the Los Pijiguaos bauxite mine will lie very close to this site. Already by the middle of 1978 the Panare had abandoned this settlement due to the increasing presence of criollos in the immediate vicinity.

a whole means that they cannot simply be abandoned, nor is there any realistic likelihood that they will be. On the other hand, it is clearly wrong that the Panare, who are unlikely to benefit from the mines except in the most minor and indirect way, should pay for them by being deprived of their means of livelihood: the land on which they live, the forest where they hunt and make their gardens, the rivers where they fish—all in theory guaranteed to them under the terms of the Agrarian Reform Law of 1960. The only way in which the interests of the Venezuelan nation could be reconciled with those of the Panare would be for the Panare's rights to be recognized to an area of land sufficient to support themselves and their descendants. Until Venezuelan society has more to offer the Panare than a miserable existence amidst the ranks of the rural poor, one can only hope that the efforts of the CVG and the other government agencies will be directed, not towards the assimilation of the Panare, but rather towards consolidating the material bases of their social and economic self-sufficiency. The legal recognition of their land rights would be the first and most fundamental step in this direction.

# APPENDIX 1: The transcription of non-English words

Generally speaking, all non-English words used in this manuscript are in italics. The only exceptions are words which are used very frequently in the text and/or which have no ready English equivalents (e.g. Llanos, criollo, sarrapia, curare, onoto, etc.). The non-English words used include Spanish, Panare and Latin words. When there is the possibility of confusion as to the linguistic origin of a word, this origin is indicated by the upper case letters S., P. or L.

Panare words are transcribed according to the system of notation given below. This system represents no more than a preliminary attempt to establish a list of the phonemes of the Panare language and further linguistic investigation is likely to lead to the modification of the list. Although I am indebted to Dr M -C. Müller for advising me on the preparation of this list, any errors in the list or in the transcription of Panare words in the text are entirely my responsibility. The method used to describe the articulation of the items in the list is taken from Gleason (1969 : 239 *et seq.*).

*Consonants*

p  =voiceless bilabial simple stop as in the English word '*p*ot'
t  =voiceless alveolar simple stop as in the English word '*t*ot'
k  = voiceless velar simple stop as in the English word '*c*ot'
c  =voiceless alveopalatal affricated stop as in the English word '*ch*op', which in certain contexts becomes a groove fricative, as in the English word '*sh*op'
g  =voiceless alveolar groove fricative, as in the English word '*s*it', which in certain contexts becomes an affricate alveolar stop as in the English word 'ha*ts*'
r  =voiced alveolar resonant that varies between a Spanish 'r' and a retroflected English 'd'
m =voiced bilabial nasal resonant, as in the English word '*m*ight'
n  =voiced alveolar nasal resonant, as in the English word '*n*ight'
h  =voiceless glottal slit fricative, as in the English word '*h*it'
'  =glottal stop. No English or Spanish equivalent.

*Semi-Vowels*

w =voiced bilabial median resonant, as in the English word '*w*et'
y  =voiced alveopalatel median resonant, as in the English word '*y*et'

*Vowels*

i  =unrounded high front vowel, as in the English word 'm*ee*t'
ë  =unrounded mid central vowel, as in the English word 'h*ur*t'
e  =unrounded mid back vowel, as in the English word 'p*e*t'
a  =unrounded low central vowel, as in the English word 'h*a*rt'
ï  =unrounded high back vowel. No English or Spanish equivalent
u  =rounded high back vowel as in the English word 'h*oo*t'
o  =rounded mid back vowel, as in the English word 'h*o*t'

In addition to these simple vowels, a number of dipthongs also occur in the Panare language.

APPENDIX 2: The organization of demographic data

The estimates of the population of Panare communities presented in Table 1 are classified into five 'levels of confidence'. These levels of confidence were defined as follows:

(A) estimates based on complete genealogies collected in communities whose members were all, or almost all, known to me personally. To the best of my knowledge, therefore, these estimates are entirely accurate.

(B) estimates based either on genealogies I collected myself but involving certain individuals who were not known to me personally, or on genealogies collected by individuals who although not anthropologists by training were sufficiently familiar with Panare culture to be able to do so. The genealogies on which these estimates are based rely to a large degree on the accuracy of the Panare informants who provided the data. But in collecting genealogies from the Panare, I found that they sometimes omitted to mention some members of their community, particularly if they were very young. Furthermore, the Panare have limited patience for retailing genealogical information, and informants would often break off or truncate discussions about genealogical matters. By cross-checking genealogies, it has been possible to identify and eliminate some of these lacunae, but probably by no means all. The estimates based on genealogies I collected myself have therefore been rounded up to the nearest unit of five. The estimates marked (3) in the penultimate column of the Table are based on a combination of the genealogical material I collected myself with material collected by Padre Gonzalo Tosantos, who during the period of my fieldwork was more or less permanently resident in the community of Portachuelo. The estimate in the Table marked (2), is taken from a publication by Cauty (1974 : 5 – 7). This author provides a genealogical chart of the community in question. However there is some discrepancy between the chart and the accompanying text. The largest figure given is the one recorded in the Table. Estimates at this level of confidence will be assumed to involve a margin of error of up to 10 per cent.

(C) estimates based on partial genealogies, combined with indirect indices of population size such as the number and dimensions of houses in a permanent settlement, the number of hearths and hammocks, etc. These estimates probably involve a margin of error of up to 15 per cent.

(D) the estimates marked (1) in the penultimate column of the Table were given by Dr W. Coppens of the Fundación La Salle, who visited these communities at various points during the period 1972 to 1976. Dr Coppens emphasizes that these are only rough estimates. It will be assumed that they involve a margin of error of at least 20 per cent.

(E) estimates given by Panare informants or local criollos. When it comes to exact figures, neither of these sources are reliable. An attempt was made to control the figures they gave by asking the size of communities relative to communities whose population were known more exactly, and by cross-checking from genealogies collected in other communities. Even so these figures must be regarded as no more than approximate, involving a margin of error of at least 25 per cent.

Figure 1 (p.21) shows the age structure of the Colorado Panare population. The ages of the individuals in this sample were established principally on the basis of external morphological characteristics. This impressionistic procedure was then checked against a number of indirect indices of age in the Panare population in general:

(1). The offspring of presently reproductive women tend to be spaced by a minimum of two years. This feature, morphological criteria, and in some cases the individuals' own testimony, were used to rank known full siblings by relative age.

(2) Panare women tend to marry shortly after they reach puberty, at approximately fifteen years of age, while men tend to marry somewhat later, at about twenty. Thus a woman with married daughters is unlikely to be less than thirty years old and a woman with married sons is unlikely to be less than thirty-five years old.

(3) Panare children are not given names until they are about two years old. Their first name is a child name. In the case of males, this name is replaced by an adult name not long after their initiation, which usually takes place when they are between ten and twelve years old. In the case of females, adult names are adopted more or less simultaneously with the onset of puberty.

# APPENDIX 3: Panare kinship terms

It is conventional in the anthropological literature for kinship terms to be glossed by means of a list of genealogical specifications, for example: father = F, FB, FFBS, or mother = M, MZ, MMZD, and so on. However I suspect that, in practice, very few anthropologists' informants have ever glossed kinship terms in this way. Rather I imagine that the great majority have explained the meaning of kinship terms in the manner described long ago by Rivers (1906 : 491): the anthropologist identifies a particular relative and the informant explains that he calls him 'x' because his father, mother or some other close relative calls him 'y'. Certainly this is the method that the Panare use. For example, a male speaker will explain that he calls his FB 'yim' because F calls him his 'yako'. It is this method that I have attempted to reproduce in the following list. To my mind, this method has two advantages over the conventional one: firstly, it brings out more clearly the principles underlying the system of kinship terms; secondly, it does not give the impression that the terms in the list correspond to a finite number of genealogical specifications.

NB: the terms given here are those used in Western Panare territory. A list of the terms used in other parts of Panare territory would be somewhat different. All the terms in the list are ascriptive reference terms (see pp. 89-92).

Key: m.s. = male speaker; f.s. = female speaker.

| | |
|---|---|
| *yako* | = same-sex sibling; same-sex offspring of anyone whom either or both of Ego's parents call *yako* |
| *nyasu* | = (m.s.) sister; female offspring of anyone whom either or both of Ego's parents call *yako* |
| *ipin* | = (f.s.) brother; male offspring of anyone whom either or both of Ego's parents call *yako* |
| *yim* | = father; anyone whom Ego's father calls *yako*. |
| *sanë* | = mother; anyone whom Ego's mother calls *yako* |
| *nëwan* | = (m.s.) son; son of a *yako* |
| *yinsin* | = (m.s.) daughter; daughter of a *yako* |
| *-nkin* | = child; (f.s.) own children and those of a *yako* |

| | |
|---|---|
| *yawon* | = anyone who is *pamo* or *tamun* to someone whom Ego calls *yim*; or, anyone who is *ipin* to someone whom Ego calls *sanë*; (f.s.) son of anyone whom Ego herself calls *ipin*; (m.s. & f.s.) spouse's father |
| *wa'nyene* | = anyone who is *nyasu* to someone whom Ego calls *yim*; (m.s.) daughter of a *nyasu*; (f.s.) daughter of an *ipin*; (m.s. & f.s.) spouse's mother |
| *pamo* | = (m.s.) son of a *yawon* |
| *pamëyim* | = (m.s.) son of a *nyasu* |
| *tamun* | = (m.s.) husband of a *nyasu*; anyone whom a *sanë* calls *yim*; (f.s.) husband |
| *wacon* | = mother's mother |
| *nahpën* | = father's father |
| *no'* | = father's mother |
| *pi"* | = (m.s.) daughter of a *wa'nyene* (unless the latter is married to a close *nëwan*); daughter of anyone whom Ego calls *yinsin*; potential spouse; wife |
| *namca* | = infant; (f.s.) all relatives in G − 2 |
| *piyaka* | = all close kin except (m.s.) those called *tamun* or *no', pamo* or *pi"* and (f.s.) those called *tamun* and their sisters, when the latter are the same age as Ego |
| *tunkonan* | = anyone who is not *piyaka* |

(This appendix is intended merely to provide necessary background
information for the discussion of the activities of government agencies
amongst the Panare in Chapter 7 of this book. It does not purport to
be comprehensive, nor the product of a detailed study of Venezuelan
indigenism. It is based largely on the following sources, from which
further details and bibliographic references should be sought: Arvelo-
Jimenez 1972a, 1980a, 1980b; Arvelo-Jimenez et al. 1977; Coppens
1971; Heinen 1975; Romero Ocando 1975; Scorza Reggio 1975;
Serbín & Gonzalez Ñañez 1980.)

During the colonial era, the aboriginal population, although often
exploited ruthlessly by means of the *encomienda* system and the various
labour-controlling legal instruments that followed it, nevertheless
enjoyed a certain degree of legal protection from the Spanish Crown.
Following Independence, however, the special legal status of the
indigenous population was abolished and a series of laws,
promulgated at various points between 1821 and 1936, eliminated
nearly all the *resguardos*, the communally-held indigenous lands
recognized by the colonial regime. The existence of *resguardos* was said
to be incompatible with the Indians' new status as full citizens of the
Republic. The laws abolishing them provided for indigenous lands to
be divided up amongst all the families of a *resguardo*, each of whom
would be given legal title to their particular plot. In actual practice,
however, very few indigenous families ever received legal titles, and
the vast majority of the lands occupied by indigenous populations
became legally classified as *tierras baldías*, uncultivated no-man's-
lands, available to be taken over by any individual, indigenous or
criollo, who had the means to do so. Clearly, this situation favoured
the most powerful elements in the national society, and large tracts of
indigenous lands passed into private hands.

Despite the fact that the indigenous population did not receive
protection from the State during the first hundred years of the
Republic, a large number of indigenous groups were still in existence
at the turn of the present century, particularly in the more isolated
areas of the country. In fact, following the collapse of the Spanish
Empire and the expulsion of the missionary orders identified with the
Spanish, the wave of colonization in the interior of the country was at
a very low ebb. Certain areas that had once been the scene of a

complex of missions, garrisons and plantations or ranches had become socio-economic backwaters of the national society, returning to their former condition as primarily indigenous areas. It was in order to rectify this situation that the dictator Juan Vicente Gomez, who ruled Venezuela from 1908 to 1935, promulgated the *Ley de Misiones* in 1915.

The first article of this law postulates the creation of 'as many missions as are necessary . . . to reduce and attract to civilized life' the indigenous groups that 'still' existed in various parts of the Republic, and at the same time to bring about 'the systematic colonization' of these areas. The rules for the implementation of this law appeared in 1921, and three subsequent conventions, signed in 1922, 1937 and 1944, gave the missions wide-ranging powers over the indigenous inhabitants of the regions where they operated. The missions were organized into four Apostolic Vicariates, which assumed all the normal functions of government in the regions they controlled.

Although they were, in theory, answerable to the federal government, the Vicariates exercised almost total legal control over the indigenous populations of their respective areas. But their practical political control of these areas was far from total: throughout this period, the indigenous groups of the Territorio Federal de Amazonas (TFA) were subject to invasions by groups of criollos led by local *caudillos* who captured Indians and took them off to criollo villages, where they were made to work virtually as slaves.

The first crack in the Catholic Church's control of indigenous areas was signalled by the establishment of a Protestant Evangelical mission in the TFA in 1946. Shortly afterwards, in 1947, another crack appeared with the creation of the Comisión Indigenista (CI). This body was created in response to the Pátzcuaro convention, signed in 1946 by the Interamerican Indigenist Institute, of which Venezuela was a member. Up until the creation of the CI, national indigenist policy had consisted of nothing more than providing financial resources for the missions. The creation of the CI appeared to testify to a concern on the part of the government to take a more active role in indigenous affairs: of the ten members of the Comisión, only one was a representative of the Catholic missions, the other nine being representatives of the various government ministries that held some sort of responsibility for the administration of the areas in which indigenous groups were to be found. In the initial phase of its operations, however, the CI acted mainly as an investigative body, promoting scientific studies that could 'serve as a basis for the practical solution of the economic and social problems of the Indiands'. Otherwise the CI's main function was to act as a consultative body to the Ministry of

Internal Affairs. But although it was supposedly independent of the missions, the CI was legally constrained by the prior contracts between the State and the missionaries and it failed to develop a new indigenist policy. In effect, Venezuelan indigenism continued to be dominated by the Roman Catholic Church.

Evidence of a more active concern on the part of the government to intervene directly in indigenous affairs was the creation in 1952, of the *Oficina Central de Asuntos Indígenas* (OCAI). At about the same time, the CI passed from being a consultant to the Ministry of Internal Affairs to being responsible to the Ministry of Justice. OCAI was conceived as the technical arm of the CI and it was charged with the practical implementation of policy decisions made by the latter. But OCAI's operations were subservient to the missions, just as the CI's policy was, and a large part of OCAI's budget was simply handed over to them. For most of the decade of the 1950s, Venezuela was ruled by the dictator Pérez Jiménez, and it was not the time for initiatives in indigenist administration (or any other sphere of government) that would upset the political *status quo*.

It was only in 1959 that the State, following the overthrow of Pérez Jiménez, promulgated Decree Law No.20, which, more by implication than direct statement, empowered the CI to formulate an independent indigenist policy. At the same time, OCAI began to extend its range of practical control inside indigenous areas by establishing five regional centres. But after an energetic start, the efforts of OCAI were curtailed by budgetary cuts. Moreover, its operations were hampered by a lack of trained personnel and by the fact that although Decree Law No.20 had suggested the need for an independent indigenist policy, it laid down no clear principles as to what this policy should be. Consequently, the employees of OCAI working in the new centres had very little idea of what they were supposed to be trying to achieve.

It was also shortly after the fall of Pérez Jiménez that the newly-formed *Acción Democrática* (AD) government passed the Agrarian Reform Law. This law represented a major landmark in Venezuelan indigenist legislation (as well as, of course, in Venezuelan law generally), because it represented the first time since the colonial era that the rights of the indigenous population to land and other natural resources had been recognized. The most important clause from the point of view of indigenism was Article 2(d):

> This Act guarantees and recognizes the right of indigenous populations which *de facto* retain their communal or extended family status—without prejudice to the privileges to which they are entitled as Venezuelans, according to previous paragraphs—to hold

the lands, woods and waterways which they occupy or which belong to them in those sites where they customarily dwell, without detriment to their incorporation to the national society according to this and other laws.

But even though this law represented an important advance, it was deficient as a legal instrument insofar as the indigenous population was concerned in two critical respects. Firstly, the law was designed primarily for the peasant population and contained no provisions by which it could be accommodated to the specific needs of indigenous groups on such important matters as patterns of land use, forms of organizing production, concepts of property ownership, etc. Secondly, the legal status of the indigenous population remained unclear. On the one hand, the law recognized that certain special rights should accrue to the Indians *qua* Indians; on the other hand, it declared that these rights should not stand in the way of their rights as full citizens nor prevent their incorporation into national life. In this latter respect, Article 2(d) is clearly formulated in such a way as to avoid a recurrence of the colonial situation in which the indigenous population were provided with a certain degree of legal protection but only at the expense of being deprived of certain other rights. Yet neither this, nor any other clause of the law lays down guidelines for official indigenist policy in situations where the rights of the indigenous population *qua* Indians conflict with their rights, or duties, as full citizens — as they are inevitably bound to do.

Although the attempt made by the State to wrest control over the indigenous population from the missions led to a cooling of relations in the early 1960s, the climate improved with the signing of a convention between the Holy See and Venezuela in 1964, by which the latter undertook to 'provide special support and protection' to the Catholic missions. A subsequent convention, signed in 1967 imposed certain restrictions on the powers accorded to missionaries by the *Ley de Misiones* which, despite the Decree Law No.20, remained in force and, moreover, continues to do so to this day. However, these conventions merely served to exacerbate the general confusion as to the legal powers of the missions within the Apostolic Vicariates. At the same time, other religious groups, both Catholic and Protestant, had begun to operate freely in other areas, under a number of different and independent agreements. This confused legal situation persists.

The confusions inherent in the legal instruments regulating Venezuelan indigenist activities are mirrored by the state of affairs on the ground in indigenous areas, where, despite, or perhaps because of, all the laws and decrees that have been passed in the last twenty years,

OCAI's impact on indigenous affairs has remained slight and far less significant than the impact of the missions.

The late 1960s saw the beginning of a new phase in Venezuelan indigenism when a number of other government bodies, some newly-created and others long-established, became directly involved in indigenous affairs. The involvement of these agencies was symptomatic of a new interest in the Amazonian hinterland of the country as, firstly, a source of raw materials and/or hydroelectric power and, secondly, a security risk which could only be effectively countered by the establishment of frontier garrisons and by programmes of colonization and economic development.

One of the most important of these agencies was the *Comisión para el Desarrollo del Sur* (CODESUR), a development agency attached to the Ministry of Public Works that was set up by the newly-formed Christian Democrat government (COPEI) in 1969. CODESUR was put in control of the economic development of the so-called 'Región Sur', i.e. the TFA and the Distrito Cedeño of Bolivar State. Since an estimated 40 per cent of the population of this area are Indians, it was clear that CODESUR would soon become involved in indigenous affairs. Indeed, the goals of CODESUR as outlined in the Fourth National Plan (1970–4) included the 'awakening' of a sense of Venezuelan nationality amongst the inhabitants of the area and the 'progressive elevation' of the socio-cultural and economic level of the population by means of educational programmes and economic development schemes. As far as the indigenous population was concerned, the sociocultural changes envisaged by CODESUR would be achieved with the collaboration of *promotores indígenas,* members of the indigenous communities themselves, in practice usually young, bilingual men, who would act as intermediaries between government 'experts' and the other members of their communities. Their efforts would be backed up by radio broadcasts from a station in San Juan de Manapiare, in a number of indigenous languages, on 'educational' themes, including agriculture and animal husbandry, health and hygiene, history and geography of Venezuela, and civic education.

Another government body to become more directly involved in indigenous affairs than it had been before was the *Instituto Agrónomo Nacional* (IAN), which is the body responsible for the implementation of the Agrarian Reform Law. In the early 1970s, an Office of Indigenous Development was set up within IAN, which was staffed largely by a group of individuals whose policies were, in effect, an attempt to put into practice the principles of the so-called *Nuevo Indigenismo,* the New Indigenism. This form of indigenist policy was based on the precepts laid down in the Declaration of Barbados of

1971 which stressed, above all, the need to recognize the right of indigenous groups to self-determination in political, social and economic affairs, and called for all nation-states in South America to accept the principle of cultural pluralism within their boundaries. In practice, the activities of the Office of Indigenous Development revolved around three poles: the granting of land titles, the formation of economic co-operatives and the creation of indigenous political federations, both on a local and on a national level. All these goals it sought to achieve by careful manipulation of the provisions laid down, essentially for peasant communities, in the Agrarian Reform Law.

By the end of 1978, land titles had been granted to ninety-five indigenous communities, involving well over a million hectares; eighty co-operatives had been established; six local federations and one national indigenous federation had been formed. Moreover, the IAN group had contributed actively to a national debate within the press, government institutions and the universities as to what the goals of Venezuelan indigenism should be. But over the last two or three years, much of the impetus has gone out of this movement, following the dispersal of the group that originally set up the Office of Indigenous Development. Furthermore, their record has been exposed to severe criticism by other indigenists. It has been claimed that the federations either do not exist, except on paper or that, if they do, they do not represent indigenous feeling, being merely an instrument for the manipulation of indigenous communities by IAN bureaucrats; that all the co-operatives, with one exception, have been an economic disaster; and that the land titles granted to indigenous communities have not taken into account their need for large quantities of land if their traditional subsistence techniques are to be viable.

CODESUR's activities in the field of indigenism has also declined in recent years. Following the replacement of COPEI by *Acción Democrática* (AD) in 1974, its activities were severely curtailed and it became little more than a research body. In any case, it had never had much practical impact on the indigenous affairs of the Región Sur. Recently, it has been abolished entirely. The position of CODESUR as the development agency responsible for Southern Venezuela was taken over during the AD administration by the *Corporación Venezolana de Guayana* (CVG). During the first years of its existence, CVG did very little in the field of indigenous affairs. In March 1979, just as CVG was beginning to show some signs of becoming involved, the national government changed once again after AD lost the election. It still remains to be seen what effect the Christian Democrat (COPEI) administration will have on the CVG's policy towards the indigenous groups living in the area for which it is responsible.

Ever since the other agencies of the government began to take an interest in indigenous affairs in the late 1960s, OCAI, the agency specifically responsible for indigenous affairs, has found itself somewhat pushed out of the limelight. The involvement of these other agencies has served to increase the general confusion as to the goals of Venezuelan indigenism, since each agency tends to operate independently, pursuing objectives in conformity with its own particular interests. By 1975, it was estimated by OCAI that there were thirty-two bodies, both public and private, that held some official brief to intervene in indigenous affairs. Although some effort is made to co-ordinate the activities of these bodies through the CI, there is still a regrettable lack of collaboration between them.

As in the case of the other agencies, the last few years have also seen major changes in OCAI. In 1975, the budget of OCAI was dramatically increased following the accession to power of AD, and a new indigenist policy was formulated which recognized, in principle at least, the cultural pluralism of the Venezuelan nation and the right of the indigenous population to some degree of self-determination. But the extent of this self-determination was never precisely stipulated, whilst the performance of OCAI at a grass-roots level, despite the budgetary increase, continued to be disappointing. Moreover, little more than a year after the formulation of the new policy, a major change in indigenist administration took place: ultimate responsibility for indigenous affairs was transferred from the Ministry of Justice to the Ministry of Education, whilst, at a lower level, OCAI was dissolved and replaced by the *Oficina Ministerial de Asuntos Fronterizos e Indígenas* (OMAFI). The CI continued to act as an intermediary between OMAFI, the Ministry of Education and all the other agencies of the government concerned with indigenous affairs.

Symptomatic of the transferal of responsibility for indigenous affairs from the Ministry of Justice to the Ministry of Education was the decree published by the COPEI administration in September 1979, six months after taking office, which called for the gradual implementation of bilingual education programmes in indigenous communities. The decree clearly recognizes the principle of cultural pluralism and the need to preserve the cultural patrimony of the indigenous communities through educational programmes adapted to the socio-cultural characteristics of each particular ethnic group. But other than this and the usual re-shuffling of appointments that attends any change of administration in Venezuela, so far the COPEI administration has brought no major change to the general course of Venezuelan indigenism. Its policy seems to be merely to continue the rather ill-defined, rule-of-thumb policy of its predecessor. However, one would expect the activities of OMAFI under COPEI to be guided by the declared interests of Venezuelan Christian Democracy, which in the particular sphere of indigenous affairs are likely to mean increased support for the Roman Catholic missions, and for investment both by the State and by private enterprise in the social and economic development of the Región Sur.

The government's apparent reluctance to take any major new step in indigenous affairs has been demonstrated in relation to two particular issues that assumed importance towards the end of 1979: the investigation of the activities of the New Tribes Mission (NTM) in Venezuela and the creation of a Yãnomamö 'park'. The investigation into the activities of the NTM were carried out independently by three different bodies—the office of the Attorney-General, a military tribunal and a special commission of the Chamber of Deputies. These investigations were implemented in response to serious charges, on the one hand by a naval captain formerly based in Puerto Ayacucho, who claimed that the NTM had been engaged in para-military activities there, and on the other by a group of anthropologists and other intellectuals, who accused the NTM of practising ethnocide. Part of the evidence for this latter charge was a film entitled *Yo hablo a Caracas*, in which a Ye'kuana ritual specialist relates and criticizes the attempts of the NTM to destroy the traditional way of life of his people. To this chorus of criticism was added the influential voice of the Roman Catholic missions, who have always regarded the intervention of Protestant missions in their Apostolic Vicariates as illegal. But, although the various commissions heard evidence that would be extremely compromising for the New Tribes Mission if proved to be true, the government has neither taken the decisive step of expelling the missionaries, nor, on the other hand, cleared them of the charges made against them.

The question of the creation of a Yãnomamö 'park' became a contentious issue in Caracas following the international campaign, in Western Europe and the United States, as well as in Brazil, for the creation of such a park on the Brazilian side of the border in order to protect the Yãnomamö from the various economic interests intent on invading the area. It was argued that since half the Yãnomamö live within Venezuela, the Brazilian park would not be viable unless a similar park were created on the Venezuelan side of the border also. It was suggested that the terms of the newly-signed 'Amazon Pact' would be an appropriate vehicle for securing international collaboration on the matter. But the various groups lobbying for a Yãnomamö park within Venezuela soon found themselves confronted by the fact that Venezuelan law, unlike its Brazilian counterpart, does not provide a well-established precedent for indigenous parks. Two alternatives have therefore been proposed: one lobby is in favour of creating a reserve for the protection of natural species (for which, ironically, there is stronger precedent) which could also provide protection for the Yãnomamö since it would effectively prevent the invasion of the area; the other lobby, however, is strongly opposed to this idea, proposing instead that the whole area be legally made over to the various Yãnomamö sub-groups by means of collective land titles granted by IAN under the terms of the Agrarian Reform Law. So far, however, the government has not acted on these suggestions.

As this account would suggest, the history of Venezuelan indigen-smi since the mid-1940s has been largely a story of legal, bureaucratic and frankly political adjustments of a piecemeal kind rather than the progressive development of a coherent and practicable indigenist policy. Broadly speaking, the official policy of the Venezuelan government today, whatever its formal political credo, could be said to be integrationist (as opposed to assimilationist) in the sense that although it envisages the eventual incorporation of the indigenous population into the national society, it recognizes at the same time, in principle at least, the right of indigenous groups to preserve their own cultural traditions. What is not clear however is the degree to which the government is prepared to make the practical, political provisions necessary for them to be able to do so.

It may be that the absence of a clearly defined indigenist policy in Venezuela is nothing more than a result of the fact that up until now the country has derived most of its foreign exchange from oil and other mineral deposits outside the areas currently occupied by indigenous groups (although the Los Pijiguaos bauxite deposits on the edge of Panare territory may well change that). Thus there has never been such a direct clash between the interests of national economic development and those of the indigenous groups as there has been, for example, in Brazil or in Peru. Consequently, there has never been such a pressing political need, as there has been in these other countries, for a clear definition of indigenous rights within the law. On the other hand, it could equally well be that the government perceives certain advantages to the present situation, for, in the absence of a coherent indigenist policy, it can leave effective control of indigenous affairs to economic development agencies, private enterprise and the missions, whilst simultaneously remaining uncommitted itself to any particular course of action in the future. In other words, the very absence of a systematic policy may in fact be a policy in itself.

# BIBLIOGRAPHY

ANTOLINEZ, Gilberto (1944) 'Características típicas de la vivienda Panare' *América Indígena* IV, 3 : 201 – 10. México.

ANTOLINEZ, Gilberto (1952) 'Interesantes aspectos de la cultura Panare' *Venezuela Misionera* XIV : 279 – 84. Caracas.

ARANGO MONTOYA, Padre Francisco (1979) 'Desde Caicara del Orinoco en el Distrito Cedeño, Estado Bolivar, Venezuela'. *Venezuela Misionera*. No. 482 : 285 – 7.

ARCAND, Bernard (1972) 'The urgent situation of the Cuiva indians of Columbia' *International Workgroup for Indigenous Affairs Document*, No.7, 28 pp. Copenhagen.

ARVELO – JIMENEZ, Nelly (1971) *Political relations in a tribal society: a study of the Ye'cuana Indians of Venezuela* (Cornell University Latin American Studies Program dissertation series, No.31.) Ithaca.

ARVELO – JIMENEZ, Nelly (1972a) 'An analysis of official Venezuelan policy in regard to the Indians' in W. Dostal (ed.) *The Situation of the Indians in South America* Geneva/World Council of Churches.

ARVELO – JIMENEZ, Nelly, Walter COPPENS, Roberto LIZARRALDE, H. Dieter HEINEN (1977) 'Indian Policy' in John D. Martz and David J. Myers (eds.) *Venezuela : the democratic experience*, pp. 323 – 34. Praeger.

ARVELO–JIMENEZ, Nelly (1980a) 'Programs among indigenous populations of Venezuela and their impact: a critique' in F. Scazzocchio (ed.) *Land, people and planning in contemporary Amazonia*. Cambridge Centre of Latin American Studies, pp. 210–221.

ARVELO – JIMENEZ, Nelly (1980b) 'Una perspectiva analítica : la antropología en el caso Nuevas Tribus'. Unpublished manuscript.

BARTH, Fredrik, ed. (1969) *Ethnic groups and boundaries : the social organization of culture difference.* Universitetsforlaget/Allen and Unwin.

BUENO, Fr. Ramón (1933) *Apuntes sobre la provincia misionera de Orinoco e indígenas de su territorio.* Caracas. (Written between 1801 and 1804.)

BUTT, Audrey (1965/6) 'The shaman's legal role' *Revista do Museu Paulista*, XVI : 152 – 86.

CAULDER, Wynona (1976) 'Going to God's House' *Brown Gold*, XXXIV, 1 : 2–3.

CARDOSO DE OLIVEIRA, Roberto (1968) *Urbanização e tribalismo : a integração dos índios Terêna numa sociedade de classe*. Rio de Janeiro, Zahar.

CARDOSO DE OLIVEIRA, Roberto (1972a) *O índio e o mundo dos brancos : uma interpretação sociológica da situaçã dos Tukúna*. Sao Paulo, Livraria Pioneira Editôra. (Second edn. Originally published in 1964.)

CARDOSO DE OLIVEIRA, Roberto (1972b) *A sociologia do Brasil indígena*. Rio de Janeiro, Tempo Brasileiro.

CARDOSO DE OLIVEIRA, Roberto and Luiz de CASTRO FARIA (1971) 'Interethnic contact and the study of populations' in Francisco M. Salzano (ed.) *The ongoing evolution of Latin American populations*. Springfield, Illinois, Thomas.

CARNEIRO, Robert (1973) 'Slash-and-burn cultivation among the Kuikuru and its implications for cultural development in the Amazon Basin' in D. Gross (ed.) *Peoples and Cultures of Native South America*, pp. 98 – 123. New York, Doubleday. (Originally published in 1961.)

CAUTY, André (1974a) 'Reflexiones sobre 'las formas flexionales' del idioma panare' *Antropológica*, 37 : 41 – 50. Caracas.

CAUTY, André (1974b) 'Reflexiones sobre denominación y designación en el idioma panare' *Antropológica*, 39 : 3 – 24. Caracas.

CHAFFANJON, Jean (1889) *L'Orénoque et le Caura*. Paris, Hachette.

CHAGNON, Napoleon (1973) 'The culture-ecology of shifting (pioneering) cultivation among the Yanomamö Indians' in D. Gross (ed.) *Peoples and cultures of Native South America*. pp. 126 – 32. New York, Doubleday. (Originally published in 1968.)

CODAZZI, Agustín (1940) *Geografía de Venezuela* (3 vols.) Caracas, Biblioteca Venezolana de Cultura. (2nd edn.Originally published in 1841.)

CODESUR (1970) *Informe preliminar*. Caracas, Ministerio de Obras Públicas.

COPPENS, Walter (1971) 'La tenencia de tierra indígena en Venezuela : aspectos legales e antropológicos' *Antropológica* 29 : 3 – 37. Caracas.

CRUXENT, José Maria (1948) 'Datos demográficos' *Memoria de la Sociedad de Ciencias Naturales La Salle*, 21 : 64 – 8. Caracas.

CVG (1978) 'Feasibility study on the bauxite deposits of Los Pijiguaos'. Swiss Aluminium Ltd/CADAL, México.

CVG (n.d.) *Corporación Venezolana de Guayana : informe quinquenal, 1974 – 1978*. Caracas, Gráficas Armitano.

DA MATTA, Roberto (1976) *Um mundo dividido : a estrutura social dos índios apinayé*. Petropolis, Vozes.

DEL CARMEN PEREZ, María; Maria Lucina REYES, Deisy ROJAS, José RODRIGUEZ, Freddy ROSALES (1973) *Estudio socio-demográfico del Distrito Cedeño, Estado Bolivar.* Caracas, Min. de Obras Públicas.

DEL REY FAJARDO, José (1971) *Aportes jesuíticos a la filiología colonial venezolana* (2 vols.) Caracas, Univ. Católica Andrés Bello.

DELGADO, Rafael (1949) 'Notas etnográficas de los panare de Las Vegas' *Memoria de la Sociedad de Ciencias Naturales La Salle*, 23 : 11 – 22. Caracas.

DOLE, Gertrude E. (1973) 'Shamanism and political control among the Kuikuru' in D. Gross (ed.), *Peoples and cultures of native South America* pp.294 – 307. New York, Doubleday. (Originally published in 1964.)

DUMONT, J. -P. (1971) 'Compte-rendu de mission chez les Indiens Panare' *L'Homme*, XI, 1 : 83 – 8.

DUMONT, J. -P. (1972) 'Rapport pour la Commission Indigéniste Nationale du Venezuela sur la situation actuelle des Indiens Panare' in R. Jaulin (ed.), *De l'ethnocide*, pp. 79 – 98. Paris, 10.18.

DUMONT, J. -P. (1974a) 'L'alliance substituée; la communication entre créoles vénézuéliens et Indiens Panare' *L'Homme*, XIV, 1 : 43 – 56.

DUMONT, J. -P. (1974b) 'Espacements et déplacements dans l'habitat Panare' *Journal de la Société des Américanistes*, 41 : 17 – 30.

DUMONT, J. -P. (1974c) 'Of dogs and men : naming among the Panare Indians' *Atti del XL Congresso Internazionale degli Americanisti*, 2 : 645 – 51. Gcnoa, Tilgher.

DUMONT, J.-P. (1976) *Under the rainbow : nature and supernature among the Panare Indians.* Austin and London, Univ. of Texas Press.

DUMONT, J.-P. (1977) 'From dogs to stars : the phatic function of naming among the Panare' in Ellen B. Basso (ed.), *Carib-speaking Indians : culture, society and language.* Tuscon, Univ. of Arizona Press.

DUMONT, J.-P. (1977b) 'Le sens de l'espace chez les Panare' *Actes du XLIIe Congres International des Américanistes* (Paris, Sept. 1976), Vol. II : 47 – 53.

DUMONT, J.-P. (1977c) 'Musical politics : on some symbolic aspects of the musical instruments of the Panare Indians' in Stanley A. Freed (ed.) *Anthropology and the climate of opinion*, Annals of the New York Academy of Sciences, 293 : 206 – 14.

DUMONT, J.-P. (1978) *The headman and I : ambiguity and ambivalence in the fieldworking experience.* Austin and London, University of Texas Press.

DUMONT, Louis (1953) 'The Dravidian kinship terminology as an expression of marriage' *Man*, LIII, (54) : 34 – 9

DUMONT, Louis (1971) *Introduction á deux théories d'anthropologie sociale : groupes de filiation et alliance de mariage*. Mouton.

DURBIN, Marshall (1977) 'A survey of the Carib language family' in Ellen B. Basso (ed.), *Carib-speaking Indians : culture, society and language*. pp.23 – 38. Tuscon, University of Arizona Press.

EWEL, John J. and Arnaldo MADRIZ (1968) *Zonas de vida de Venezuela*. Caracas, Min. de Agricultura y Cría.

FERRER PEREZ, Loraida, Tomás GARRIDO, Luis GASCON, Ramón QUILADA, Nelida QUINTERO, Briscelda TOVAR (1975) *Diagnóstico socio-económico del sub-sector pecuario, Distrito Cedeño, Estado Bolívar*. Caracas, Min. de Obras Públicas.

GILIJ, Felipe Salvador (1965) *Ensayo de historia americana*. Biblioteca de la Academia Nacional de la Historia, Caracas, Nos. 72 – 4. (Originally published in 1782.)

GINES, Hno. and Ramón AVELEDO (1958) *Aves de caza de Venezuela* Caracas, Sucre.

GLEASON, H.A. (1969) *An introduction to descriptive linguistics* (rev. edn). Holt, Rinehart and Winston.

GOODY, Jack (1976) *Production and reproduction : a comparative study of the domestic domain*. Cambridge University Press.

GRANT, S.C.N. (1898) *Atlas to accompany the case presented on the part of Her Britannic Majesty to arbitral tribunal between Great Britain and the United States of Venezuela* . . . London.

HAMES, Raymond B. and Irene L. HAMES (1976) 'Ye'kwana basketry : its cultural context' *Antropológica*, 44 : 3 – 58. Caracas.

HARNER, Michael J. (1968) 'Technological and social change amongst the Eastern Jivaro' *Proceedings of the 37th International Congress of Americanists*, vol.1, pp. 363 – 88. Mar de Plata.

HEINEN, Dieter H. (1975) 'The Warao Indians of the Orinoco Delta : an outline of their traditional economic organization and inter-relation with the national economy' *Antropologica*, 40 : 25 – 55. Caracas.

HENLEY, Paul (1975) 'Wánai: aspectos del pasado y del presente del grupo indígena mapoyo' *Antropológica*, 42 : 29 – 55. Caracas.

HENLEY, Paul (1978) 'Os índios e a civilização : a critical appreciation' *Cambridge Anthropology*. IV, 3 : 88 – 111. Cambridge.

HENLEY, Paul (1980) Review of J.-P. Dumont, *The headman and I : ambiguity and ambivalence in the fieldworking experience* in *Man*, vol. 15, No.1 : 206.

HENLEY, Paul and Marie-Claude MULLER (1978) 'Panare basketry : means of commercial exchange and artistic expression' *Anthropológica*, 49 : 29 – 130. Caracas.

HERNANDEZ-BRETON, Armando (1969) *Ley de Reforma Agraria* (Novena Edn). Caracas, La Torre.

HOLLAND, Luke (1980) *Indians, missionaries and the Promised Land : photographs from Paraguay.* Survival International. London.

HUMBOLDT, Alexander von (1942) *Viaje a las regiones equinocciales del nuevo continente.* (5 vols.) Caracas, Min. de Educación. (Originally published in 1821.)

HURTADO IZQUIERDO, R. (1961) 'La incorporación de los indígenas de Guayana al progreso nacional' Instituto Agrónomo Nacional publication, Cuidad Bolivar.

KAPLAN, J.O. (1975) *The Piaroa, a people of the Orinoco basin : a study in kinship and marriage.* Oxford, Clarendon Press.

KLOOS, Peter (1971) *The Maroni River Caribs of Surinam.* Assen, Van Gorcum.

KRISOLOGO, Pedro (1965) 'Antropología cultural del pueblo panare' *Boletín Indigenista Venezolano,* 9 : 161 – 86. Caracas.

LARAIA, Roque de Barros and Roberto DA MATTA (1967) *Indios e castanheiros: a impresa extrativa dos índios do médio Tocantins.* São Paulo, Difusão Europeia do Livro.

LEACH, Edmund (1976) *Culture and communication : the logic by which symbols are connected.* Cambridge University Press.

LOPEZ RAMIREZ, Tulio (1944) 'Visita a los indios Panare en Venezuela' *Acta Americana,* II, 3 : 254 – 5.

LAYRISSE, Miguel and Johannes WILBERT (1966) *The indian societies of Venezuela : their blood group types.* Caracas, Fundación La Salle.

MATTEI – MULLER, Marie-Claude and Paul HENLEY (1978) *Wapa : la comercialización de artesanía indígena y su innovación artística. El caso de la cestería panare.* Caracas, Litografía Tecnocolor.

MAZIAREK, Stanislaw (1975) *El diamante en Venezuela.* Caracas, Editorial Arte.

MELATTI, Júlio César (1967) *Indios e criadores : a situação dos Krahó na área pastoril do Tocantins.* Rio de Janeiro, Univ. Federal.

MELATTI, Júlio César (1970) *Indios do Brazil* Brasília, Editôra de Brasília.

MULLER, Marie-Claude (1974) 'El sistema de posesión en la lengua panare' *Antropológica,* 38 : 3 – 14. Caracas.

MULLER, Marie-Claude (1975) 'La diferenciación linguística panare-mapoya' *Antropológica* 42 : 79 – 91. Caracas.

MURDOCK, George P. (1949) *Social Structure.* New York, Macmillan.

PEREZ-ARBELAEZ, E. (1956) *Plantas útiles de Colombia.* Bogotá, Camacho Roldán.

PETRICEKS, Janis (1968) 'Shifting cultivation in Venezuela'. Ph. D. thesis. Syracuse University. University Microfilms, Ann Arbor (69 – 804).

PRICE, Jana (1976) 'Rewards' *Brown Gold,* XXXIV, 1 : 4–5.

PRICE, Jana (1980) 'The Panares need the bread of life' *Brown Gold,* XXXVII, 10 : 6–7.

PURSEGLOVE, J.W. (1972) *Tropical crops : monocotyledons.* London, Longmans.

PURSEGLOVE, J.W. (1974) *Tropical crops : dicotyledons.* London, Longmans. (First published 1968.)

RIBEIRO, Darcy (1970) *Os índios e a civilização : a integração das populaçoes indígenas no Brasil moderno.* Rio de Janeiro, Civilização Brasileira.

RILEY, Carrol L. (1952) 'Trade Spanish of the Piñaguero Panare' in *Trager's Studies in Linguistics,* X,1 : 6 – 11.

RILEY, Carrol L. (1953) 'Noticias sobre los indios Panare de Venezuela' *Boletín Indigenista Venezolano,* I : 265 – 86. Caracas.

RILEY, Carrol L. (1959) 'Some observations on the Panare language' *Boletín del Museo de Ciencias Naturales,* IV-V, 1-4 : 87 – 96. Caracas.

RIVERS, W.H.R. (1906) *The Todas.* London, Macmillan.

RIVIERE, Peter (1969) *Marriage among the Trio : a principle of social organization.* Oxford Univ. Press.

RIVIERE, Peter (1972) *The forgotten frontier : ranchers of North Brazil.* Holt, Rinehart and Winston.

RIVIERE, Peter (1977) 'Some problems in the comparative study of Carib societies' in Ellen B. Basso (ed.) *Carib-speaking Indians : culture, society and language* pp. 39–42. Tucson, University of Arizona Press.

ROHL, Eduardo (1949) *Fauna descriptiva de Venezuela.* Caracas, Tipografía Americana.

ROMERO OCANDO, Eddie (1975) *Un nuevo enfoque en el indigenismo venezolano.* Caracas, Oficina Central de Asuntos Indígenas.

ROZE, Janis (1970) *Ciencia y fantasía sobre las serpientes de Venezuela* Caracas, Fundación la Salle.

SAHLINS, Marshall (1974) *Stone Age Economics.* Tavistock.

SANDNER MONTILLA, Fernando (1975) *Manual de las serpientes ponzoñosas de Venezuela.* Caracas. (2nd edn.)

SCHNEE, Ludwig (1973) *Plantas comunes de Venezuela.* Caracas, Univ. Central de Venezuela.

SCORZA REGGIO, Juan V. (1975) *Analisis de los últimos cien años de indigenismo oficial en Venezuela.* Caracas, Universidad Católica Andrés Bello.

SERBIN, Andrés and Omar GONZALEZ NANEZ, eds., (1980) *Indigenismo y autogestión.* Caracas, Monte Avila.

SILVERWOOD-COPE, Peter (1972) 'A contribution to the ethnography of the Colombian Maku' Unpublished Ph.D. thesis, Cambridge University.

SISKIND, Janet (1973) 'Tropical forest hunters and the economy of sex' in D. Gross (ed.) *Peoples and cultures of native South America,* pp. 226 – 40. New York, Doubleday.

STUCKY, Maurice (1979) 'Panare outreach' *Brown Gold,* XXXVII, 4 : 8.

TAVERA ACOSTA, Bartolomé (1930) *Venezuela pre-coloniana.* Caracas.

TELLO, Jaime (1979) *Mamíferos de Venezuela.* Caracas, Fundación La Salle.

THOMAS, David J. (1973) 'Pemon demography, kinship and trade' University of Michigan Ph.D. dissertation. Ann Arbor, University Microfilms.

TOSANTOS, Gonzalo (1977) *Apuntes sobre el idioma panare.* Cumaná, Editorial Universitaria de Oriente.

VILA, Pablo (1969) *Geografía de Venezuela : el territorio nacional y su ambiente físico.* (2nd edn.) Caracas, Min. de Educación.

VILLALON, María Eugenia (1978) 'Aspectos de la organización social y la terminología de parentesco e'nyapa (vulg. Panare)' *Colección de Lenguas Indígenas* (Serie menor), No.5 Caracas, Univ. Católica Andrés Bello.

VILLASMIL FEBRES, Leopoldo *et al.* (1976) *Indios, diamantes y fronteras.* Caracas, Comisión Presidencial de Guaniamo.

WAVRIN, Marquis de (1937) *Moeurs et coutumes des indiens sauvages de l'Amérique du Sud.* Paris, Payot.

WILBERT, Johannes (1959) 'Aspectos sociales de la cultura panare' *Antropológica,* 7 : 47 – 62. Caracas.

WILBERT, Johannes (1961) *Indios de la región Orinoco-Ventuari.* Caracas, Fundación La Salle.

YANES, Francisco Javier (1943) *Relación documentada de los principales sucesos ocurridos en Venezuela desde que se declaró el Estado Independiente hasta el año de 1821.* (2 vols.) Caracas, Academia Nacional de la Historia. (Written in the early nineteenth century.)

# INDEX OF AUTHORS AND OTHER SOURCES

# GENERAL INDEX